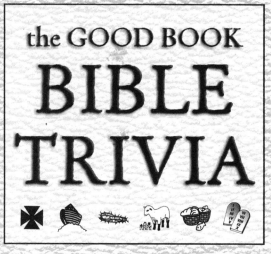

the GOOD BOOK

BIBLE
TRIVIA

Over 4,300
Questions & Answers
about the Bible

J. STEPHEN LANG

TYNDALE and Tyndale's quill logo are registered trademarks of Tyndale House Publishers, Inc.

Copyright © 1988, 2008 by J. Stephen Lang. All rights reserved.

The Good Book Bible Trivia: Over 4,300 Questions & Answers about the Bible

Previously published as *The Complete Book of Bible Trivia* under ISBN 978-0-8423-0421-4.

Cover photograph copyright © by iStockphoto. All rights reserved.

Designed by Mark Anthony Lane II

ISBN-13: 978-1-4143-1974-2

ISBN-10: 1-4143-1974-6

Printed in the United States of America

14 13 12 11 10 09 08
7   6   5   4   3   2   1

To Mark Fackler,
who is a friend of the Bible
and who understands laughter

TABLE OF CONTENTS

PART FOURTEEN: . . . AND THINGS LEFT OVER

INTRODUCTION

CAN WE SPEAK of the Bible and trivia in the same breath?

I think we can. As I began writing this book, I became more and more convinced that the Bible, that divine book through which God's Truth shines, is an earthy, human collection of people and incidents. I believe, as most Christians do, that the Bible has come down to us through God's initiative. I also believe that God chose to present his truth through stories, oracles, and letters that not only inspire us but also captivate us as any good stories do. Even people unfamiliar with the Bible have recognized for centuries that it is a veritable treasure trove of stories, as attested by the many poems, plays, novels, films, paintings, and sculptures that are based on the Scriptures.

This is not the first collection of questions and answers about the Bible, and it won't be the last. However, most books have focused on the seriousness of the text, with questions arranged in neat Genesis-to-Revelation sequence.

I have arranged things topically, with such titles as "Strange Ways to Die," "Hairy and Hairless" (yes, really), "All Kinds of Villains," "The Women on the Throne," and so on. The topics are arranged under fourteen sections but this book is for browsing. Want to fill up your time commuting on the train? How about the hour you spend waiting at the dentist's office or the few minutes before dinner is on the table? In other words, the book is designed to be read randomly, anywhere, and with no preparation of any kind. It is designed to entertain the person who unashamedly likes to be entertained—and challenged. By the way, to avoid the hassle of having all the answers in one section at the back of the book, we've placed the answer in a logical place—upside down at the bottom of the page where the questions appear.

I believe that asking questions can lead us deeper into the Bible and make us appreciate and (it is hoped) study more deeply this fascinating treasure of stories. In doing the research for this book, I learned quite a bit, but not enough to answer every question correctly—at least, not yet.

Happy reading! I hope you enjoy getting better acquainted with the divine—and very human—Book of books.

PART ONE
A CAST OF THOUSANDS

LAUGHERS AND DANCERS

1 Whose entrancing dance proved fatal for John the Baptist?

2 Who held a feast with dancing when his son returned?

3 Who laughed at Nehemiah's plans to rebuild Jerusalem?

4 Who danced with all his might when the Ark of the Covenant was brought to Jerusalem?

5 Who laughed when she heard she would bear a son in her old age?

6 Who was snickered at for claiming that a dead girl was only asleep?

7 What prophetess led the women of Israel in a victory dance?

8 Whose ill-fated daughter came out dancing after his victory over the Ammonites?

9 Who had his decree for a Passover celebration laughed at by the men of Israel?

10 From the choices listed, what tribe took wives from among the dancers at Shiloh?

A Issachar B Judah C Benjamin

11 Who came out dancing after David killed Goliath?

12 What is the only book in the Bible to mention God laughing?

13 What epistle tells Christians to turn their laughter to mourning?

14 What old woman said, "God has brought me laughter. All who hear about this will laugh with me"?

15 Who told Job that God would certainly fill a righteous man with laughter?

(More Laughers on the next page)

Laughers and Dancers

1 The daughter of Herodias (Matthew 14:6-8).   2 The father of the Prodigal Son (Luke 15:25).
3 Sanballat, Tobiah, and Geshem (Nehemiah 2:19).   4 David (2 Samuel 6:14).   5 Sarah (Genesis 18:10-12).   6 Jesus (Matthew 9:23-24).   7 Miriam (Exodus 15:20).   8 Jephthah's (Judges 11:34).
9 Hezekiah (2 Chronicles 30:5, 10).   10 C: Benjamin (Judges 21:20, 23).   11 The women of Israel (1 Samuel 18:6-7).   12 Psalms (2:4; 37:13; 59:8).   13 James (4:9).   14 Sarah (Genesis 21:6).
15 Bildad (Job 8:21).

LAUGHERS AND DANCERS (CONTINUED)

16 According to Psalm 126, what caused laughter among the Jews?

17 What old man laughed at God's promise that he would father a child in his old age?

18 What group of people were busy dancing and partying when David caught up with them?

19 What graven image did the Israelites dance in front of?

20 What book says there is a time to weep and a time to laugh?

21 Who, in the Beatitudes, does Jesus promise laughter to?

22 What book says that laughter is foolishness?

23 What book says that even in laughter the heart is sorrowful?

24 Whom did Jesus speak of as dancing in the streets?

25 Who danced around the altar of their false god?

26 Whose wife despised him for dancing in the streets?

27 From the choices listed, what instrument is usually associated with dance in the Bible?

   A Harp **B** Tambourine **C** Lyre

28 What book says, "Our dancing has turned to mourning"?

29 According to Job, whose children dance around and make music?

30 What Old Testament character's name means "laughter"?

More Laughers and Dancers

16 Bringing the captives back to Jerusalem (Psalm 126:2). 17 Abraham (Genesis 17:17). 18 The Amalekites (1 Samuel 30:16-18). 19 The golden calf made by Aaron (Exodus 32:19). 20 Ecclesiastes (3:4). 21 Those who weep (Luke 6:21). 22 Ecclesiastes (2:2). 23 Proverbs (14:13). 24 Children (Luke 7:32). 25 The priests of Baal (1 Kings 18:26). 26 David's wife, Michal (1 Chronicles 15:29). 27 B: The tambourine or timbrel (Exodus 15:20; Judges 11:34; Job 21:12; Psalm 150:4). 28 Lamentations (5:15). 29 The children of the wicked (Job 21:7-12). 30 Isaac (Genesis 21:3-6).

THEY DID IT FIRST

1 What king had the first birthday party in the Bible?

2 Where was the first beauty contest in the Bible, and who won?

3 Who was the first Christian martyr?

4 What is the first dream mentioned in the Bible?

5 What is the first war mentioned in the Bible?

6 Who was the first drunk?

7 Where was the first piggy bank?

8 Who was the first person to fall asleep during a sermon?

9 What is the first commandment in the Bible?

10 What is the first purchase of land in the Bible?

11 What was the first instance of book burning?

12 What was the first military coup in Israel?

13 Who used the first pseudonym?

14 Who built the first city?

15 Who was the first hunter?

16 Who was the first murderer?

17 What is the first book of the Bible named after a woman?

(More Firsts on the next page)

They Did It First

1 Pharaoh, at the time Joseph was in Egypt (Genesis 40:20). 2 The one at the court of Persian ruler Ahasuerus; the winner was Esther (Esther 2). 3 Stephen (Acts 6:7–8:2). 4 The dream of Abimelech, in which he was told to return Sarah to Abraham (Genesis 20:3-8). 5 The war of the kings of the north, led by Chedorlaomer, king of Elam (Genesis 14). 6 Noah, who planted a vineyard after leaving the ark (Genesis 9:21). 7 In the Temple at Jerusalem; it was a chest, ordered by King Joash, who had a hole bored in the lid to keep priests from stealing funds (2 Kings 12). 8 Eutychus, who dozed off and fell out of a window during Paul's sermon (Acts 20:9). 9 "Be fruitful and multiply" (Genesis 1:28). 10 Abraham bought the Cave of Machpelah as a tomb for Sarah (Genesis 23:3-20). 11 Jeremiah's scroll, sent to King Jehoiakim, was burnt piece by piece as it was being read to the king (Jeremiah 36:21-23). 12 Absalom led an attempt to overthrow his father, David (2 Samuel 15–18). 13 Esther, whose real name was Hadassah (Esther 2:7). 14 Cain (Genesis 4:17). 15 Nimrod (Genesis 10:9). 16 Cain (Genesis 4:8). 17 Ruth.

THEY DID IT FIRST (CONTINUED)

18 Who is the first prophet mentioned in the Bible?

19 Where did Jesus work his first miracle?

20 What was the first of the ten plagues of Egypt?

21 Who was the first king of Israel?

22 Who were the first foreign missionaries?

23 Who was the first shepherdess?

24 Who was the first single man to be exiled?

25 Who was the first judge of Israel?

26 Who was the first disciple chosen by Jesus?

27 Who wore the first bridal veil?

28 From the choices listed, who told the first lie?

   A The serpent   B Eve   c Adam

29 Who was the first priest mentioned in Scripture?

30 Who wore the first ring?

31 What was the first city called?

32 What was the first animal out of the ark?

33 Where were the disciples first called Christians?

34 Who took the first census of the Hebrews?

(More Firsts on the next page)

They Did It First

18 Abraham (Genesis 20:7).   **19** Cana (John 2:1-11).   **20** The river turns to blood (Exodus 7:14-24).
21 Saul (1 Samuel 10:1).   **22** Paul and Barnabas (Acts 13).   **23** Rachel (Genesis 29:9).   **24** Cain
(Genesis 4:12).   **25** Othniel (Judges 3:9).   **26** Simon Peter (John 1:42).   **27** Rebekah (Genesis 24:65).
28 A: The serpent (Genesis 3:4).   **29** Melchizedek (Genesis 14:18).   **30** Pharaoh (Genesis 41:42).
31 Enoch, named after Cain's son (Genesis 4:17).   **32** The raven (Genesis 8:7).   **33** Antioch (Acts
11:26).   **34** The priest Eleazar (Numbers 26:1-2).

35 Who was the first shepherd?

36 Who were the first exiles?

37 Who were the first twins?

38 Who constructed the first altar?

39 Who built the first Jerusalem Temple?

40 From the choices listed, who planted the first garden?

    A Adam **B** Cain **C** God **D** Noah

41 Who was the first metal craftsman?

42 Who was the first farmer?

43 Who was the first polygamist?

44 What is the first commandment with a promise attached to it?

45 Who was the first apostle to be martyred?

46 Who was the first child mentioned in the Bible?

47 Who was the first daughter mentioned by name?

48 What is the first color mentioned in the Bible?

49 Who planted the first vineyard?

They Did It First

35 Abel (Genesis 4:2). **36** Adam and Eve, driven from the garden (Genesis 3:24). **37** Jacob and Esau (Genesis 24:23-26). **38** Noah (Genesis 8:20). **39** Solomon (1 Kings 6). **40** C: God (Genesis 2:8). **41** Tubal-cain (Genesis 4:22). **42** Cain (Genesis 4:2). **43** Lamech (Genesis 4:19). **44** "Honor your father and mother" (Deuteronomy 5:16; Ephesians 6:2-3). The promise is that the person will have a long, full life if he honors his parents. **45** James (Acts 12:1-2). **46** Cain (Genesis 4:1). **47** Naamah, daughter of Lamech (Genesis 4:22). **48** Green: "I have given every green plant" (Genesis 1:30). **49** Noah (Genesis 9:20).

6   THE GOOD BOOK BIBLE TRIVIA

SECOND IN LINE

1 At 969 years, Methuselah was the longest-lived man. Who came in second at 962 years?
2 Saul was the first king of Israel. Who was the second? (Hint: It wasn't David.)
3 The first covenant God made with man was his covenant with Noah. With whom did he make the second covenant?
4 In John's Gospel, Jesus' first miracle is turning water into wine. What is the second miracle?

The answers to the next three questions are hidden in the puzzle that follows the questions. Can you find them?

5 Stephen was the first Christian martyr. What apostle was the second?
6 Paul's first traveling companion was Barnabas. Who was the second?
7 The first plague in Egypt was the turning of the Nile waters to blood. What was the second plague?

F	V	T	M	J
W	R	I	X	A
K	C	O	N	M
G	A	U	G	E
S	I	L	A	S
H	O	P	Z	T

(More Seconds on the next page)

Second in Line

1 Jared (Genesis 5:20). 2 Ishbosheth (2 Samuel 2:8-10). 3 Abraham (Genesis 15-17). 4 Healing an official's son in Cana (John 4:43-54). 5–7 The names hiding in the puzzle are James, brother of John (Acts 12:1-2); Silas (Acts 15:36-41); and frogs (Exodus 8:1-8).

8 Othniel was the first judge of Israel. Who was the second?

9 Jacob's firstborn was Reuben. Who was his second son?

10 David's first capital city was Hebron. Name his second, and more famous, capital by filling in the blanks.

— — — — — — — — — —

11 The serpent in Eden was the first talking animal in the Bible. What was the second?

12 Eve is the first woman in the Bible. Who is the second?

13 Solomon led the way in constructing the first temple in Jerusalem. Who led in the building of the second temple?

14 Esther is the first book in the Bible not to mention the name of God. What is the second book with this omission?

EXTRA CREDIT

The Bible was originally written in what three languages?

Hebrew and Aramaic (Old Testament) and Greek (New Testament)

Second in Line (continued)
8 Ehud (Judges 3:15). 9 Simeon (Genesis 29:33). 10 Jerusalem (2 Samuel 5:6-10). 11 Balaam's donkey (Numbers 22:28-30). 12 Cain's wife, who is not named (Genesis 4:17). 13 Zerubbabel and Joshua (Ezra 3). 14 Song of Songs (Song of Solomon).

8 THE GOOD BOOK BIBLE TRIVIA

KINGS, PHARAOHS, AND OTHER RULERS (I)

1 What king hosted a banquet where a phantom hand left a message on the palace wall?

2 What king of Israel was murdered while he was drunk?

3 What king of Salem was also a priest of the Most High God?

4 What king of Gerar took Sarah away from Abraham?

5 What Hebrew captive interpreted the dreams of the Egyptian pharaoh?

6 What three kings listened to the prophet Elisha as he prophesied to the accompaniment of a harp?

7 What king attacked the Israelites on their way into Canaan, only to be completely destroyed later?

8 What king of Sidon gave his daughter Jezebel as a wife to Ahab?

9 What king of Bashan was famous for having an enormous iron bed?

10 Who was the last king of Judah?

11 What king of Hazor organized an alliance against Joshua?

12 What military man captured 31 kings?

13 What king of Moab sent the prophet Balaam to curse Israel?

14 What king of Mesopotamia was sent by God to conquer the faithless Israelites?

15 What Canaanite king of the time of the judges was noted for having nine hundred iron chariots?

16 What son of Gideon was proclaimed king in Shechem?

(More Kings on the next page)

Kings, Pharaohs, and Other Rulers (I)

1 Belshazzar (Daniel 5:1-9). 2 Elah (1 Kings 16:8-10). 3 Melchizedek (Genesis 14:18). 4 Abimelech (Genesis 20:2). 5 Joseph (Genesis 41:1-36). 6 Joram of Israel, Jehoshaphat of Judah, and the king of Edom (2 Kings 3:11-19). 7 The king of Arad (Numbers 21:1-3). 8 Ethbaal (1 Kings 16:31). 9 Og (Deuteronomy 3:11). 10 Zedekiah (2 Kings 25:1-7). 11 Jabin (Joshua 11:1-5). 12 Joshua (12:9-24). 13 Balak (Numbers 22:2-6). 14 Cushan-Rishathaim (Judges 3:8). 15 Jabin (Judges 4:2-3). 16 Abimelech (Judges 9:6).

A CAST OF THOUSANDS 9

17 What king of the Amalekites was captured by Saul and cut into pieces by Samuel?

18 What much-married king is considered the author of the Song of Songs?

19 What Philistine king did David seek refuge with when he fled from Saul?

20 What shepherd boy, the youngest of eight sons, was anointed by Samuel in front of his brothers?

21 What king wanted to see miracles when the arrested Jesus was sent to him?

22 What king of Tyre sent cedar logs and craftsmen to King David?

23 What prophet had a vision of a time when the Lord would gather the kings of the earth together and put them all in a pit?

24 From the choices of David's sons, what man (David's oldest), tried to make himself king of Israel?

A Absalom   B Adonijah   C Amnon

25 What wise king made an alliance with Egypt when he married the pharaoh's daughter?

26 What Egyptian king gave refuge to Jeroboam when he fled from Solomon?

27 What king had a strange dream about an enormous, fruitful tree that was suddenly chopped down with only a dry stump left?

28 What man, one of Solomon's officials, had his reign over Israel foretold by the prophet Ahijah?

(More Kings on the next page)

(More Kings on the next page)

17 Agag (1 Samuel 15:8, 32). 18 Solomon (Song of Songs (Song of Solomon) 1:1). 19 Achish of Gath (1 Samuel 21:10). 20 David (1 Samuel 16:6-13). 21 Herod (Luke 23:8). 22 Hiram (2 Samuel 5:11). 23 Isaiah (24:21-22). 24 B: Adonijah (1 Kings 1:5-53). 25 Solomon (1 Kings 3:1). 26 Shishak (1 Kings 11:40). 27 Nebuchadnezzar (Daniel 4:10-18). 28 Jeroboam (1 Kings 11:26-40).

Kings, Pharaohs, and Other Rulers (I)

29 What king of Judah was constantly at war with King Jeroboam of Israel?

30 What king was confronted by the prophet Nathan because of his adulterous affair?

31 What king of Israel reigned only two years and was murdered while he was fighting against the Philistines?

32 Spell out the name of the man who violently protested having a king in Israel, though he himself anointed the first two kings.

— — — — —

33 What city did King Jeroboam use as his capital when the northern tribes split from the southern tribes?

34 What king of Israel reigned only seven days and killed himself by burning down his palace around him?

35 What king of Ethiopia was supposed to aid Hezekiah in breaking the power of the Assyrians?

36 What king led Israel into sin by allowing his evil wife to introduce Baal worship into the country?

37 Who was the last king of Israel?

(More Kings on the next page)

Kings, Pharaohs, and Other Rulers (I)
29 Abijam, or Abijah (1 Kings 15:6). **30** David (2 Samuel 12:1-15). **31** Nadab (1 Kings 15:26-27). **32** Samuel (1 Samuel 8-10). **33** Tirzah (1 Kings 14:17). **34** Zimri (1 Kings 16:15, 18). **35** Tirhakah (2 Kings 19:9). **36** Ahab (1 Kings 16:29-33). **37** Hoshea (2 Kings 17:4).

38 What king of the Amorites refused to let the Israelites pass through his kingdom?

39 What king called Elijah the worst troublemaker in Israel?

40 What king of Syria was Elijah told to anoint?

41 What evil king of Judah was humbled and repentant after being taken to Babylon in chains?

42 What king was told by the prophet Micaiah that his troops would fall in battle?

43 What saintly king had a fleet built to sail for gold, though the ships never sailed?

44 What king of Israel consulted the god Baal-zebub after falling off his palace balcony?

45 What king of Moab was famous as a sheep farmer?

46 From the choices listed, what king refused to let the Israelites pass through his country on their way to Canaan?

      A King of Edom   **B** King of Arad   **c** King of Moab

47 What king had the prophet Uriah murdered for opposing him?

48 Who became king of Syria after he smothered King Ben-hadad with a wet cloth?

49 What king of Judah led the country into sin by marrying the daughter of the wicked Ahab?

50 Who is the only king in the Bible referred to as "the Mede"?

Kings, Pharaohs, and Other Rulers (I)

38 Sihon (Numbers 21:21-26). **39** Ahab (1 Kings 18:17). **40** Hazael (1 Kings 19:15). **41** Manasseh (2 Chronicles 33:10-13). **42** Ahab (1 Kings 22:17). **43** Jehoshaphat (1 Kings 22:48). **44** Ahaziah (2 Kings 1:2). **45** Mesha (2 Kings 3:4). **46** A: The king of Edom (Numbers 20:14-20). **47** Jehoiakim (Jeremiah 26:20-23). **48** Hazael (2 Kings 8:15). **49** Jehoram (2 Kings 8:16-18). **50** Darius (Daniel 5:31).

12   THE GOOD BOOK BIBLE TRIVIA

SO MANY DREAMERS

1 Who told Pilate that a worrisome dream made it clear that Pilate was to have nothing to do with Jesus?

2 According to one Old Testament prophet, there will come a day when young men will see visions and old men will dream dreams. Which prophet?

3 Who repeats the words of this prophet in an early Christian sermon?

4 Joseph, Mary's husband, was warned in dreams to do four things. What?

5 In Nebuchadnezzar's famous tree dream, who is symbolized by the majestic tree that is cut down?

6 Daniel had a dream of four beasts rising out of the sea. What did they look like?

7 In Nebuchadnezzar's dream of the statue, what four metals are mentioned as composing the statue?

A Bronze **B** Gold **C** Lead **D** Silver

E Brass **F** Copper **G** Iron

8 One of Gideon's soldiers dreamed of a Midianite tent being overturned by an unlikely object. What was it?

9 When God came to the young Solomon in a dream and asked him what he desired, what did Solomon ask for?

10 What three Egyptian officials did Joseph interpret dreams for?

11 God protected Jacob by sending a dream of warning that Jacob should not be pursued or harmed. Who received this dream?

12 Who irritated his brothers by telling them of his dreams?

13 Who slept on a stone pillow at Bethel and had a dream of a stairway to heaven?

So Many Dreamers

1 His wife (Matthew 27:19). 2 Joel (2:28). 3 Peter, at Pentecost (Acts 2:17). 4 Go ahead and marry Mary, take a different route out of Bethlehem, flee to Egypt, and return from Egypt (Matthew 1:18–2:23). 5 Nebuchadnezzar (Daniel 4:5–17). 6 A lion, a bear, a leopard, and a monster with iron teeth (Daniel 7). 7 B, D, E, and G: Gold, silver, brass, and iron (Daniel 2:31–35). 8 A cake of barley bread (Judges 7:13). 9 An understanding heart and good judgment (1 Kings 3:5–10). 10 The pharaoh, his baker, and his butler (Genesis 40–41). 11 Laban, Jacob's father-in-law (Genesis 31:29). 12 Joseph (Genesis 37:1–11). 13 Jacob (Genesis 28:10–15).

CHANGE OF LIFE, CHANGE OF NAME

Match these renamed biblical characters with their original names.

1 Abraham and Sarah	Daniel
2 Israel	Oshea
3 Joshua (Jehoshua)	Saul
4 Solomon	Eliakim
5 Peter	Mattaniah
6 Paul	Joseph
7 Mara	Jacob
8 Zaphenath-paneah	Jedidiah
9 Belteshazzar	Simon or Simeon
10 Jehoiakim	Abram and Sarai
11 Zedekiah	Naomi

EXTRA CREDIT

Q&A

What were the first manuscripts of the New Testament written on?

Papyrus, a material made from strips of reeds

WHAT'S IN A NAME?

Most biblical names had specific meanings. Below are the meanings of the names of several biblical characters. Can you name the person in each case? *(This isn't as hard as it looks. Except for 1, 2, 4, 6, 9-14, and 35, all the names are also the titles of books of the Bible. The other names are familiar.)*

1 beloved
2 prosperous
3 God is strong
4 God is Savior
5 help
6 great warrior
7 love's embrace
8 salvation of the Lord
9 God has helped
10 red earth
11 eagle
12 enlightened
13 the Lord sustains
14 the Lord is gracious
15 messenger
16 worshiper of the Lord
17 the Lord has consoled
18 star
19 something wrong seeing
20 asked of God
21 exalted of God
22 dove
23 he that weeps
24 peace
25 honored of God
26 honorable
27 God is judge
28 the Lord is salvation
29 salvation
30 one with a burden; to carry
31 gift of the Lord
32 light-giving
33 rock
34 the Lord remembers
35 little
36 the Lord hides
37 the Lord has been gracious
38 praise of the Lord
39 festive
40 who is the Lord
41 compassionate
42 affectionate
43 the Lord is God
44 polite
45 supplanter

NAMES MADE IN HEAVEN

1 What did God change Jacob's name to?

2 Who was told by God to name his son Maher-shalal-hash-baz?

3 Who told Joseph what Jesus' name would be?

4 What prophet was told by God to name his son Lo-ammi?

5 Who told Hagar to name her son Ishmael?

6 What did God change Abram's name to?

7 Who was told by an angel that his son was to be named John?

8 What prophet told the priest Pashhur that his new name was to be Magor-missabib?

9 What did God call his human creation?

10 What new name did Jesus give to Simon?

11 What was Hosea told to name his daughter?

12 What was Sarai's name changed to?

13 Who was told to name his son Solomon?

14 Who was told to name his firstborn son Jezreel?

15 Who told Mary that her son was to be named Jesus?

HAIRY AND HAIRLESS

1 What prophet was a very hairy man?

2 Who is the only man mentioned in the Bible as being naturally bald?

3 What grief-stricken Old Testament man shaved his head after he learned his children had been destroyed?

4 What king of Babylon, driven from his palace, lived in the wilderness and let his hair grow long and shaggy?

5 Shave off the correct letters in the puzzle below to reveal who is mentioned first in the Bible as being very hairy.

NOHESAULOT

6 What prince had his hair cut only once a year?

7 What apostle purified himself, along with four other men, by shaving his head?

8 As a Nazarite, this judge of Israel never shaved or had a haircut until his mistress shaved his head. Who was he?

9 What leader plucked out his own hair and beard when he heard the Jews had intermarried with other races?

10 What smooth-skinned man had a hairy twin brother?

(More Hairy and Hairless on the next page)

11 What sort of person had to shave all his hair twice, six days apart?

12 Who was forbidden to "trim off the hair on your temples"?

13 What class of people could not shave their heads nor let their hair grow long?

14 What prophet did God tell to shave his head and beard?

15 Shave off the correct letters in the puzzle below to reveal the man who was so incensed at the intermarriage of Jews with foreigners that he pulled out the hair of some men.

JONAHNEHEMIAHCAIN

16 What prophet told the people of Jerusalem to cut off their hair as a sign the Lord had rejected them?

17 Who had to shave their whole bodies as part of the ceremony of consecrating themselves to the Lord?

18 If an Israelite man took a female prisoner of war as his wife, what did she have to do to her hair?

19 What group of consecrated men never cut their hair?

20 What Christian shaved his head at Cenchrea in connection with a vow?

Hairy and Hairless

11 A leper (Leviticus 14:7-9). 12 Jews (Leviticus 19:27). 13 Priests (Ezekiel 44:20). 14 Ezekiel (5:1-4). 15 Nehemiah (13:23-27). 16 Jeremiah (7:29). 17 The Levites (Numbers 8:5-7). 18 Shave it off (Deuteronomy 21:10-12). 19 The Nazarites (Numbers 6:5, 13, 18). 20 Paul (Acts 18:18).

18 THE GOOD BOOK BIBLE TRIVIA

THE RUNNERS

1 What bizarre person saw Jesus from far off and ran to worship him?

2 What belligerent man ran to meet his brother and kissed him after a long time of separation?

3 Who outran a team of horses?

4 What evangelist ran to meet a foreign official in his chariot?

5 What disciple outran Peter to Jesus' tomb?

6 Who ran to the priest Eli, thinking Eli had called him in the night, though it was actually God who called?

7 What cousin of Jacob's ran to tell her father when she found she and Jacob were related?

8 What boy ran into the Philistine camp to confront their best warrior?

9 What servant of the prophet Elisha ran to meet the woman of Shunem?

10 Fill in the blanks on the first line to spell the name of the short man who ran to see Jesus but could not see him because of his height. Then fill in the blanks on the second line to spell out what the short man climbed to get a bird's-eye view.

— — — — — — — — —

— — — —

11 Who ran to meet the Lord in the plains of Mamre?

12 Who sent Cushi to run to David with the news of Absalom's death?

(More Runners on the next page)

13 According to Isaiah, what sort of people can run and not be weary?

14 What prophet ran after another prophet to accept the appointment as his successor?

15 What usurper to the throne of Israel gathered up 50 men to run before him?

16 When the man of Benjamin saw the Ark of the Covenant captured by the Philistines, what Israelite did he run to tell?

17 What judge's mother ran to tell her husband Manoah that an angel had appeared to her?

18 What beautiful woman caused Abraham's servant to run to meet her?

19 What did a man at Jesus' crucifixion run to find for the dying Jesus?

20 Who ran into the midst of the Israelites carrying incense to stop a plague?

21 Who had a vision of one angel running to meet another?

22 What two women ran from Jesus' empty tomb to tell the disciples what had happened?

23 What man ran to meet Abraham's servant at the well?

NOTABLE WOMEN, AND SOME LESS NOTABLE (I)

1 The only female judge of Israel, she judged the tribes from under a palm tree. Her victory song is famous. Who was she?

2 What widowed prophetess was 84 years old when she saw the young Jesus in the Temple?

3 What wife of David had been married to Nabal, who died when she told him of the gifts she had given to David?

4 What elderly cousin of Mary became the mother of John the Baptist?

5 What prophetess, active during the reign of Josiah, consoled the king while chastising the people of Judah?

6 What scheming princess of Tyre married and manipulated the weak Ahab and imposed her pagan religion on Israel?

7 What Israelite woman aided the people by murdering the Canaanite captain Sisera in her tent?

8 What Jewish girl married a Persian emperor and helped save her exiled people from extermination?

9 What two sisters from Bethany had a brother named Lazarus and were close friends of Jesus?

10 What prophetess was the sister of two great leaders and was once afflicted with leprosy for being rebellious?

11 What harlot became a hero for saving the life of Joshua's spies and was so honored in later days that she is listed in the genealogy of Jesus?

(More Women on the next page)

Notable Women, and Some Less Notable (I)
1 Deborah (Judges 4–5). 2 Anna (Luke 2:36-38). 3 Abigail (1 Samuel 25:18-20). 4 Elizabeth (Luke 1). 5 Huldah (2 Kings 22:14-20). 6 Jezebel (1 Kings 16–19). 7 Jael (Judges 4:17-22). 8 Esther. 9 Mary and Martha (Luke 10:38-42; John 11). 10 Miriam (Exodus 15; Numbers 12). 11 Rahab (Joshua 2, 6).

NOTABLE WOMEN, AND SOME LESS NOTABLE (I)
(CONTINUED)

12 What loving woman, a concubine of Saul, watched over the corpses of her slaughtered children, protecting them from birds and animals?

13 Though her profession was condemned by an official decree of King Saul, the king disguised himself in order to get help from her. Who was she?

14 What Persian queen upset the king and his counselors by refusing to appear before them at their drunken banquet?

15 What dancer so enchanted Herod that he offered her anything she wished?

16 Who was turned into a pillar of salt?

17 What king of Judah was Abi the wife of?

18 Spell out the name of David's sister who had the same name as one of his wives.

— — — — — — — —

19 What woman was given as a wife after her future husband brought in two hundred Philistine foreskins as a gift to her father?

20 Who offered a bottle of milk to an enemy soldier and then killed him?

21 After Eve, who is the first woman mentioned in the Bible?

22 What Old Testament woman had children named Lo-ruhamah, Lo-ammi, and Jezreel?

23 What was Saul's wife's name?

24 What wife of David was also given as a wife to a man named Palti?

Notable and Less Notable Women (I)
12 Rizpah (2 Samuel 21:1-10). 13 The witch of Endor (1 Samuel 28). 14 Vashti (Esther 1). 15 The daughter of Herodias, known to us from the writings of Josephus as Salome, though her name does not appear in the Bible (Matthew 14:1-11). 16 Lot's wife (Genesis 19:26). 17 Ahaz (2 Kings 18:2). 18 Abigail (1 Chronicles 2:16-17). 19 Michal (1 Samuel 18:27). 20 Jael (Judges 4). 21 Adah (Genesis 4:19). 22 Gomer, wife of Hosea (Hosea 1). 23 Ahinoam (1 Samuel 14:50). 24 Michal (1 Samuel 25:44).

22   THE GOOD BOOK BIBLE TRIVIA

LATE-NIGHT CALLERS

1 Who came to Peter late at night and released him from prison?

2 Who had a late-night visit from an angel, who assured him that he would be safe aboard a storm-tossed ship?

3 Who led some officers of the chief priests to pay a late-night call on Jesus?

4 What Pharisee came to Jesus late at night?

5 Who met a man with whom he engaged in an all-night wrestling match?

6 Who came through Egypt on a late-night visit to almost every household?

7 Arrange the letters in the correct order to spell out where shepherds received angels as late-night visitors.

HEMTEBELH

— — — — — — — — —

8 Who took Saul's spear after sneaking into his camp late one night?

9 Who visited a medium at night?

10 Who attacked a Midianite camp late at night?

11 Who paid the young Samuel a late-night call?

12 Who frightened his followers, who thought he was a ghost when he passed by them late at night?

Late-Night Callers

1 An angel (Acts 12:6-17). 2 Paul (Acts 27:23-24). 3 Judas (John 18:3, 12). 4 Nicodemus (John 3:1-2). 5 Jacob (Genesis 32:22-31). 6 The Lord (Exodus 12:29-31). 7 Bethlehem (Luke 2:8-16). 8 David and Abishai (1 Samuel 26:7-12). 9 Saul (1 Samuel 28:8). 10 Gideon and his men (Judges 7:19). 11 The Lord (1 Samuel 4:1-14). 12 Jesus, when he walked on the lake (Mark 6:48).

MOST MENTIONED MEN

If you like crossword puzzles, complete the intersecting boxes to reveal the answers to the first five questions, then continue on with the other questions.

1 **(1 Across)** What patriarch has 306 mentions, ranking him sixth?

2 **(1 Down)** What priest ranks fourth, with a total of 339 references?

3 **(2 Down)** What leader, with 740 mentions, ranks third?

4 **(3 Across)** What man, as if you didn't know, is the most mentioned man in the Bible?

5 **(4 Across)** What king's name appears 338 times and ranks fifth?

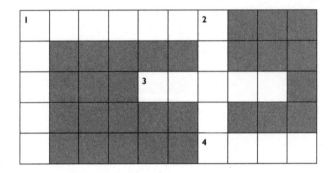

6 What king, mentioned 1,118 times in the Bible, is the second most mentioned man?

7 What wise king ranks seventh with his 295 mentions?

(More Men on the next page)

MOST MENTIONED MEN (CONTINUED)

8   What man would, if his famous nickname were considered a real personal name, outrank all the others in this list? (As it stands, using his usual name, he ranks eighth with 270 mentions.)

9   What government leader in a foreign land ranks ninth, with 208 references?

10 What military man ranks tenth, with 197 references?

11 What apostle ranks eleventh, with 185 references?

12 What apostle ranks twelfth, with 166 references?

13 What military commander in the reign of David ranks thirteenth, with 137 mentions?

14 What prophet ranks fourteenth and has only one less mention than the answer to question 13?

15 What prophet and judge has one less reference than the person in question 14 and ranks fifteenth?

16 What patriarch, though he is mentioned much less than his father or son, ranks sixteenth, with 127 mentions?

17 What kinsman of Jesus ranks seventeenth, with 86 references?

18 What government official is, with 56 references, the most mentioned unbeliever in the New Testament?

19 How many times is Adam mentioned in the Bible?

20 After Peter and Paul, which apostle is mentioned the most times (35 references)?

MOTHERS AND DAUGHTERS

1 Who was the mother of the Levitical priesthood?

2 What daughter of a pharaoh married one of the descendants of Judah?

3 What Egyptian woman was the mother of two of the tribes of Israel?

4 What wife of Lamech was the mother of the founder of music?

5 Who had a daughter named Jemima?

6 What daughter of a priest married a king who became a leper?

7 Who had a daughter named Keren-happuch?

8 What prophet had a daughter named Lo-ruhamah? From the choices listed, do you know what her name means?

A God's favor   B A voice in the wilderness

c God has departed   D Not loved

9 What wife of David was mother of the handsome—but rebellious—Absalom?

10 What daughter of Absalom married her cousin, King Rehoboam?

11 What daughter of Saul was promised as a wife to David for slaying Goliath?

12 Who was the mother of Huz, Buz, and Pidash?

13 Who is the first daughter mentioned by name in the Bible?

14 What Ammonite woman, a wife of Solomon, became the mother of the royal dynasty of Judah?

15 What man's daughters involved him in incestuous relations when they believed there were no other men around?

TEACHER, TEACHER

1 What famous rabbi was Paul's teacher?

2 Who commissioned Ezra to teach the law to Israel?

3 According to Jesus, who would teach his followers all they needed to know?

4 What two men were to instruct the people involved in the construction of the tabernacle?

5 Who was the godly king of Judah who sent his princes throughout the land to teach the law to the people?

6 What learned Greek taught in the synagogue at Ephesus but was himself instructed by Aquila and Priscilla?

7 What king sent an exiled priest back to Samaria to teach the Gentiles there how to follow God?

8 Shave off and rearrange the correct letters in the puzzle below to reveal the apostle's name who taught in Tyrannus's lecture hall.

KODLUAPIZ

— — — —

9 Who was supposed to teach the Israelites how to deal with lepers?

10 What New Testament word means "teacher"?

THE NAKED TRUTH

1 What prophet walked around naked for three years?

2 Who went naked as a way of wailing over the fate of Jerusalem?

3 What king of Israel, struck with the power to prophesy, stripped off his clothes and lay naked for a whole day and night?

4 What father lay naked and intoxicated in his tent, which so disturbed his sons that they came and covered him?

5 In war, what persons were often humiliated by being stripped?

6 What prophet threatened to publically strip his wife naked?

7 What disciple, busy at his daily work, was caught naked by Jesus?

8 Who embarrassed his wife when he danced for joy when the Ark of God was returned?

9 Where did a follower of Jesus escape an angry mob by running away naked?

10 What prophet spoke of a woman (merely a symbol) who committed sexual sins while naked?

EXTRA CREDIT

According to tradition, which Gospel was written first?

The Gospel of Mark

The Naked Truth

1 Isaiah (20:3).   2 The prophet Micah (1:8).   3 Saul (1 Samuel 19:24).   4 Noah (Genesis 9:21-23).
5 Captives (2 Chronicles 28:15).   6 Hosea (2:3, 9).   7 Simon Peter (John 21:7).   8 King David
(2 Samuel 6:20).   9 Gethsemane (Mark 14:51-52).   10 Ezekiel (23:10, 29).

28   THE GOOD BOOK BIBLE TRIVIA

NOTABLE WOMEN, AND SOME LESS NOTABLE (II)

1 What woman of Corinth had a household that Paul described as being full of strife among Christian leaders?

2 What woman was, in Ezekiel, used as a symbol of wicked Jerusalem?

3 What woman with a cumbersome name was the Hittite wife of Esau?

4 Who is the only woman mentioned in Paul's letter to Philemon?

5 What Egyptian woman was the wife of Joseph?

6 What king of Judah was the husband of Azubah?

7 What Hittite woman married Esau, causing grief to Isaac and Rebekah?

8 What handmaid of Rachel bore Jacob the sons Dan and Naphtali?

9 What woman was, in Ezekiel, used as a symbol of wicked Samaria?

10 What woman of Rome was mentioned by Paul as sending her greetings to Timothy?

11 What wife of David was the mother of the rebellious Adonijah?

12 What was the name of Sarah's Egyptian maid?

13 What woman of Midian was killed by being run through with a javelin?

14 What woman of Athens became a Christian because of Paul's teaching?

15 What two women of Philippi were asked by Paul to stop their quarreling?

16 Who were the first two women to be the wives of the same man?

(More Women on the next page)

Notable Women, and Some Less Notable (II)

1 Chloe (1 Corinthians 1:11). 2 Oholibah (Ezekiel 23:4, 11). 3 Oholibamah (Genesis 36:2, 5).
4 Apphia, a Christian of Colosse (Philemon 2). 5 Asenath (Genesis 41:45). 6 Asa (1 Kings 22:41-42).
7 Bashemath (Genesis 26:34). 8 Bilhah (Genesis 29:29; 30:3-7; 35:22, 25; 37:2). 9 Oholah (Ezekiel
23:4-5). 10 Claudia (2 Timothy 4:21). 11 Haggith (2 Samuel 3:4). 12 Hagar (Genesis 16:1).
13 Cozbi (Numbers 25:15-18). 14 Damaris (Acts 17:34). 15 Euodia and Syntyche (Philippians 4:2).
16 Adah and Zillah, wives of Lamech (Genesis 4:19-24).

17 What was Esther's Hebrew name?

18 Who was wife to godly King Josiah?

19 What evil woman is associated with the church of Thyatira?

20 What Midianite woman was slain by the priest Phinehas for marrying an Israelite?

21 By eliminating letters in the first line of scrambled letters below, find what Naomi called herself after suffering great tragedy; do the same in the second line and reveal what that name means.

MXAYRZAM

IBJIKTLTMENR

— — — —

— — — — —

22 What queen of Judah was the wife of godly King Hezekiah and mother of evil King Manasseh?

23 What courageous woman was wife of the priest Jehoiada?

24 What Egyptian servant woman was insolent to Sarah?

25 What woman, the wife of a servant of Herod, was healed by Jesus?

26 What woman of the Roman church is commended by Paul for her hard work?

27 Who had a wife named Judith?

(More Women on the next page)

NOTABLE WOMEN, AND SOME LESS NOTABLE (II)
(CONTINUED)

28 What church was Julia part of?

29 Who was Abraham's wife after Sarah died?

30 What two Hebrew women did God make houses for?

31 What servant woman was ordered out of the house by Sarah?

32 What wife of a palace official went to embalm the body of Jesus?

33 Who was Mehetabel?

34 What Israelite woman lived in Moab but returned to Israel after her husband's death?

35 What false prophetess made attempts to keep Nehemiah from rebuilding the walls of Jerusalem?

36 Who was Ruth's sister-in-law?

37 From the choices listed, what church was the faithful Persis a part of?

       A Rome   **B** Ephesus   **C** Philippi   **D** Galatia

38 Who were Puah and Shiprah?

39 What four women in the early church were described as prophetesses?

40 What servant girl in Jerusalem came to the door when Peter escaped from prison?

41 What Hebrew woman married an Egyptian and later saw their half-breed son stoned to death?

MORE KINGS, PHARAOHS, AND OTHER RULERS

1 What king of Israel had a reputation as a fast and furious chariot driver?

2 What Syrian king besieged Samaria, causing great famine that led to cannibalism?

3 What Egyptian king fought against Judah and murdered King Josiah?

4 What king of Judah had to be hidden as a boy to protect him from the wrath of wicked Queen Athaliah?

5 Who set up golden bulls at Dan and Bethel so that his people would not go to Jerusalem to worship?

6 What king of Judah was stricken with leprosy?

7 This Persian king had a beauty contest to pick a bride. In the crossword, fill in the two names he was known by (1 down and 2 across) and the name of his head-turning Jewish queen (3 across). We've given you a one-letter hint for each name.

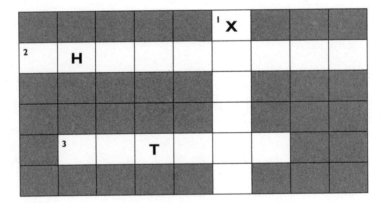

(More Kings on the next page)

More Kings, Pharaohs, and Other Rulers
1 Jehu (2 Kings 9:20). 2 Ben-hadad (2 Kings 6:24-30). 3 Neco (2 Kings 23:29). 4 Joash (2 Kings 11:1). 5 Jeroboam (1 Kings 12:26-31). 6 Uzziah, also called Azariah (2 Kings 15:5). 7 Ahasuerus, or Xerxes; Esther (Esther 1:1; 2:1-18).

8 What king of Israel made Elisha angry by not striking the ground enough with his arrows?

9 What king of Judah showed mercy when he executed his father's murderers but spared their families?

10 What good king of Judah was murdered by two of his court officials?

11 What king of Israel was assassinated by Shallum after a six-month reign?

12 What cruel king of Israel assassinated King Shallum and ripped open the pregnant women of Tappuah?

13 What king of Egypt received an appeal for help from Hoshea of Israel, who wanted to throw off the Assyrian yoke?

14 What king of Israel had much of his territory taken away by the Assyrian king?

15 What evil king of Judah sacrificed his son as a burnt offering and built a Syrian-style altar in Jerusalem?

16 What king of Israel experienced a long famine and drought during his reign?

17 What Assyrian king brought about the fall of Samaria and the deportation of the Israelites to other countries?

18 What godly king of Judah tore down the idols in the country and broke the power of the Philistines?

19 What king of Gezer opposed Joshua's army and was totally defeated, with no soldiers left alive?

20 What Assyrian king was killed by his sons while worshiping in the temple of his god Nisroch?

21 What king was criticized by the prophet Isaiah for showing Judah's treasure to Babylonian ambassadors?

(More Kings ahead!)

More Kings, Pharaohs, and Other Rulers

8 Jehoash (2 Kings 13:18-19).   9 Amaziah (2 Kings 14:5-6).   10 Joash (2 Kings 12:20-21).
11 Zechariah (2 Kings 15:8-10).   12 Menahem (2 Kings 15:16).   13 So (2 Kings 17:4).   14 Pekah
(2 Kings 15:29).   15 Ahaz (2 Kings 16:3, 10).   16 Ahab (1 Kings 18:1-2).   17 Shalmaneser (2 Kings
17:3-6).   18 Hezekiah (2 Kings 18:1-8).   19 Horam (Joshua 10:33).   20 Sennacherib (2 Kings
19:36-37).   21 Hezekiah (2 Kings 20:12-18).

22 What king of Syria joined the king of Israel in attacking Judah?

23 What Assyrian king received 38 tons of silver as tribute money from Menahem of Israel?

24 What king of Assyria had his army of 185,000 soldiers destroyed by the angel of the Lord?

25 What cruel king lied to the wise men about his desire to worship the infant Jesus?

26 What king of Judah had the worst reputation for killing innocent people?

27 What king of Judah reigned for only two years and was murdered by his court officials?

28 What godly king began his reign at age eight and led a major reform movement in Judah?

29 Who had a dream about a statue composed of different materials?

30 What king reinstituted the celebration of Passover in Judah and invited the people of Israel to participate?

31 What king of Judah was killed at the Battle of Megiddo by the forces of Egypt?

32 What king repented because of the preaching of the prophet Jonah?

33 What king of Israel tricked the worshipers of Baal by gathering them together in a temple and slaughtering all of them?

34 What king of Israel built the city of Samaria and made it his capital?

35 What Babylonian king sent his ambassadors to the court of Hezekiah, where they were shown all his treasures?

(More Kings on the next page)

More Kings, Pharaohs, and Other Rulers
22 Rezin (2 Kings 16:5). **23** Tiglath-Pileser (2 Kings 16:7-8) **24** Sennacherib (2 Kings 19:35).
25 Herod (Matthew 2:7-8). **26** Manasseh (2 Kings 21:16). **27** Amon (2 Kings 21:19-23). **28** Josiah
(2 Kings 22-23). **29** Nebuchadnezzar (Daniel 2). **30** Hezekiah (2 Chronicles 30:1-12). **31** Josiah
(2 Kings 23:29-30). **32** The king of Nineveh (Jonah 3:6). **33** Jehu (2 Kings 10:18-27). **34** Omri
(1 Kings 16:24). **35** Merodach-Baladan (2 Kings 20:12-13).

36 What son of Josiah was taken prisoner by Pharaoh Neco and never left Egypt?

37 Who reigned in Jerusalem when the Babylonian king's forces first attacked Judah?

38 Who was reigning in Judah when the Babylonians besieged Jerusalem and carried the nobles of the city away to Babylon?

39 What king of Judah saw the country threatened by the Assyrian army of Sennacherib?

40 What king of Babylon burned down the temple, palace, and city walls of Jerusalem?

41 What king of Judah was blinded and taken away in chains to Babylon?

42 Who was taken prisoner to Babylon, though he came to enjoy the favor of the Babylonian king?

43 What Babylonian king gave the deposed king of Judah a place of great honor in Babylon?

44 What king burned in his fireplace the letter sent to him by the prophet Jeremiah?

45 What king ordered Jezebel's servants to toss her out of a window?

46 What king of Persia issued the decree that the people of Judah could rebuild their temple?

47 What king of Assyria had sent foreigners to settle in Israel after the Israelites had been taken away?

48 What Persian king received a letter complaining about the Jews rebuilding their temple in Jerusalem?

49 What soldier was anointed king of Israel by one of Elisha's followers?

More Kings, Pharaohs, and Other Rulers

36 Joahaz, or Jehoahaz (2 Kings 23:33-34). **37** Jehoiakim (2 Kings 24:1). **38** Jehoiachin (2 Kings 24:15-16). **39** Hezekiah (2 Kings 18:13). **40** Nebuchadnezzar (2 Kings 25:8-11). **41** Zedekiah (2 Kings 25:7). **42** Jehoiachin (2 Kings 25:27-30). **43** Evil-merodach (2 Kings 25:27-30). **44** Jehoiakim (Jeremiah 36:23). **45** Jehu (2 Kings 9:31-33). **46** Cyrus (Ezra 1:1-4). **47** Esarhaddon (Ezra 4:2). **48** Artaxerxes (Ezra 4:6-7). **49** Jehu (2 Kings 9:1-13).

A CAST OF THOUSANDS   35

WOMEN ON THE THRONE

1 Who plotted the execution of John the Baptist?

2 Bernice was the consort of what ruler?

3 The Ethiopian eunuch that Philip witnessed to was the servant of what queen?

4 Whose wife brought Daniel's gift of prophecy to her husband's attention?

5 What Jewish girl became queen of Persia?

6 Who defied her royal husband and was replaced by a foreign woman?

7 What daughter of Ahab tried to destroy the entire royal line of Judah?

8 Who was removed from her position as queen mother because she had made an idol?

9 What Baal-worshiping princess led Ahab into idolatry?

10 During the reigns of David and Solomon, Tahpenes was the queen of what country?

11 What queen traveled far to meet Solomon face-to-face?

12 What wife of the soldier Uriah became David's wife and bore him Solomon?

13 Rizpah was the wife of what king of Israel?

14 Who became David's wife after her husband, Nabal, died?

15 Who nagged at David for dancing in the streets?

MOST MENTIONED WOMEN

1 What Old Testament woman bore a child at age 90 and is the most mentioned woman in the Bible (56 mentions)?

2 What wife of a patriarch ranks second, with 47 mentions?

3 What relative of number 2 ranks third, with 34 mentions?

4 What mother of twins ranks fourth, with 31 mentions?

5 Spell out the name of this evil woman who ranks fifth, with 23 mentions.

— — — — — — —

6 What New Testament woman ranks sixth, with 19 mentions?

7 What wife of both Nabal and David ranks seventh, with 15 mentions?

8 What sister of a famous leader ties with number 7?

9 What follower of Jesus is mentioned 14 times?

10 What servant woman is also mentioned 14 times?

11 Solve the math problem below and find out how many times Eve, the first woman, is mentioned.

$$50 \times 2 \div 5 - 19 + 3 = \underline{}$$

Most Mentioned Women

1 Sarah. 2 Rachel. 3 Leah. 4 Rebekah. 5 Jezebel. 6 Mary, Jesus' mother. 7 Abigail. 8 Miriam. 9 Mary Magdalene. 10 Hagar. 11 Only four.

A CAST OF THOUSANDS   37

STILL MORE KINGS, PHARAOHS, AND OTHER RULERS

1 Who built pagan temples to please all his foreign wives?

2 Which Gospel claims that Pilate had the plaque "The King of the Jews" fastened on Jesus' cross?

3 What Persian king was embarrassed by his disobedient wife?

4 What king of Judah was murdered after he fled to Lachish?

5 What king had a sinister prime minister named Haman?

6 What king is supposed to have written Ecclesiastes?

7 What two kings are mentioned as the authors of Proverbs?

8 What future king of Israel was out hunting for his donkeys when Samuel came to anoint him?

9 What much-loved and much-quoted prophet was active in the reigns of Uzziah, Jotham, Ahaz, and Hezekiah, and, according to tradition, was executed by Manasseh?

10 What king had the apostle James executed with a sword and had Peter arrested?

11 What fat king of Moab was murdered by the judge Ehud?

12 What king of Babylon went insane and lived in the fields, where he ate grass and let his hair and fingernails grow long?

13 What king made a famous judgment about a baby that two women claimed was theirs?

14 What king ordered Daniel thrown into the lions' den?

15 What king of Judah tore down the pagan shrines and stamped out child sacrifice in Judah?

16 What king of Judah sacrificed his sons in the fire but later became repentant?

17 What cruel king had the infant boys of Bethlehem slaughtered?

(More Kings on the next page)

18 What king broke his own law when he called on a spiritualist to bring up the ghost of Samuel?

19 Who was the only king of Israel to kill both a king of Judah and a king of Israel?

20 What king was referred to by Jesus as "that fox"?

21 What son of Saul was made king of Israel by Abner?

22 What king executed John the Baptist after his wife's daughter asked for the head of John on a platter?

23 What Assyrian king attacked the Philistines, leading Isaiah to walk around naked for three years?

24 What king, dressed in royal finery, was hailed as a god but then struck down by the angel of the Lord?

25 What king did Paul tell the story of his conversion to?

26 What king gave his daughter as a wife for David?

27 What Hebrew was given the daughter of the pharaoh as a wife?

28 According to Luke's Gospel, what Roman ruler ordered a census in the empire?

29 Who was the first king to reign at Jerusalem?

30 What saintly king of Judah was crippled with a foot disease in his old age?

31 What king was reprimanded by his military commander for weeping too long over his dead son?

32 What son of David tried to make himself king after David's death?

33 Who was king of Judah when the long-lost Book of the Law was found in the Temple?

34 Who received a visit from the Queen of Sheba, whom he impressed with his wisdom?

(More Kings on the next page)

35 Who is the only king who is said to have neither mother nor father?

36 What king of Judah became king at age seven and was aided in his reign by the saintly priest Jehoiada?

37 What king had the misfortune of his worst enemy being his son-in-law and the best friend of his son?

38 What king is considered to be the author of 73 of the Psalms?

39 What king built the first temple in Jerusalem?

40 What army commander made Saul's son Ishbosheth king over Israel?

41 What evil king of Israel pouted when he couldn't get a man to sell his plot of land?

42 What psalm is supposed to be David's expression of guilt after his affair with Bathsheba?

43 What king suffered from an almost-fatal illness but was promised fifteen more years of life by Isaiah?

44 Which of the ten plagues finally convinced the Egyptian pharaoh to let the Israelites leave?

45 Who reigned in Persia when Nehemiah heard the sad news about the walls of Jerusalem?

46 What king of Judah purified the Temple and rededicated it to God?

47 What apostle fled the soldiers of King Aretas in Damascus?

48 What king of Israel was told by the prophet Jehu that the royal family would be wiped out because of its destruction of Jeroboam's dynasty?

49 What son of Solomon caused the kingdom to split when he threatened the people of Israel?

50 What king sent his son to David with expensive presents that David decided to use in worship?

(2 Samuel 8:9-12).

Still More Kings, Pharaohs, Rulers (continued)
35 Melchizedek, king of Salem (Hebrews 7:3). 37 Saul (1 Samuel 18:1, 28). 38 David. 39 Solomon (2 Chronicles 2:1). 40 Abner (2 Samuel 2:8-10). 41 Ahab (1 Kings 21:1-5). 42 Psalm 51. 43 Hezekiah (2 Kings 20:1-6). 44 The death of the firstborn (Exodus 12:30-32). 45 Artaxerxes (Nehemiah 1:1). 46 Hezekiah (2 Chronicles 29). 47 Paul (2 Corinthians 11:32). 48 Baasha (1 Kings 16:1-4). 49 Rehoboam (1 Kings 12:1-17). 50 Toi, king of Hamath

A HERD OF PROPHETS

1 This bald prophet was the performer of many miracles and the successor to another great prophet.
2 This prophet, famous for his vision of the dry bones, was with the exiles in Babylon.

The answers to the next five questions are hidden in the puzzle that follows the questions. Can you find the names?

3 This elderly woman recognized the infant Jesus as being the Messiah.
4 This king of Israel was, early in his career, associated with a group of prophets.
5 This man of Tekoa was a simple laborer who had the audacity to confront the king's priest at his shrine.
6 This man prophesied against Nineveh.
7 This prophet was famous for his marriage to a prostitute.

A	N	N	A	M
P	I	R	M	U
A	E	S	O	H
B	U	C	S	A
S	A	U	L	N
E	K	T	D	Y

8 This prophet's work is quoted in the New Testament more than any other's. He is famous for his vision of God in the Temple.

(More Prophets on the next page)

9 This kinsman of Jesus ate locusts, preached repentance, and baptized penitents in the Jordan.

10 This Christian prophesied a famine in the land.

11 This New Testament character prophesied the destruction of Jerusalem.

12 This woman was sent for when the long-neglected Book of the Law was found during Josiah's reign.

13 These four young women, daughters of a Christian evangelist, were considered prophetesses.

14 This court prophet confronted King David with his adultery.

15 This man, who anointed the first two kings of Israel, was considered both a judge and a prophet.

16 This prophet of Moab had a confrontation with his talking donkey.

17 This Old Testament patriarch was revealed as a prophet to King Abimelech.

18 This Egyptian-born Hebrew leader predicted the coming of a prophet like himself.

19 This prophet took David to task for numbering the people of Israel.

20 This prophet predicted that Jeroboam would be king over 10 tribes of Israel.

21 This reluctant prophet was thrown overboard in a storm.

22 This young prophet had a vision of a statue composed of different metals.

23 This prophet, put into a hole in the ground for being too outspoken, was often called the "weeping prophet."

(More Prophets on the next page)

A Herd of Prophets
9 John the Baptist. **10** Agabus (Acts 11:27-28; 21:10-11). **11** Jesus. **12** Huldah (2 Kings 22). **13** The daughters of Philip (Acts 21:8-9). **14** Nathan (2 Samuel, 1 Kings). **15** Samuel. **16** Balaam (Numbers 22-24). **17** Abraham (Genesis 20:1-7). **18** Moses (Deuteronomy 18:15). **19** Gad (2 Samuel 24:10-14). **20** Ahijah (1 Kings 11:29-40). **21** Jonah. **22** Daniel. **23** Jeremiah.

A HERD OF PROPHETS (CONTINUED)

24 This wilderness man confronted the prophets of Baal in a famous contest. He was taken to heaven in a chariot of fire.

25 This prophet predicted the outpouring of God's Spirit upon all people.

26 This man wrote a brief book against Edom.

27 This sister of a Hebrew leader was herself a prophetess. For a time she was afflicted with leprosy.

28 The only female judge of Israel, this woman was considered a prophetess.

29 This apostle of Jesus recorded his visions of the world's end times.

30 This man, who traveled to Antioch with Paul, Silas, and Barnabas, was considered a prophet.

31 Spell the name of the prophet who spoke of the need to purify temple worship after the return from exile in Babylon. He also predicted the coming of someone like the prophet Elijah.

— — — — — — — —

32 This man of Moresheth was a contemporary of Isaiah. He spoke of the need to walk humbly with God.

33 This prophet, who posed much of his book in the form of questions and answers, concluded that "the just shall live by faith."

34 Active during Josiah's reign, this prophet spoke about judgment and the coming "day of the LORD."

35 This unlucky prophet delivered an unfavorable message to King Ahab.

(More Prophets on the next page)

36 This false prophet wore a yoke, which Jeremiah broke.

37 This traveling companion of Paul was considered a prophet.

38 Active at the time of the rebuilding of the Temple in Jerusalem, this prophet is associated with Zechariah.

39 This prophet, who lived in Jerusalem after the Babylonian exile, had visions of a flying scroll and a gold lampstand.

40 This man is spoken of as being his brother's prophet. He is also famous for having constructed a golden calf.

41 This false prophet wore iron horns and told King Ahab he would be victorious in battle.

42 This prophet told King Rehoboam that Judah would be abandoned to the forces of the Egyptian king.

43 This prophet, who lived in the reign of King Asa in Judah, was the son of the prophet Oded.

44 This false prophet was a sorcerer and an attendant of the proconsul, Sergius Paulus.

45 This prophetess is mentioned as an intimidator of Nehemiah.

46 This evil prophetess is referred to in Revelation by the name of an Old Testament queen.

NOTABLE WOMEN, AND SOME LESS NOTABLE (III)

1 Who was the mother of the Midianites?

2 What Gospel mentions Susanna, who had been healed by Jesus?

3 Who is the only Egyptian queen mentioned in the Bible?

4 What Egyptian woman found the infant Moses in the river?

5 What daughter of David was raped by her half brother?

6 What epistle mentions Tryphena, a faithful church worker?

7 Who was the wife of Haman of Persia?

8 Who were the first two women to hear that their husband had killed a man?

9 What servant of Leah's mothered two of the 12 tribes of Israel?

10 True or false: The names of Adam's daughters were Adah, Zillah, Milcah, and Iscah.

11 Whose daughters became the mothers of the Moabites and the Ammonites?

12 What priest of Midian had seven daughters, one of which became the wife of Moses?

13 Who was offered as a sacrifice by her father, one of Israel's judges?

14 What daughter of a troublemaker married a Jewish priest, a marriage that caused him to lose his post?

15 What was the name of Melchizedek's mother?

16 What little girl was referred to as "Talitha" by Jesus?

17 What two Hebrew servant women risked their lives by disobeying the command of the pharaoh?

(More Women on the next page)

18 What harlot fled from a burning city, taking her family with her?

19 Whose 10 concubines were forced to engage in public lewdness with the king's sons?

20 Whose Israelite servant girl told him about a cure for leprosy?

21 Who urged her husband to curse God and die?

22 What apostle had a sister whose son informed soldiers of a murderous plot?

23 Who was forbidden to mourn the death of his beautiful wife?

24 Eliminate the right "notes" to reveal the name of the first female singer mentioned in the Bible.

CDMIGARIFBAM

— — — — — —

25 What woman in the time of the judges had dedicated 1,100 shekels of silver to the making of idols?

26 Whose mother took refuge in Moab while her son was fleeing the wrath of Israel's king?

27 What woman put on an act to convince David to recall Absalom from exile?

28 What was the occupation of the two women who disputed over a child and asked Solomon for a decision?

29 What city suffered such a terrible famine that two women agreed to eat their sons for dinner?

30 What woman in Proverbs taught wise sayings to her son?

31 What book portrays Wisdom as a woman?

(More Women on the next page)

32 What grief-stricken woman turned away from her diseased husband because his breath was so offensive?

33 Where did the faithful mother of Rufus live?

34 What violent son of Gideon was killed by a woman who dropped a millstone on his skull?

35 Who tricked his enemies by leaving a harlot's house earlier than expected?

36 Who is the only woman in the King James Bible described as a "wench"?

37 Who helped David by hiding two of his messengers in her cistern?

38 What woman saved her city by negotiating peacefully with Joab?

39 Solve the math problem below and find out how many times Eve's name appears in the New Testament.

$$98 \div 14 \times 8 - 35 + 6 - 25 = \underline{\quad}$$

40 Who is the first female barber mentioned in the Bible?

41 Where did Paul exorcise a spirit from a girl who later became a believer?

42 Which epistle mentions "silly women" who are always learning but never aware of the truth?

43 Which epistle is addressed to a woman?

44 How many times does Eve's name appear in Genesis?

45 What prophet pictures women weeping for the god Tammuz?

(More Women on the next page)

Notable Women, and Some Less Notable (III)
32 Job's wife (Job 19:17). **33** Rome (Romans 16:13). **34** Abimelech (Judges 9:53). **35** Samson (Judges 16:1-3). **36** The woman of En-rogel who acted as a liaison between David and the high priest (2 Samuel 17:17). **37** The Bahurim woman (2 Samuel 17:19). **38** The wise woman of Abel (2 Samuel 20:16-22). **39** Twice (2 Corinthians 11:3; 1 Timothy 2:13). **40** Delilah (Judges 16:19). **41** Philippi (Acts 16:16). **42** 2 Timothy (3:6-7). **43** 2 John. **44** Twice (Genesis 3:20; 4:1). **45** Ezekiel (8:14).

A CAST OF THOUSANDS   47

NOTABLE WOMEN, AND SOME LESS NOTABLE (III)
(CONTINUED)

46 Which Gospel records Jesus saying "Remember Lot's wife"?

47 What shepherd girl became the much-loved wife of Jacob?

48 What daughter of Jacob caused major problems by venturing into strange territory?

49 What quick-witted widow secured children through her deceived father-in-law?

50 Unscramble the letters below to reveal the name of the Egyptian pharaoh whose wife caused Joseph to be thrown into prison.

HTIPROAP

— — — — — — — —

51 What Midianite woman married Moses?

52 What Moabite was an ancestor of Jesus?

53 What invading general had a loving mother who never saw her son return from battle?

54 What woman was married to a fool with a name that meant "fool"?

55 What singer was shut out of the Israelite camp for seven days when she was stricken with leprosy?

56 What five women demanded that Moses give them their deceased father's estate, though women had no property rights at the time?

57 What woman was spared when Joshua's men took Jericho?

58 What unfortunate woman was gang raped, then cut into 12 pieces and sent to the tribes of Israel?

(More Women on the next page)

Notable Women, and Some Less Notable (III)
46 Luke (17:32). **47** Rachel (Genesis 29:6). **48** Dinah (Genesis 34). **49** Tamar (Genesis 38).
50 Potiphar (Genesis 39:7-20). **51** Zipporah (Exodus 2:21). **52** Ruth (4:17). **53** Sisera (Judges 5:28). **54** Abigail (1 Samuel 25:23-25). **55** Miriam (Numbers 12). **56** The five daughters of Zelophehad (Numbers 26-27). **57** Rahab (Joshua 6:17). **58** The Levite's concubine (Judges 19-20).

NOTABLE WOMEN, AND SOME LESS NOTABLE (III)
(CONTINUED)

59 Who brought down Samson for the price of 1,100 pieces of silver from each of the Philistine chieftains?

60 At whose house did Peter confront maids who asked him if he was one of Jesus' disciples?

61 What famous Moabite woman was married to Chilion of Israel?

62 Who was the Kate Smith of the Hebrews?

63 What woman was suspected of drunkenness as she prayed in the sanctuary at Shiloh?

64 Who was David's first wife?

65 What young girl warmed the cold bones of old King David?

66 What name was borne by one of David's wives and one of his mothers-in-law?

67 Who got leprosy for speaking out against her brother?

68 What famous woman judge was married to the obscure man named Lapidoth?

69 What was Moses' mother's name?

70 What woman gave up her son to the household of an Egyptian but came to raise him in her own home anyway?

71 What Midianite woman was the daughter of a priest and the wife of a former Egyptian prince?

72 What woman of dubious character hid Israelite spies under piles of flax?

73 What woman from an idol-worshiping nation became an ancestor of Christ?

(More Women on the next page)

Notable Women, and Some Less Notable (III)
59 Delilah (Judges 16:5). **60** The high priest's (Matthew 26:69-71; Mark 14:66-69). **61** Ruth (1:2-5).
62 Miriam, who sang a patriotic song after the crossing of the Red Sea (Exodus 15:21). **63** Hannah
(1 Samuel 1:13-14). **64** Michal (1 Samuel 18:27). **65** Abishag (1 Kings 1:3, 15). **66** Ahinoam (1 Samuel
14:50; 25:43). **67** Miriam (Numbers 12). **68** Deborah (Judges 4:4). **69** Jochebed (Exodus 6:20).
70 Jochebed, Moses' mother (Exodus 2:8-10). **71** Zipporah, Moses' wife (Exodus 2:21). **72** Rahab
(Joshua 2:6). **73** Ruth (4:17).

74 What barren woman begged the Lord for a son and later gave up her only son to live in the house of the priest Eli?

75 Who took great pains to make peace between David and her foolish and obnoxious husband?

76 What woman broke the law by the king's order?

77 What wife of David took enormous pains to secure the throne for her son?

78 What son of David was called the "son of Haggith"?

79 What wife of David is part of Matthew's genealogy of Jesus?

80 Who came to Jesus at the wedding of Cana and said, "They have no wine"?

81 What queen of Israel ordered the extermination of the prophets of the Lord?

82 Who was thrown from a window by two eunuchs?

83 What woman, associated with the prophet Elijah, was mentioned by Jesus?

84 What wealthy woman had a son who died of a sunstroke?

85 What daughter of Jezebel was killed at Jerusalem's Horse Gate?

86 What wise woman was sought out by Josiah when the Book of the Law was discovered in the Temple?

87 What book of the Bible mentions a virtuous woman who is more valuable than rubies?

88 Who was the first woman to ask the Lord for help?

89 Who was Jesus speaking of when he said, "Behold your mother"?

90 Which of David's servants did his son Adonijah desire?

Notable Women, and Some Less Notable (III)
74 Hannah (1 Samuel 1:20-25). **75** Abigail (1 Samuel 25:23-35). **76** The witch of Endor (1 Samuel 28:7-25). **77** Bathsheba, mother of Solomon (1 Kings 1). **78** Adonijah (1 Kings 1:11). **79** Bathsheba (Matthew 1:6). **80** Mary (John 2:3). **81** Jezebel (1 Kings 18:4). **82** Jezebel (2 Kings 9:33). **83** The widow of Zarephath (Luke 4:25-26). **84** The woman of Shunam (2 Kings 4:19). **85** Athaliah (2 Chronicles 23:14). **86** Huldah the prophetess (2 Kings 22:14). **87** Proverbs (31:10-31). **88** Rebekah (Genesis 25:22). **89** Mary (John 19:27). **90** Abishag, the Shunammite (1 Kings 2:17).

THE INVENTORS

1 Who was the first person to practice wine making?
2 What righteous man started the practice of herding sheep?
3 What mighty man was the first hunter?
4 Who invented farming?
5 Who invented the art of working with metal?
6 Who was the first man to build a city?
7 Who invented music making?
8 Who invented tents?

EXTRA CREDIT

What epistle did Martin Luther call "an epistle of straw"?

James

The Inventors

1 Noah (Genesis 9:20-21).   2 Abel (Genesis 4:2).   3 Nimrod (Genesis 10:8-9).   4 Cain (Genesis 4:2).
5 Tubal-cain (Genesis 4:22).   6 Cain (Genesis 4:17).   7 Jubal, inventor of the harp and organ,
according to the KJV; the NIV and other Bible versions say the harp and flute (Genesis 4:21).   8 Jabal
(Genesis 4:20).

DOWN ON THE FARM

1 What was the farmer Elisha doing when Elijah threw his mantle upon him?

2 What suffering man was a farmer?

3 Who planted the first garden?

4 What judge was a wheat farmer?

5 What king of Judah loved farming?

6 Who was the first man to plant a vineyard?

7 What barley farmer married a Moabite woman and became an ancestor of David?

8 Who was the first farmer?

9 For what cripple did David order Ziba to farm the land?

10 Who had a vineyard that Ahab coveted?

11 What patriarch farmed in Gerar and received a hundredfold harvest?

12 What lieutenant of David had his barley fields destroyed by Absalom?

13 What king, famous for his building projects, also planted vineyards, gardens, and orchards?

THEY HEARD VOICES

1 What New Testament character was the "voice crying in the wilderness"?

2 What blind father recognized Jacob's voice but was deceived by his glove-covered hands?

3 When Moses was in the Tabernacle, where did God's voice come from?

4 Who heard a voice that said, "Write down what you see"?

5 Where did God speak to Moses in a voice like thunder?

6 What barren woman moved her lips in prayer but made no sound?

7 According to Deuteronomy, where did God's voice come from?

8 Who told Saul that obeying God's voice was more important than sacrificing animals?

9 Which Gospel mentions the voice of Rachel weeping for her children?

10 Who heard the voice of an angel ordering that a large tree be chopped down?

11 What book says that the divine voice sounds like a waterfall?

12 Who said, "Is that your voice, David my son"?

13 To which church did Jesus say, "If you hear my voice and open the door, I will come in"?

14 What apostle addressed the Pentecost crowd in a loud voice?

15 Who cried out at the top of her voice when she saw Samuel raised from the dead?

16 At what event did a voice from heaven say, "This is my beloved Son, in whom I am well pleased" (KJV)?

17 What boy was sleeping near the Ark of the Covenant when he heard God's voice calling to him?

(More Voices on the next page)

They Heard Voices

1 John the Baptist (Mark 1:3).   2 Isaac (Genesis 27:22).   3 Above the Ark of the Covenant (Numbers 7:89).   4 John (Revelation 1:10).   5 Mount Sinai (Exodus 19:19).   6 Hannah (1 Samuel 1:13).   7 The fire (Deuteronomy 5:24).   8 Samuel (1 Samuel 15:22).   9 Matthew (2:18).   10 Daniel (4:14).   11 Revelation (1:15).   12 Saul (1 Samuel 26:17, NIV).   13 Laodicea (Revelation 3:20).   14 Peter (Acts 2:14).   15 The witch of Endor (1 Samuel 28:12).   16 Jesus' baptism (Matthew 3:17).   17 Samuel (1 Samuel 3:3-14).

18 Where was Jesus when the divine voice said, "This is my dearly loved Son . . . listen to him"?

19 What king heard the voice of God in the Temple—although there was no Temple at the time?

20 Who heard the voice of those who had been killed for proclaiming God's word?

21 Who heard God's voice after running away from Queen Jezebel?

22 Who screamed in a loud voice, asking Jesus not to punish him?

23 What king was told by Isaiah that the king of Assyria had raised his voice up against God?

24 What was the problem of the ten men who called to Jesus in loud voices, begging him for mercy?

25 Who heard the "still, small voice" of God?

26 What criminal did the people of Jerusalem cry out for in a loud voice?

27 Who heard God speaking out of a whirlwind?

28 What bird did John hear crying in a loud voice, "Terror, terror, terror to all who belong to this world"?

29 In Psalm 19, what has a voice that goes out to all the world?

30 Who said that the bridegroom's friend is happy when he hears the bridegroom's voice?

31 In the Psalms, what trees are broken by the power of God's voice?

32 Who heard a voice telling of the fall of Babylon?

33 Which Gospel mentions the dead awakening to the voice of the Son of God?

34 What, according to Proverbs, lifts its voice up in the streets?

(More Voices on the next page)

They Heard Voices
18 On the Mount of Transfiguration (Matthew 17:5). **19** David (2 Samuel 22:7). **20** John (Revelation 6:10). **21** Elijah (1 Kings 19:13). **22** The Gadarene demoniac (Mark 5:7). **23** Hezekiah (2 Kings 19:22). **24** Leprosy (Luke 17:13). **25** Elijah (1 Kings 19:12). **26** Barabbas (Luke 23:18). **27** Job (38:1). **28** An eagle (Revelation 8:13). **29** The heavens (Psalm 19:4). **30** John the Baptist (John 3:29). **31** The cedars of Lebanon (Psalm 29:5). **32** John (Revelation 18:2). **33** John (5:25). **34** Wisdom (Proverbs 1:20).

35 What city in Revelation was seen as a place that would never again hear the voices of brides and grooms?

36 According to Jesus, whose voice do the sheep know? Herd the letters into the correct order to reveal the answer.

HET DEEPSHSRH

—— —— ——   —— —— —— —— —— —— —— —— , ——

37 What book mentions the sweet voices of lovers in the garden?

38 In Revelation, where did the voice proclaiming the new heaven and earth come from?

39 Who heard God's voice in the Temple in the year that King Uzziah died?

40 Who came forth when Jesus called to him in a loud voice?

41 What prophet predicted that Rachel's voice would be heard, wailing for her dead children?

42 Which Gospel mentions the voice of God speaking during Jesus' farewell address to his disciples?

43 What prophet mentions Jerusalem with the voice of a ghost?

44 Who heard the voice of Jesus many months after Jesus' ascension to heaven?

(More Voices on the next page)

45 What epistle mentions an archangel's voice in connection with the resurrection of believers?

46 What prophet's voice did the returned Jewish exiles obey?

47 From the choices listed, what prophet mentions a voice crying in the wilderness?

A Obadiah **B** Isaiah **C** Jeremiah **D** Haggai

48 Who heard the divine voice telling him to eat unclean animals?

49 What king heard God's voice just as he was boasting about how great Babylon was?

50 Who heard the voice of God as he watched four mysterious creatures flying under a crystal dome?

51 Who recognized Peter's voice after he was miraculously delivered from prison?

52 According to Isaiah, what noble person will not lift up his voice in the streets?

53 According to Paul, what language did the divine voice use on the Damascus road?

54 What king called to Daniel in an anguished voice?

55 Which epistle mentions the voice of Balaam's donkey?

They Heard Voices
45 1 Thessalonians (4:16). **46** Haggai's (1:12). **47** B: Isaiah (40:3). **48** Peter (Acts 10:13-15). **49** Nebuchadnezzar (Daniel 4:31). **50** Ezekiel (1:24). **51** Rhoda (Acts 12:14). **52** The Lord's servant (Isaiah 42:2). **53** Hebrew (or, in some translations, Aramaic) (Acts 26:14). **54** Darius (Daniel 6:20). **55** 2 Peter (2:16).

SLEEPERS AND NONSLEEPERS

1 Who had surgery performed on him while he slept?
2 Who was killed as he slept in the tent of Jael?
3 Who slept in the bottom of a ship as it rolled in a storm?
4 Who suggested to Jezebel's priests that Baal was sleeping on duty?
5 Who slept at Bethel and dreamed about angels?
6 Who slept at David's door while he was home on furlough?
7 From the choices listed, who could not sleep on the night after Haman built a gallows for hanging Mordecai?

   A Esther   **B** Mordecai   **C** King Xerxes

8 Who had troublesome dreams that kept him from sleeping?
9 Who was visited by an angel of the Lord while sleeping?
10 Who slept while Jesus prayed in Gethsemane?
11 Who sneaked into Saul's camp while he was asleep?
12 Who spoke to Abram while he was in a deep sleep?
13 Who did not sleep while Daniel was in the lions' den?

(More Sleepers on the next page)

Sleepers and Nonsleepers

1 Adam (Genesis 2:21).   2 Sisera (Judges 4:21).   3 Jonah (1:5).   4 Elijah (1 Kings 18:27).   5 Jacob (Genesis 28:11-15).   6 Uriah (2 Samuel 11:9).   7 C: King Xerxes (Ahasuerus) (Esther 6:1).
8 Nebuchadnezzar (Daniel 2:1).   9 Joseph (Matthew 2:13).   10 The disciples (Luke 22:45).
11 David and Abishai (1 Samuel 26:7).   12 God (Genesis 15:12-16).   13 King Darius (Daniel 6:18).

SLEEPERS AND NONSLEEPERS (CONTINUED)

14 Who slept through a haircut?

15 Who slept during a storm on the Sea of Galilee?

16 Who fell asleep during Paul's sermon and was later raised from the dead by Paul?

17 Who was sleeping between two soldiers when an angel came to release him?

18 Who was awakened from a deep sleep by an earthquake that toppled a prison?

19 According to Jesus, this person was not dead, but only sleeping. Who was it?

20 Who told Laban he had gone 20 years without a decent sleep?

21 According to Proverbs, what does it take for the wicked to sleep well?

22 Which epistle tells sleepers to rise from the dead?

23 Which epistle uses sleep as a metaphor for physical death?

24 What boy was called out of his sleep by the voice of God?

25 Which epistle urges believers to be alert, not asleep?

26 Who was in a deep sleep as the angel Gabriel explained a vision?

Sleepers and Nonsleepers

14 Samson (Judges 16:19). 15 Jesus (Luke 8:23-24). 16 Eutychus (Acts 20:9-12). 17 Peter (Acts 12:6-7). 18 The Philippian Jailer (Acts 16:27). 19 Jairus's daughter (Luke 8:52). 20 Jacob (Genesis 31:38, 40). 21 Causing trouble (Proverbs 4:16). 22 Ephesians (5:14). 23 1 Corinthians 15. 24 Samuel (1 Samuel 3:2-10). 25 1 Thessalonians (5:4-8). 26 Daniel (8:15-18).

GODLY GOVERNMENT WORKERS IN UNGODLY PLACES

1 What Hebrew governed Egypt?

2 What upright young man was made ruler over the whole province of Babylon?

3 Sergius Paulus, who became a Christian, was the deputy of what island?

4 What Persian king did Nehemiah serve under?

5 What church in Greece had believers who were workers in "Caesar's household"?

6 From what country was the eunuch that was baptized by Philip?

7 What Jewish man served as an honored official under Ahasuerus of Persia?

8 Fill in the blanks to reveal the godly Roman centurion of Caesarea who summoned Peter to his house.

__ __ __ __ __ __ __ __

9 What three Hebrew men were appointed Babylonian administrators by Nebuchadnezzar?

10 What was the occupation of the Roman who had his beloved servant healed by Jesus?

11 What Jewish girl became queen of Persia?

NOTABLE WOMEN, AND SOME LESS NOTABLE (IV)

1 What New Testament woman was married to a priest named Zachariah?

2 Who begged her sister for some mandrakes, hoping they would help her bear children?

3 To whom did Jesus say, "I am the resurrection and the life"?

4 Who sat at Jesus' feet while her sister kept house?

5 What two women witnessed Jesus' tears over their dead brother?

6 What disciple's mother-in-law was healed of a fever by Jesus?

7 What wicked woman, the wife of a wicked king, brought about the death of John the Baptist?

8 How much time did cousins Mary and Elizabeth spend together during their pregnancies?

9 Who offered to bear the guilt if her scheme to deceive her aged husband was found out?

10 Who said to her husband, "Give me children, or I'll die"?

11 What woman was called a prophetess by Luke?

12 Who died in giving birth to Benjamin?

13 What clever woman hoodwinked her father-in-law out of a signet ring and bracelets?

14 Who falsely accused her Hebrew servant of trying to seduce her?

15 What woman was the mother of two of Jesus' disciples?

16 Who asked Jesus for the special water to quench her thirst forever?

17 Who called Jesus "Rabboni"?

(More Women on the next page)

Notable Women, and Some Less Notable (IV)

1 Elizabeth (Luke 1:5). 2 Rachel (Genesis 30:14). 3 Martha (John 11:24-26). 4 Mary (Luke 10:39-42). 5 Mary and Martha (John 11:32-39). 6 Peter's (Mark 1:30-31). 7 Herodias, wife of Herod (Luke 3:19). 8 Three months (Luke 1:56). 9 Rebekah (Genesis 27:13). 10 Rachel (Genesis 30:1). 11 Anna (Luke 2:36). 12 Rachel (Genesis 35:18). 13 Tamar (Genesis 38:17). 14 Potphar's wife (Genesis 39:14). 15 Salome (Mark 15:40): while this verse does not specifically say that Salome is the mother of James and John, Matthew 27:56 mentions that two Marys and the mother of James and John were watching the crucifixion, so we may assume from Matthew and Mark that the third woman, Salome, was the mother of James and John. 16 The Samaritan woman (John 4:15). 17 Mary Magdalene (John 20:16).

NOTABLE WOMEN, AND SOME LESS NOTABLE (IV)
(CONTINUED)

18 To what earthy woman did Jesus say, "God is a spirit"?

19 Which of David's wives was described as "very beautiful to look upon"?

20 What wife, seeing her husband on the verge of death, circumcised their son?

21 Who criticized her famous brother for being married to an Ethiopian woman?

22 What Old Testament woman is mentioned in the roll of the faithful in Hebrews 11?

23 What woman gave needed courage to the fainthearted Barak?

24 Who pouted when her strongman lover kept fooling her about the source of his strength?

25 Who lay down at her future husband's feet when he was asleep?

26 Which of David's wives "despised him in her heart"?

27 What wife of a sheepherder admitted that her husband was a complete fool?

28 Who killed a fatted calf and made bread for a despairing king?

29 Who was the mother of John Mark?

30 Who was the royal mother of Nathan, Shobab, and Shimea?

31 Who came to Jerusalem with a caravan of camels and loads of jewels?

32 Who ran to tell people that she had met the Christ by a well?

33 What woman set up a special apartment for the prophet Elisha?

34 What book mentions an industrious woman who plants a vineyard with her own hands?

(More Women on the next page)

Notable Women, and Some Less Notable (IV)

18 The Samaritan woman (John 4:24). **19** Bathsheba, or Bath-shua (2 Samuel 11:2). **20** Zipporah (Exodus 4:25). **21** Miriam (Numbers 12:1). **22** Rahab (Hebrews 11:31). **23** Deborah (Judges 4:8). **24** Delilah (Judges 16). **25** Ruth (3:4-9). **26** Michal (2 Samuel 6:16). **27** Abigail (1 Samuel 25:25). **28** The witch of Endor (1 Samuel 28:24). **29** Mary (Acts 12:12). **30** Bathsheba (1 Chronicles 3:5). **31** The queen of Sheba (1 Kings 10:2). **32** The Samaritan woman (John 4:29). **33** The woman of Shunem (2 Kings 4:9). **34** Proverbs (31:16).

35 Who was the angel Gabriel speaking to when he said, "Blessed art thou among women" (KJV)?

36 Where was Mary the last time she is mentioned in the New Testament?

37 Who was the first woman to tell Jesus she believed he was the Messiah?

38 What was the affliction of the woman who touched the hem of Jesus' robe?

39 To whom did Jesus say, "I was sent only to help God's lost sheep—the people of Israel"?

40 Who asked if her two sons could have places of priority in Jesus' Kingdom?

41 Who had had five husbands and was living with another man?

42 What woman accused Elijah of murdering her son, a son that Elijah then raised from the dead?

43 What woman had been healed of seven demons by Jesus?

44 How many Marys are in the New Testament?

45 Who was the first woman to go against Jesus' words "You cannot serve God and money"?

46 What woman had Tabitha as a pet name?

47 What woman had the same name as an old kingdom of Asia?

48 What daughter of Job had a 12-letter name?

49 What woman instructed the brilliant Apollos in theology?

50 Who was probably the carrier of Paul's epistle to the Romans?

(More Women on the next page)

Notable Women, and Some Less Notable (IV)

35 Mary (Luke 1:28).   **36** With the apostles in the upper room in Jerusalem (Acts 1:13-14).
37 Martha (John 11:24-27).   **38** An issue of blood (Mark 5:31).   **39** The Syro-Phoenician woman of
Canaan (Matthew 15:24).   **40** The mother of John and James (Matthew 20:21).   **41** The Samaritan
woman (John 4:18).   **42** The widow of Zarephath (1 Kings 17:18).   **43** Mary Magdalene (Mark
16:9).   **44** Six—Jesus' mother, Mary of Bethany, Mary Magdalene, Mary mother of James and Joses,
Mary mother of John Mark, and Mary of Rome.   **45** Sapphira, wife of Ananias (Acts 5).   **46** Dorcas
(Acts 9:36, 39).   **47** Lydia (Acts 16:14).   **48** Keren-happuch (Job 42:14).   **49** Priscilla (Acts 18:26).
50 Phoebe (Romans 16:1-2).

NOTABLE WOMEN, AND SOME LESS NOTABLE (IV)
(CONTINUED)

51 What pastor was the son of the devout Eunice?

52 Who was with David when Bathsheba and Nathan pleaded with him to designate Solomon as his successor?

53 Who was given by her Egyptian father as a reward to a Hebrew servant?

54 What evil woman lived in the Valley of Sorek?

The answers to the next four questions are hidden in the puzzle that follows the questions. Can you find the names?

55 Who was better to her widowed mother-in-law than any seven sons could be?

56 Who was the first woman to be ashamed of her clothing?

57 Who said, "Your father and I have been frantic, searching for you everywhere"?

58 Who was Timothy's devout grandmother?

R	O	T	E	R
D	U	N	K	S
K	Y	T	P	I
I	R	V	H	O
B	A	B	E	L
C	M	E	V	E

(More Women on the next page)

Notable Women, and Some Less Notable (IV)
51 Timothy (2 Timothy 1:5). 52 Abishag (1 Kings 1:15). 53 Asenath, wife of Joseph (Genesis 41:45). 54 Delilah (Judges 16:4). 55 Ruth (4:15). 56 Eve; actually, she was ashamed of her lack of clothing (Genesis 3:7). 57 Mary (Luke 2:48). 58 Lois (2 Timothy 1:5).

59 What wealthy woman made her living selling purple cloth?

60 What woman, wife of wicked King Amon, gave birth to the future godly king Josiah?

61 What courageous woman risked her life to keep her royal nephew alive?

62 What woman had such an influential life that Israel had 40 years of peace?

63 What Jewish-Christian woman had lived at Rome, Corinth, and Ephesus?

64 Who bore three sons and two daughters after giving up her first son to serve the Lord at Shiloh?

65 What wife of David had no children because she had criticized her husband's jubilant dancing?

66 Who married David after her stupid husband died out of fear?

67 Who was the last woman to have dinner with King Saul?

68 Who called herself Mara, a name meaning "bitter"?

69 Who was given a miraculous supply of food by the prophet Elijah?

70 What faithful woman did Elisha warn of a coming famine?

71 Who asked her royal son to surrender his father's concubine to another son?

72 Who referred to Mary as the "mother of my Lord"?

73 Who anointed Jesus' feet with precious ointment?

74 Who had her conversation with Jesus interrupted by his disciples, who criticized him for speaking with a woman?

75 Who was the first woman to see Jesus' empty tomb?

(More Women on the next page)

Notable Women, and Some Less Notable (IV)

59 Lydia (Acts 16:14). **60** Jedidah (2 Kings 22:1). **61** Jehosheba, Joash's aunt (2 Kings 11:2-3). **62** Deborah (Judges 5:31). **63** Priscilla (Acts 18:2, 18, 24-26). **64** Hannah (1 Samuel 2:21). **65** Michal (2 Samuel 6:23). **66** Abigail (1 Samuel 25:36-42). **67** The witch of Endor (1 Samuel 28:25). **68** Naomi (Ruth 1:19-21). **69** The widow of Zarephath (1 Kings 17:16). **70** The woman of Shunem (2 Kings 8:1). **71** Bathsheba (1 Kings 2:20-21). **72** Elizabeth (Luke 1:41-43). **73** Mary of Bethany (John 12:3). **74** The Samaritan woman (John 4:27). **75** Mary Magdalene (John 20:1).

NOTABLE WOMEN, AND SOME LESS NOTABLE (IV)
(CONTINUED)

76 What two tribes of Israel were descended from an Egyptian woman?

77 What pagan woman of the Gospels is traditionally identified with the Christian woman Claudia mentioned in 2 Timothy?

78 What Christian woman was the first to see the risen Christ?

79 What woman's absence made the Israelites pause in their journey to the Promised Land?

80 What woman was the first Christian convert in Europe?

81 What woman has been proposed as the author of the Epistle to the Hebrews?

82 What devout woman was described by Paul as "our sister" and "a servant of the church"?

83 What book features a dark Shulamite woman who sings to her loved one?

84 Solve the math problem below to find out how many husbands the hypothetical woman had in the riddle the Sadducees asked.

$$100 \div 50 \times 33 - 66 + 15 - 8 = \underline{}$$

85 What was the proposed punishment for the woman taken in adultery, later forgiven by Jesus?

86 Where did Paul cast demons out of a girl who was a spiritualist?

87 What was the hometown of Mary and Martha and Lazarus?

88 What beautiful woman of Israel was married to a Hittite warrior?

89 What distraught woman failed at first to recognize the resurrected Jesus?

(More Women on the next page)

Notable Women, and Some Less Notable (IV)

76 Manasseh and Ephraim, their father, Joseph, was married to Asenath of Egypt (Genesis 41:50-52). **77** Pilate's wife (Matthew 27:19). **78** Mary Magdalene (John 20:14). **79** Miriam's (Numbers 12:15). **80** Lydia (Acts 16:14). **81** Priscilla. **82** Phoebe (Romans 16:1-2). **83** The Song of Songs (Song of Solomon). **84** Seven (Mark 12:20-25). **85** Stoning (John 8:3-11). **86** Philippi (Acts 16:16). **87** Bethany (John 11:1). **88** Bathsheba, wife of Uriah (2 Samuel 11:3). **89** Mary Magdalene (John 20:14-15).

NOTABLE WOMEN, AND SOME LESS NOTABLE (IV)
(CONTINUED)

If you like crossword puzzles, complete the intersecting boxes to reveal the answers to the first five questions, then continue with the last three.

90 (1 Across) Who worked hard gleaning grain for herself and her mother-in-law?

91 (2 Down) Which of Jacob's wives was the first to bear children?

92 (3 Down) What New Testament woman holds the record for widowhood with 84 years?

93 (4 Across) What doting mother made her absentee son a new coat each year?

94 (5 Across) What Christian woman was noted for helping the poor in the early church?

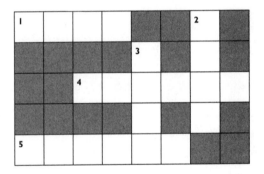

95 What book speaks of the "sons of God" taking the "daughters of men" as wives?

96 What woman is significant for keeping her own name when she married instead of taking her husband's name?

97 What book has a chorus of girls of Jerusalem as characters?

PART TWO
CRIMES AND PUNISHMENTS

ALL KINDS OF VILLAINS

1 Who plotted to have the entire Hebrew nation completely exterminated?

2 Who committed the first murder?

3 Who acknowledged the innocence of Jesus but allowed him to be crucified anyway?

4 Spell out the name of the ruler who had John the Baptist beheaded. During Jesus' trial, Pontius Pilate sent him to this same ruler.

— — — — —

— — — — — — —

5 What king was constantly making oaths of love and loyalty to David while frequently trying to kill him?

6 What evil king of Israel was led into even more wickedness by his beautiful and scheming wife?

7 Who ordered the killing of infant boys in Bethlehem?

8 What treacherous son led a revolt against his father, the king of Israel?

9 Who made numerous attempts to swindle Jacob, who ultimately prospered?

10 What two traitorous army captains murdered their king as a favor to David and were then executed by David for treachery?

THIEVING TYPES

1 Who stole idols from her father?
2 What robber was released from prison at the time of the Passover?
3 According to Malachi, what were the people of Judah stealing from God?
4 Unscramble the letters to reveal (in three words) what Joseph accused his brother Benjamin of stealing.

HIPRUSELVISC

— — —   — — — — — —
— — —

5 Which epistles say that the Day of the Lord will come like a thief?
6 What disciple stole from the treasury?
7 In the time of the judges, what man stole 1,100 pieces of silver from his own mother?
8 Who was stoned for stealing booty during the battle for Ai?
9 Unscramble the letters to reveal the prophet who condemned people who piled up stolen goods.

KAKAHUKB

— — — — — — — —

PLAYING WITH FIRE

1 What group of converts burned their books of magic?

2 Who burned Joab's barley field just to get his attention?

3 Who burned the Philistines' grain by tying torches to the tails of foxes?

4 What king of Babylon burned Jerusalem?

5 What Canaanite city was burned down by the men of Dan?

6 What Israelite had his goods burned after he had been stoned to death?

7 What nation burned David's city of Ziklag?

8 What king committed suicide by burning down his palace with himself inside?

9 What judge killed about a thousand people when he burned down the tower of Shechem?

10 What Israelite city was burned up by Pharaoh?

11 What tribe of Israel sacked Jerusalem and burned it?

12 In the days of the judges, what tribe had its cities burned by the other tribes?

PEOPLE IN EXILE

1 What apostle was exiled to Patmos?

2 How many years were the Israelites in Egypt?

3 What prophet was exiled in Egypt with other people from Judah?

4 What was the first instance of exile in the Bible?

5 Who was brought down to Egypt and sold to a man named Potiphar?

6 Who chose to go into exile rather than constantly quarrel with his brother?

7 Who was exiled from the rest of the world?

8 Whom did Abraham banish to the desert?

9 Who stayed in Egypt until Herod died?

10 Who carried the people of Jerusalem off to Babylon?

11 What future king of Israel fled from Solomon and hid in Egypt?

12 What nation carried Israel into exile?

13 Who was in exile three years after killing his brother Amnon?

14 What land did Moses flee to when he left Egypt?

15 Who was exiled to the land of Nod?

16 What judge fled from his kin and lived in the land of Tob?

17 Christians were scattered throughout Judea and Samaria because of a persecution that began after whose death?

(More Exiles on the next page)

People in Exile

1 John (Revelation 1:9). 2 430 years (Exodus 12:40). 3 Jeremiah (43:5-7). 4 God drove Adam and Eve out of the Garden (Genesis 3:24). 5 Joseph (Genesis 39:1). 6 Jacob (Genesis 27:41-45). 7 Noah and his family, since everyone else died (Genesis 7:23). 8 Hagar and Ishmael (Genesis 21:14). 9 Joseph, Mary, and Jesus (Matthew 2:13-15). 10 Nebuchadnezzar (2 Kings 24:14-15). 11 Jeroboam (1 Kings 11:40). 12 Assyria (2 Kings 17:6). 13 Absalom (2 Samuel 13:37-38). 14 Midian (Exodus 2:15). 15 Cain (Genesis 4:13-16). 16 Jephthah (Judges 11:3). 17 Stephen's (Acts 8:1).

18 What exiled king of Judah became a friend of the king of Babylon?

19 Who predicted the Babylonian exile to Hezekiah?

20 Who was king in Israel when the Assyrians deported the people?

21 What king of Judah was temporarily exiled in Assyria, where he repented of his evil ways?

22 Who was king when Jerusalem fell to the Babylonians?

23 What prophet went into exile in Babylon?

24 Who was appointed governor of Judah after the people went into exile?

25 When the Assyrians deported the people of Israel, how many of the 12 original tribes were left?

26 What blind king died in exile in Babylon?

27 What king issued an edict ending the exile of the Jews?

28 What Assyrian king carried the people of Israel into exile?

29 What interpreter of dreams was in exile in Babylon?

30 What prophet warned the wicked priest Amaziah that Israel would go into exile?

31 Which epistles are addressed to God's people in exile?

32 Which psalm is a lament of the exiles in Babylon?

People in Exile

18 Jehoiachin (2 Kings 25:27-30). 19 Isaiah (2 Kings 20:12-19). 20 Pekah (2 Kings 15:29).
21 Manasseh (2 Chronicles 33:11-13). 22 Zedekiah (2 Chronicles 36:11-20). 23 Ezekiel (1:1-2).
24 Gedaliah (2 Kings 25:22). 25 One—Judah (2 Kings 17:18). 26 Zedekiah (Jeremiah 52:11).
27 Cyrus of Persia (2 Chronicles 36:22-23). 28 Tiglath-pileser (2 Kings 15:29). 29 Daniel (1:1-6).
30 Amos (7:17). 31 James and 1 Peter. 32 Psalm 137.

A COLLECTION OF TRAITORS

1 What infamous Philistine woman tricked Samson into revealing the secret of his strength?

2 Hazael of Syria usurped the throne after he murdered the king, Ben-hadad. What unusual method did he use for the murder?

3 When Pekah the usurper reigned in Israel, who murdered him and took over the throne?

4 What fiery chariot driver slew the king of Israel and the king of Judah and later had Jezebel murdered, after which he reigned as king in Israel?

5 Find the letters that spell two synonyms for the word "traitor," cross them out, and you will see the name of David's son who led a major revolt against his father.

ATURBNCSOAATLSOPMY

6 What traitor murdered Elah, king of Israel, and then later, after a seven-day reign, committed suicide?

7 Who murdered Shallum and took his place on the throne of Israel?

8 When Judas appeared in Gethsemane to betray Jesus, he was accompanied by a crowd. What were the people of the crowd carrying?

A Collection of Traitors:
1 Delilah (Judges 16). 2 He took a thick cloth, dipped it in water, and smothered the king (2 Kings 8:15). 3 Hoshea (2 Kings 15:30). 4 Jehu (2 Kings 9). 5 Absalom (2 Samuel 15); the synonyms are turncoat and spy. 6 Zimri (1 Kings 16:8-10). 7 Menahem (2 Kings 15:14). 8 Swords and clubs (Mark 14:43).

A GALLERY OF PRISONERS

1 Who was put in prison as a political enemy of the Philistines?

2 What king of Israel was imprisoned for defying Assyrian authority?

3 What kinsman of Jesus was imprisoned for criticizing King Herod's marriage to Herodias?

4 What famous dreamer was imprisoned after being accused of trying to seduce Potiphar's wife?

5 Whose brothers were imprisoned after being falsely accused of being spies in Egypt?

6 Who was imprisoned for prophesying the destruction of the kingdom of Judah?

7 What king of Judah was blinded and imprisoned because he defied Babylonian authority?

8 Who prophesied doom for King Asa and was put in prison?

9 What king of Judah was sent into exile in Babylon and put in prison but was later released and treated as a friend of the king of Babylon?

10 Who prophesied doom and defeat for King Ahab and was put in prison for his harsh words?

11 What two apostles were put into prison in Jerusalem for preaching the gospel?

12 Who remained in the prison at Philippi even after an earthquake opened the prison doors?

A Gallery of Prisoners
1 Samson (Judges 16:24). 2 Hoshea (2 Kings 17:4). 3 John the Baptist (Matthew 14:3-5). 4 Joseph (Genesis 39:7-19). 5 Joseph's (Genesis 42). 6 Jeremiah (37–38). 7 Zedekiah (2 Kings 25:6-7). 8 Hanani (2 Chronicles 16:10). 9 Jehoiachin (2 Kings 24:12, 27-30). 10 Micaiah (1 Kings 22:26-27). 11 Peter and John (Acts 4:3). 12 Paul and Silas (Acts 16:16-24).

COURTS, COUNCILS, AND TRIALS

1 When Jesus was brought before the council, how many false witnesses were brought in to accuse him?

2 Who suggested to Moses that he appoint judges so that he would not have to judge all cases himself?

3 According to the Law, how many witnesses are necessary before a man could be tried and put to death?

4 What cynical king asked Jesus questions and then allowed him to be mocked?

5 According to Jesus, when his followers were dragged into court, they would not need to worry about their defense, for someone else would speak through them. Who?

6 What stinging accusation of the Jews finally convinced Pilate to allow Jesus to be executed?

7 What person's presence at the trial of Peter and John kept the rulers and priests from punishing the two apostles?

8 Find the name of a famous trial lawyer in the line of letters, then cross them out to reveal the name of the Roman official who gave Paul a centurion as a guard and told the centurion to allow Paul freedom to see whomever he wished.

CLAFRENECELDARIROWX

9 In what city were Paul and Silas tried, flogged, and jailed after they cast a demon out of a fortune-teller?

10 When Paul was mobbed in the Temple, who rescued him?

11 When Stephen was brought to trial, what was the charge laid against him?

12 What three rulers, hearing Paul defend himself in Caesarea, agreed that he deserved no punishment?

Courts, Councils, and Trials

1 Two (Matthew 26:57-66). 2 His father-in-law, Jethro (Exodus 18). 3 At least two (Deuteronomy 17:6). 4 Herod (Luke 23:1-11). 5 The Spirit (Matthew 10:16-20). 6 They claimed that Pilate was no friend of Caesar (John 19:12). 7 The lame man Peter and John had healed (Acts 4:14). 8 Felix (Acts 24:23); Clarence Darrow is the famous lawyer. 9 Philippi (Acts 16:16-22). 10 The chief Roman captain (Acts 22:30; 23:1-10). 11 That he had taught that Jesus had aimed to change the customs taught by Moses (Acts 6:11-14). 12 Festus, Agrippa, and Bernice (Acts 25:23–26:32).

LIES AND MORE LIES

1 Who was the first person to lie to God about a murder?

2 Who was probably the most deceptive father-in-law in the Bible?

3 What doting mother lied to procure a blessing for her favorite son?

4 Who was the only animal that lied?

5 What frustrated Egyptian wife claimed her Hebrew servant tried to seduce her?

6 What lying prophet put Jeremiah in the stocks and was later told that he and his whole household would die in exile?

7 Who was turned into a leper for lying to the prophet Elisha?

8 Fill in the blanks to reveal the owner of a vineyard who was executed by Ahab because lying witnesses claimed he had blasphemed against God and the king.

— — — — —

9 What king of Israel claimed to be a devout worshiper of Baal in order to gather together Baal-worshipers and butcher them?

10 Who died after lying to Peter about the value of the possessions they had sold?

11 What godly prophet lied to Ahab about the outcome of a battle?

12 Who is the father of lies?

13 What two men—father and son—claimed at different times that their wives were actually their sisters?

Lies and More Lies
1 Cain (Genesis 4:8-9). 2 Laban, father-in-law of Jacob (Genesis 29). 3 Rebekah, mother of Jacob and Esau (Genesis 27). 4 The serpent (Genesis 3:1-5). 5 The wife of Potiphar, Joseph's master (Genesis 39). 6 Pashhur (Jeremiah 20:1-3, 6). 7 His servant, Gehazi (2 Kings 5:20-27). 8 Naboth (1 Kings 21). 9 Jehu (2 Kings 10). 10 Ananias and Sapphira (Acts 5:1-9). 11 Micaiah (1 Kings 22). 12 The devil (John 8:44). 13 Abraham (Genesis 12:11-13) and Isaac (Genesis 26:6-7).

VIOLENT PEOPLE AND THINGS

1 What oversized warrior had bronze armor weighing over 125 pounds?

2 What Roman official in Jerusalem bowed to the wishes of an uncontrollable mob?

3 In what city in Greece did a group of Jews whip up a company of thugs in an anti-Paul riot?

4 Who carried five smooth stones as his weapons?

5 What did Ehud use to kill fat King Eglon of Moab?

6 Who killed six hundred Philistines with an ox goad?

7 What did Jael use to murder Sisera?

8 What rebel was killed by three darts, shot into his heart by Joab?

9 What prophet was commanded to make a model of Jerusalem and set battering rams against it?

10 Who threw a javelin at David?

11 In what city was Jesus almost killed by an angry mob?

12 What city had a riot on behalf of the goddess Artemis?

13 What king fortified Jerusalem with catapults for throwing stones?

14 What apostle was almost done in by 40 men waiting to ambush him at Jerusalem?

15 Who drew the army of Ai out of the city while another group ambushed the city and destroyed it?

16 What paranoid king ordered the execution of the infants in Bethlehem?

17 Who killed Abner?

(More Violence on the next page)

Violent People and Things

1 Goliath (1 Samuel 17:4-6). 2 Pilate (Matthew 27:23-24). 3 Thessalonica (Acts 17:5). 4 David (1 Samuel 17:40). 5 A two-edged dagger (Judges 3:16-21). 6 Shamgar (Judges 3:31). 7 A tent peg through his temple (Judges 4:21). 8 Absalom (2 Samuel 18:14). 9 Ezekiel (19:34). 10 Saul (1 Samuel 18:11). 11 Nazareth (Luke 4:29). 12 Ephesus (Acts 19:28-29). 13 Uzziah (2 Chronicles 26:14-15). 14 Paul (Acts 23:21-23). 15 Joshua (8:12-22). 16 Herod (Matthew 2:16). 17 Joab (2 Samuel 3:26).

CRIMES AND PUNISHMENTS   77

VIOLENT PEOPLE AND THINGS (CONTINUED)

18 What evil king of Judah was killed by his servants?

19 What Christian witness was killed by the people of Pergamum?

20 Who killed Ben-hadad with a wet cloth?

21 What two women brought about the execution of John the Baptist?

22 What king of Israel had the whole dynasty of Ahab murdered?

23 What former member of the Egyptian court killed an Egyptian official?

24 Whom did Rechab and Baanah murder to get in good with David?

25 What king of Assyria was murdered at worship by his two sons?

26 What good king of Judah was murdered by his court officials?

27 What saintly deacon was murdered by the Jewish elders for his testimony?

(More Violence on the next page)

EXTRA CREDIT

What U.S. president cut out all the supernatural references for his version of the Gospels?

Thomas Jefferson

Violent People and Things

18 Amon (2 Kings 21:23). **19** Antipas (Revelation 2:13). **20** Hazael (2 Kings 8:7, 15). **21** Herodias and her daughter (Mark 6:25, 27). **22** Jehu (2 Kings 9). **23** Moses (Exodus 2:12). **24** Ishbosheth (2 Samuel 4:6). **25** Sennacherib (2 Kings 19:37). **26** Joash (2 Kings 12:20-21). **27** Stephen (Acts 7:58-59).

VIOLENT PEOPLE AND THINGS (CONTINUED)

28 Who had one of his army men killed in order to cover up an adulterous affair?

29 Who killed Hamor and Shechem for offending their sister Dinah?

30 What Old Testament figure boasted to his two wives that he had killed a young man?

31 What son of Abraham was supposed to have been against everyone, and everyone against him?

32 Who caused a riot when people thought he had taken a Gentile into the Temple?

33 What tribe was ambushed at Gibeah by the other tribes of Israel?

34 In the time of the judges, what did the Levite do when his concubine had been savagely abused by the men of Gibeah?

35 Who killed Amasa after holding his beard and kissing him?

36 What rebel killed Gedaliah, the governor of Judah, after the fall of Judah to the Babylonians?

37 Where did Cain kill Abel?

38 What king was critically wounded by Philistine arrows?

39 Who slew a thousand men with the jawbone of an ass?

40 Who carried a staff that was as big as a weaver's beam?

41 Who pelted King David with stones while telling him what a violent king he was?

Violent People

28 David (2 Samuel 12:9). 29 Levi and Simeon (Genesis 34:26). 30 Lamech (Genesis 4:23). 31 Ishmael (Genesis 16:12). 32 Paul (Acts 21:30-35). 33 Benjamin (Judges 20:29-33). 34 He cut her into 12 pieces and sent to each tribe of Israel (Judges 19). 35 Joab (2 Samuel 20:9-10). 36 Ishmael (2 Kings 25:25). 37 Out in the fields (Genesis 4:8). 38 Saul (1 Samuel 31:3). 39 Samson (Judges 15:15). 40 Goliath (1 Samuel 17:7). 41 Shimei (2 Samuel 16:5-8).

THE IMPERSONATORS

1 What king disguised himself in order to consult with a sorceress?

2 Who fooled Jacob by posing as her sister?

3 Who pretended to be a madman in order to escape from King Achish?

4 Who disguised himself while going to battle against the forces of Pharaoh Neco of Egypt?

5 Who posed as her husband's sister while in Egypt?

6 What king's wife disguised herself in order to consult the prophet Ahijah?

7 What smooth-skinned man disguised himself so well that he passed himself off as his hairy brother?

8 Who persuaded the clever woman of Tekoa to pretend to be a widow in order to play on David's sympathy?

9 Who posed as Isaac's sister?

10 From the choices listed, who fooled Joshua by pretending to be ambassadors from a distant country?

    A The Philistines   **B** The Gibeonites   **c** The Amalekites

11 What evil king of Israel disguised himself while going against the armies of Syria?

12 Who sent spies to act as followers of Jesus and to try to trap him?

13 What king was confronted by a prophet posing as a wounded soldier?

14 According to Paul, who masquerades as an angel of light?

TAXES, EXTORTION, AND BRIBES

1 What noble prophet's sons were notorious for taking bribes?
2 What tax collector climbed a tree to see Jesus?
3 Fill in the blanks to reveal who kept Paul in prison, hoping Paul would try to bribe him for release.

— — — — —

4 Who advised that the Egyptians be taxed 20 percent of their produce in order to prepare for famine?
5 Who taxed the Israelites in order to pay off Pul, the king of Assyria?
6 Whom did Jesus send fishing in order to get money for taxes?
7 Who warned the people of Israel that having a king would mean having taxation?
8 What figure did Jesus use as a contrast to the humble tax collector?
9 Fill in the blanks to reveal what the hungry Esau gave up to Jacob in exchange for food.

— — —

— — — — — — — —

10 What was Judas given to betray Jesus?

(More Taxes on the next page)

TAXES, EXTORTION, AND BRIBES (CONTINUED)

11 By what other name was the tax collector Matthew known?

12 What did John the Baptist tell the tax collectors who came to him for baptism?

13 Who offered Delilah silver if she could find out the secret of Samson's strength?

14 Who bribed the guards at Jesus' tomb to say that the disciples had stolen the body?

15 According to the law, how much tax did all adult Israelites have to pay when the census was taken?

16 What ruler imposed tribute in Jesus' day?

17 Who taxed his subjects in order to pay tribute to Pharaoh Neco of Egypt?

18 What king is remembered as placing a "heavy yoke" of taxation on Israel?

19 What king of Israel paid tribute money to King Shalmaneser of Assyria?

20 Who laid a tax on the whole Persian Empire?

21 To what king of Judah did the Philistines bring tribute?

22 What Persian king exempted the priests and Levites from paying taxes?

23 What empire's taxation led to Jesus being born in Bethlehem?

24 Whose wife was threatened with having her family's house burned down unless she would find the answer to a riddle?

25 Who prepared a feast and invited Jesus, along with a group of tax collectors?

Taxes, Extortion, and Bribes

11 Levi (Luke 5:29-32). 12 To collect no more than was legal (Luke 3:12-13). 13 The lords of the Philistines (Judges 16:5). 14 The chief priests (Matthew 28:11-15). 15 A half shekel each (Exodus 30:12-16). 16 Caesar (Matthew 22:17-22). 17 Jehoiakim (2 Kings 23:33-35). 18 Solomon (1 Kings 12:1-14). 19 Hoshea (2 Kings 17:3-4). 20 King Ahasuerus (Esther 10:1). 21 Jehoshaphat (2 Chronicles 17:11). 22 Artaxerxes (Ezra 7:24). 23 Rome (Luke 2:1-7). 24 Samson's (Judges 14:15). 25 Levi (or Matthew) (Luke 5:29-32).

PART THREE
MILITARY MATTERS

THEY SPIED

1 Who sent spies to watch Jesus?

2 Who sent two spies to Jericho?

3 Who sent spies to see if Saul had followed him?

4 What tribe sent out five spies to check out its land?

5 What counselor of Absalom was actually a spy for David?

6 Solve the math problem below and find out how many spies Moses sent into Canaan.

$$4 \times 4 - 10 + 14 - 8 = \underline{\quad}$$

7 What epistle warns against people sent in to "spy out our liberty"?

8 What rebel sent his spies throughout Israel, telling them to wait till they heard the sound of the trumpet?

9 What Canaanite city did spies find the entrance of?

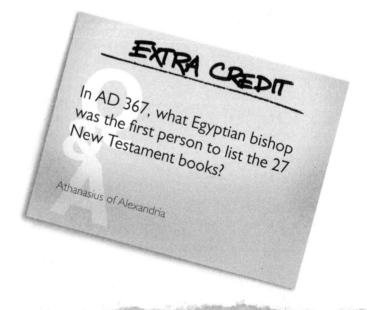

EXTRA CREDIT

In AD 367, what Egyptian bishop was the first person to list the 27 New Testament books?

Athanasius of Alexandria

They Spied

1 The chief priests and scribes (Luke 20:20). 2 Joshua (2:1). 3 David (1 Samuel 26:3-4). 4 Dan (Judges 18:2-28). 5 Hushai (2 Samuel 15:32-37). 6 Twelve—one from each tribe (Numbers 13:1-16). 7 Galatians (2:4). 8 Absalom (2 Samuel 15:10). 9 Bethel (Judges 1:23-25).

84   THE GOOD BOOK BIBLE TRIVIA

MILITARY MEN

1 Who was sleeping between two soldiers when he was miraculously delivered?

2 What captain of the palace guard did Joseph serve under?

3 What loyal Israelite soldier gave Moses a positive report about the land of Canaan?

4 What Hittite soldier was put on the front lines of battle so David could take his wife?

5 Which Gospel is the only one to mention the Roman soldiers piercing Jesus' body with a spear?

6 What Gittite soldier supported David during the rebellion of Absalom?

7 What leper was commander of the Syrian troops?

8 What soldier led a revolt against King Elah, made himself king, and then committed suicide after a seven-day reign?

9 From the choices listed, what Roman soldier treated Paul kindly on his voyage to Rome?

   A Cornelius   B Julius   C Aristarchus   D Publius

10 What foreign king had Nebuzaradan as commander of his troops?

11 Who was commander of the rebel army when Absalom rebelled against David?

12 What Roman soldier was led to Christ by Peter?

(More Soldiers on the next page)

Military Men
1 Peter (Acts 12:6). 2 Potiphar (Genesis 39:1). 3 Caleb (Joshua 14:6-13). 4 Uriah (2 Samuel 11:3). 5 John (19:34). 6 Ittai (2 Samuel 15:19). 7 Naaman (2 Kings 5:1). 8 Zimri (1 Kings 16:9-20). 9 B: Julius (Acts 27:1-3). 10 Nebuchadnezzar (2 Kings 25:8). 11 Amasa (2 Samuel 17:25). 12 Cornelius (Acts 10:1).

13 Which Gospel does not mention the Roman soldier at Jesus' crucifixion who realized that Jesus was the son of God?

14 Where was Jesus when a Roman officer asked him to heal a beloved servant?

15 Who had a nephew that informed the Roman soldiers of a plot to kill a prisoner?

16 Unscramble the letters to spell out the name of the military commander who sent Paul under guard from Jerusalem to Caesarea.

UDALISUC SYLSIA

— — — — — — —

— — — — — —

17 What soldier was in charge of David's bodyguard?

18 Where was Paul when a Roman soldier stopped him from being murdered by an angry mob?

19 What cousin of Saul was commander of the king's troops?

20 What Canaanite commander was murdered by Jael?

21 Who was commander of the Israelites under Moses?

22 Who was the commander of Abimelech's army?

23 What was the title of the Assyrian field commander who tried to intimidate King Hezekiah by speaking propaganda to the people of Jerusalem?

MILITARY MEN (CONTINUED)

24 What judge from Gilead was called to be a commander against the Ammonites?

25 What irate soldier falsely accused Jeremiah of deserting to the Babylonians and arrested him?

26 What Philistine soldier was slain by a boy carrying a bag of stones?

27 Who was commander of Solomon's army?

28 Who was commander of David's army?

29 What commander led a successful revolt against the ill-fated King Zimri?

30 What army commander was anointed by a prophet and told that he was to stamp out Ahab's dynasty?

31 Who met the commander of the Lord's army?

32 Who was commander of the troops during the rebuilding of the walls of Jerusalem?

33 What Babylonian soldier was ordered to execute Daniel and his friends?

34 What soldier, David's oldest brother, picked on David for coming to the battle lines?

35 What brother of Joab was famous for having killed 300 enemy soldiers in battle?

36 Who told Roman soldiers to be content with their pay and to avoid taking money by force?

Military Men

24 Jephthah (Judges 11:6). **25** Irijah (Jeremiah 37:13). **26** Goliath (1 Samuel 17:48-54). **27** Benaiah (1 Kings 4:4). **28** Joab (2 Samuel 8:16). **29** Omri (1 Kings 16:16). **30** Jehu (2 Kings 9:1-11). **31** Joshua (5:14). **32** Hananiah (Nehemiah 7:2). **33** Arioch (Daniel 2:14). **34** Eliab (1 Samuel 17:28). **35** Abishai (1 Chronicles 11:20). **36** John the Baptist (Luke 3:14).

BATTLES WON SUPERNATURALLY

1 What prophet's word caused the Syrian soldiers to be struck blind?

2 What nation's army was destroyed in the Red Sea?

3 What nation was Israel fighting when Moses' arms, held aloft, caused Israel to win?

4 From the choices listed, what weather phenomenon did the Lord use to defeat the Amorites when Joshua and his men were fighting them?

    A Large Hailstones   B Earthquake   c Sandstorm

    D Drought

5 What army was defeated when an angel of the Lord struck down 185,000 soldiers?

6 When Samuel was offering a sacrifice, what did the Lord do to rattle the Philistines?

7 What occurred when Jonathan and his armor-bearer attacked the Philistines?

8 What made the Syrians flee, thinking the Israelites had joined forces with Egyptians and Hittites?

9 Who were the Judeans fighting when God helped them slaughter a half million soldiers?

10 What king led the people in singing and praising God, leading God to destroy the armies of the Ammonites, Moabites, and Edomites?

PART FOUR
RELIGIOUS MATTERS

A BOOK OF COVENANTS

1   The covenant after the Flood was made not only between God and man but also between God and the animals and the earth. What did God give as the sign of this covenant?

2   In God's covenant with Abraham, what ceremonial rite was made mandatory for all Abraham's male descendants?

3   In the covenant between God and Israel at Sinai, the agreement was broken almost immediately afterward by the Israelites. What did they do that was an infringement of the covenant?

4   Fill in the blanks to reveal where the new covenant between God and man would be written, according to Jeremiah's vision.

    __ __   __ __ __ ,
    __ __ __ __ __

5   In the New Testament, a new covenant is instituted by Jesus. What does he use to symbolize this new covenant?

A Book of Covenants

1 A rainbow (Genesis 9:13)   2 Circumcision (Genesis 17:9-14).   3 They built and worshiped a graven image, the golden calf (Exodus 32).   4 On men's hearts (Jeremiah 31:33).   5 Wine, which symbolizes the blood of sacrifice (Mark 14:24).

90   THE GOOD BOOK BIBLE TRIVIA

THE ANOINTED ONES

1 Who anointed a stone and dedicated it to God?

2 What holy man was anointed by an immoral woman?

3 What substance was usually used for anointing in Israel?

4 Who, according to James, should anoint the sick believer with oil?

5 Whom did Moses anoint with the blood of a ram?

6 What New Testament word means "anointed"?

7 What revered judge anointed Saul?

8 What priest anointed Solomon king?

9 Who was anointed by the Holy Spirit?

10 What Persian king was considered to be God's anointed one?

11 What Old Testament word means "anointed"?

12 What apostle told the early Christians that all believers were anointed by the Holy Spirit?

13 Who anointed the Tabernacle with oil?

14 What leader anointed David as king?

15 What person was, prior to his fall, anointed by God?

16 Where did the men of Judah gather to anoint David as their king?

HOUSES OF WORSHIP

1 What gruesome object did the Philistines fasten in the temple of Dagon?

2 Which goddess had a notorious temple at Ephesus?

3 Why did John not see a temple in the new Jerusalem?

4 Whose temple did Abimelech burn while the people of Shechem were hiding inside?

5 From the choices listed, who received a vision of the Jerusalem Temple while he was in exile in Babylon?

   A Daniel   **B** Nehemiah   **c** Ezekiel   **D** Isaiah

6 According to Paul, who is called to be the temple of God?

7 What Assyrian emperor was assassinated by his sons while he was worshiping in his pagan temple?

8 Who was told in a vision to measure the Temple in Jerusalem?

9 Who carried away furnishings from the Jerusalem Temple and put them in the temple at Babylon?

10 What was Jesus talking about when he spoke of destroying the temple and raising it up in three days?

(More Houses of Worship on the next page)

Houses of Worship

1 Saul's head (1 Chronicles 10:10).   2 Diana (or Artemis) (Acts 19:27-28).   3 God and the Lamb are the temple (Revelation 21:22).   4 The temple of the god Berith (Judges 9:46-49).   5 C: Ezekiel (40-42).   6 All believers (1 Corinthians 6:19).   7 Sennacherib (2 Kings 19:37).   8 John (Revelation 11:1-2).   9 Nebuchadnezzar (2 Chronicles 36:7).   10 His body (John 2:19-21).

92   THE GOOD BOOK BIBLE TRIVIA

11 What holy object was taken by the Philistines into the temple of Dagon, causing Dagon's image to fall down?

12 Who built the first Temple in Jerusalem?

13 Who built a temple for Baal in Samaria?

14 Fill in the blanks to reveal where the Philistines carried Saul's armor after he died.

THE TEMPLE OF

— — — — — — — — —

15 Who asked Elisha's forgiveness for worshiping in the temple of the god Rimmon?

16 What king issued an order allowing the Jews to rebuild the Temple in Jerusalem?

17 Fill in the blanks to reveal who was taken to the highest point of the Jerusalem Temple.

— — — — —

18 What king tricked the followers of Baal by gathering them in Baal's temple and then slaughtering them?

19 Who had an Assyrian-style altar made for the Jerusalem Temple?

20 Whom did Solomon hire to take charge of building the Temple?

Houses of Worship

11 The Ark of God or the Ark of the Covenant (1 Samuel 5:2-4). 12 Solomon (1 Kings 6).
13 Ahab (1 Kings 16:32). 14 The temple of Ashtoreth (1 Samuel 31:10). 15 Naaman the Syrian
(2 Kings 5:18). 16 Darius (Ezra 6:1-12). 17 Jesus (Matthew 4:5). 18 Jehu of Israel (2 Kings
10:18-27). 19 King Ahaz (2 Kings 16:10-17). 20 Huram of Tyre (1 Kings 7:13-14).

HORNS OF THE ALTAR

1 What book of the Bible mentions a talking altar?

2 Who almost sacrificed his much-loved son on an altar but was stopped by an angel?

3 What kind of stone was, according to the law, not supposed to be used in making an altar?

4 What was the altar in the Tabernacle made of? What was that material covered with?

The answers to the next four questions are hidden in the puzzle that follows the questions. Can you find the names?

5 Who built the first altar?

6 What military leader was killed while holding on to the horns of the altar?

7 What king of Judah tore down Jeroboam's altar at Bethel and pounded the stones into dust?

8 Who built an altar and called it "The LORD is my banner"?

C	W	J	B	L
U	N	O	A	H
S	E	S	O	M
A	X	I	J	K
D	R	A	T	N
Y	E	H	I	S

(More Horns on the next page)

Horns of the Altar
1 Revelation (16:7). 2 Abraham (Genesis 22:9). 3 Cut stones (Exodus 20:25). 4 Acacia wood covered with bronze (Exodus 27:1). 5 Noah (Genesis 8:20). 6 Joab (1 Kings 2:28-34). 7 Josiah (2 Kings 23:15). 8 Moses (Exodus 17:15).

94 THE GOOD BOOK BIBLE TRIVIA

9 Which of the 12 tribes caused civil war when they built a magnificent altar on the banks of the Jordan?

10 What judge built an altar and called it "The LORD is peace"?

11 What king of Israel built a Baal altar to please his pagan wife?

12 What judge's parents saw an angel going up to heaven in the flames on the altar?

13 What judge and prophet built an altar to the Lord at Ramah?

14 What king was told to build an altar in a threshing place?

15 What rebellious son of David sought refuge from Solomon by holding on to the horns of the altar?

16 Who took bones out of tombs and burned them on an altar to defile it?

17 Who had a vision of the Lord standing beside the altar?

18 What king of Israel changed the religious institutions of the country by building an altar at Bethel?

19 What good king's birth was foretold hundreds of years before the fact by a prophet standing before the altar at Bethel?

20 What happened to Jeroboam's altar when he ordered his men to seize a prophet in front of it?

21 What leader was told to tear down his father's altar to Baal?

22 What god's priests danced around the altar while they cut themselves with knives and daggers?

23 What prophet triumphed when God consumed the offering on the altar and shamed the prophets of Baal?

24 What priest of Judah placed a money box near the Temple's altar?

(More Horns on the next page)

Horns of the Altar

9 Reuben, Gad, and part of Manasseh (Joshua 22:1). **10** Gideon (Judges 6:24). **11** Ahab (1 Kings 16:32). **12** Samson's (Judges 13:20). **13** Samuel (1 Samuel 7:17). **14** David (2 Samuel 24:18). **15** Adonijah (1 Kings 1:50). **16** Josiah (2 Kings 23:16). **17** Amos (9:1). **18** Jeroboam (1 Kings 12:32). **19** Josiah's (1 Kings 13:2). **20** It fell apart and the ashes scattered (1 Kings 13:5). **21** Gideon (Judges 6:25). **22** Baal's (1 Kings 18:26-29). **23** Elijah (1 Kings 18). **24** Jehoiada (2 Kings 12:9).

25 Who built an altar and named it for El, the God of Israel?

26 What evil king of Judah built an altar modeled on the altars of Syria?

27 Who rebuilt the Jerusalem altar when the exiles returned to Israel?

28 Who had his lips touched by a coal from the altar in the Temple?

29 What prophet had a vision of an idol near the altar of God?

30 What prophet foresaw the destruction of the altars of Bethel?

31 Who constructed the first altar covered with gold?

32 What prophet spoke of the Jews weeping and wailing in front of the altar because God would not accept their offerings?

33 What patriarch built an altar after he arrived in Canaan for the first time?

34 What priest saw an angel standing beside the incense altar?

35 Where did Paul see an altar inscribed "To an Unknown God"?

36 Who had a vision of the souls of the martyrs underneath the altar?

37 Who told people to make peace with their brothers before they made a sacrifice on the altar?

38 In what book does the Lord tell Moses to tear down all the pagan altars he finds?

39 What priest led a movement in which the people tore down the Baal altars and killed Mattan, the priest of Baal?

40 What wicked king of Judah built altars for the worship of Baal and the stars?

Horns of the Altar
25 Jacob (Genesis 33:20). 26 Ahaz (2 Kings 16:10). 27 The priest Joshua (Ezra 3:2). 28 Isaiah (6:6).
29 Ezekiel (8:5). 30 Amos (3:14). 31 Solomon (1 Kings 6:20). 32 Malachi (2:13). 33 Abraham
(Genesis 12:7). 34 Zacharias (Luke 1:11). 35 Athens (Acts 17:23). 36 John (Revelation 6:9).
37 Jesus (Matthew 5:24). 38 Exodus (34:13). 39 Jehoiada (2 Kings 11:18). 40 Manasseh
(2 Kings 21:3-5).

A BEVY OF PRIESTS

1 What priest is mentioned as having no mother or father?

2 What Hebrew married the daughter of an Egyptian priest?

3 What was the penalty in Israel for disobeying a priest?

4 What priest was made mute because he did not believe the prophecy given by an angel?

5 What oil was supposed to be used to anoint Israel's priests?

6 Who made the first Temple piggy bank, placed near the altar?

7 What righteous king fired all the priests that had been appointed to serve pagan gods?

8 What are the only books of the Bible named after priests?

9 What kind of head covering did the priest wear?

10 What book mentions the priest of Israel more than any other?

11 Which of Aaron's sons were killed because they offered "strange fire" to the Lord?

12 What priest was the first head of the Levites?

13 What priest was the "king of peace"?

14 What priest of Midian taught Moses how to administer justice among the Hebrews?

15 What priest in the Old Testament was also a king?

16 Who was the priest during Joshua's conquest of Canaan?

17 What priest had the boy Jehoash proclaimed king, causing the death of the wicked Queen Athaliah?

18 What priest scolded a distressed woman because he thought she had been drinking at the Tabernacle?

19 What was on the 12 stones in the high priest's breastplate?

(More Priests on the next page)

A Bevy of Priests

1 Melchizedek (Hebrews 7:3).   **2** Joseph (Genesis 41:45).   **3** Death (Deuteronomy 17:12).
4 Zacharias (Luke 1:20).   **5** Olive oil (Exodus 30:24).   **6** Jehoiada (2 Kings 12:9).   **7** Josiah (2 Kings 23:5).   **8** Ezra and Ezekiel.   **9** A turban (Exodus 28:39).   **10** Leviticus.   **11** Nadab and Abihu (Numbers 3:4).   **12** Eleazar, Aaron's son (Numbers 3:32).   **13** Melchizedek (Hebrews 7:2).
14 Jethro, also called Reuel (Exodus 18:13-27).   **15** Melchizedek (Genesis 14:18).   **16** Eleazar (Joshua 17:4).   **17** Jehoiada (2 Kings 11:9-16).   **18** Eli, who scolded Hannah, future mother of Samuel (1 Samuel 1:9).   **19** Engravings of the names of the tribes of Israel (Exodus 28:21).

20 What two gluttonous priests were notorious for keeping the sacrificial meat for themselves?

21 What reform priest was killed by the orders of King Joash, a pupil of his father?

22 What priest had a son named Ichabod, a name meaning "the glory has departed"?

23 Aaron was called to be the first priest of Israel, joined by his sons. Unscramble the letters to spell the names of Aaron's priestly sons.

DANBA

— — — — —

HIBUA

— — — — —

LEERZAA

— — — — — — —

HITRAMA

— — — — — — —

24 What king ordered the execution of Ahimelech and other priests because they had conspired with David?

25 Who was the only priest to escape Saul's slaughter at Nob?

26 What priest found the Book of the Law in the Temple during Josiah's reign?

27 When Adonijah tried to grab the throne of Israel, what priest took his side?

(More Priests on the next page)

A Bevy of Priests
20 Hophni and Phinehas (1 Samuel 1:3; 2:12-17).   **21** Zechariah (2 Chronicles 24:21).   **22** Phinehas (1 Samuel 4:21).   **23** Nadab, Abihu, Eleazar, and Ithamar (Exodus 28:1).   **24** Saul (1 Samuel 22:18).
25 Abiathar (1 Samuel 22:20).   **26** Hilkiah (2 Kings 22:8).   **27** Abiathar (1 Kings 1:7).

98   THE GOOD BOOK BIBLE TRIVIA

A BEVY OF PRIESTS (CONTINUED)

28 What high priest had John and Peter arrested after the two disciples had healed a lame man?

29 What priest was told by Jeremiah that he would be taken to Babylon as a prisoner?

30 What king of Israel sinned by appointing priests that had not been chosen by God?

31 What priest served as a witness when Isaiah gave his son the bizarre name Maher-shalal-hash-baz?

32 What priest led a reform movement in Judah, so that the people tore down their Baal temple and idols?

33 What priest of Baal was killed in Jerusalem when a reform movement threw out all the idols?

34 What were the names of the two stones worn in the high priest's breastplate and used to determine God's will?

35 What evil priest had Jeremiah beaten and placed in chains?

36 What two men were high priests during David's reign?

37 What priest received the boy Samuel as a servant?

38 When Jerusalem fell, what priest was taken prisoner to Babylon?

39 What priest was banished by Solomon, fulfilling a prophecy that Eli's descendants would be stripped of the priesthood?

40 What fat priest died when he heard the Ark had been captured?

41 What priest scolded King Uzziah for offering incense to God?

42 What priest received a letter criticizing him for not putting an iron collar on Jeremiah's neck?

43 What objects were around the hem of the priest's robe?

44 During Nehemiah's ministry, what priest dedicated the newly rebuilt walls of Jerusalem?

45 Who is the first priest mentioned in the Bible?

(More Priests on the next page)

If you like crossword puzzles, complete the intersecting boxes to reveal the answers to the first five questions, then continue to answer the last three.

46 **(1 Across)** What Old Testament book of the Bible mentions a "priest forever in the order of Melchizedek"?

47 **(2 Down)** What king ordered the priest Uriah to make a copy of a pagan altar he had seen in Damascus?

48 **(3 Down)** What king reversed the reform policies of Jehoiada the priest immediately after Jehoiada died?

49 **(4 Across)** In the time of the judges, what man was brassy enough to set up one of his sons as priest, though he had no authority to do so?

50 **(5 Across)** What leader after the exile traced his ancestry back to the high priest Aaron?

51 What priest, a prisoner in Babylon, was also a prophet?

52 What is the only parable of Jesus to have a priest as a character?

53 What prophet locked horns with the wicked priest Amaziah at Bethel?

(More Priests on the next page)

A BEVY OF PRIESTS (CONTINUED)

54 What miracle of Jesus led the priests to conspire to have him executed?

55 What prophet was sent to encourage the rebuilding of the Temple under the priest Joshua?

56 Who had a vision of the high priest Joshua standing beside Satan?

57 What was the affliction of the man who was healed by Jesus and then was sent to the priest?

58 In what priest's home did the enemies of Jesus meet to plot against him?

59 What disciple angrily cut off the ear of the high priest's servant when Jesus was arrested?

60 What New Testament book says that God has made his people to be a kingdom of priests?

61 What crime did the high priest charge Jesus with?

62 What priest was the father of John the Baptist?

63 What priest gave David the ritual bread when David fled from Saul?

64 According to Ezekiel, what was the one kind of woman a priest could not marry?

65 What priest announced that Jesus should die because it was appropriate for one man to die for the people?

66 What priest was told by the prophet Amos that his wife would become a prostitute?

67 According to John's Gospel, what priest was the first to examine the arrested Jesus?

68 What priest anointed Solomon as king?

69 What man asked the high priest for letters of commendation so he could work in the synagogues of Damascus?

(More Priests on the next page)

A Bevy of Priests

54 The raising of Lazarus (John 11:47). **55** Haggai. **56** Zechariah (3:1). **57** Leprosy (Matthew 8:4). **58** Caiaphas's (Matthew 26:3). **59** Peter (Matthew 26:51). **60** Revelation (1:6). **61** Blasphemy (Matthew 26:65). **62** Zechariah (Luke 1:5). **63** Ahimelech (1 Samuel 21:1-6). **64** A divorcée (Ezekiel 44:22). **65** Caiaphas (John 11:49). **66** Amaziah (Amos 7:17). **67** Annas (John 18:13). **68** Zadok (1 Kings 1:45). **69** Paul (Acts 9:2).

RELIGIOUS MATTERS   101

A BEVY OF PRIESTS (CONTINUED)

70 What two apostles were met by a priest of Zeus, who tried to offer sacrifices to them?

71 What priest had seven sons who were casting out demons in the name of Jesus?

72 What high priest ordered his men to slap Paul, which caused Paul to call him a "whitewashed wall"?

73 According to the Epistle to the Hebrews, who is the present High Priest of Israel?

74 From the choices listed, what Old Testament priest is Jesus like, according to the Epistle to the Hebrews?

A Aaron   B Levi   C Samuel   D Melchizedek

75 What kinsman of Moses was a priest of Midian?

76 What priest was responsible for taking the first census of Israel?

77 What New Testament epistle mentions the priesthood more than any other?

78 What tribe of Israel did all the priests spring from?

79 What New Testament epistle tells Christians that they are all priests?

80 What priest examined Jesus before the council?

BAPTISMS

1 What magician came to be baptized by Philip?

2 Who referred to the Israelites' crossing of the Red Sea as a baptism?

3 What businesswoman was baptized by Paul and Silas?

4 How many people were baptized on the day of Pentecost?

5 Who baptized Paul?

6 What Roman official did Peter baptize?

7 What kind of baptism did John promise the Christ would administer?

8 What foreign dignitary did Philip baptize?

9 What man of Philippi took Paul and Silas home and was baptized by them?

10 In what city did Crispus, the synagogue ruler, believe Paul's message and submit to baptism?

11 Where did Paul baptize 12 men who had received the baptism of John?

12 Which Gospel opens with John the Baptist preaching in the desert?

13 In which Gospel does John try to dissuade Jesus from being baptized?

14 What did John the Baptist tell the tax collectors who came to him for baptism?

15 Which epistle mentions "one Lord, one faith, one baptism"?

16 Which epistles compare baptism to burial?

17 Which epistle says that the flood waters at the time of Noah symbolize baptism?

THE COMPANY OF APOSTLES

1 Who was the first apostle to be martyred?

2 Who succeeded Judas Iscariot as an apostle?

3 What apostle was a tax collector from Capernaum?

4 According to tradition, which apostle was a missionary to India?

5 What apostle was probably crucified in Rome, head downward?

6 Who was the only one of the 12 apostles not from Galilee?

7 According to tradition, how did Simon the Zealot die?

8 Who was called the beloved disciple?

9 Who, according to tradition, preached in Assyria and Persia and died a martyr in Persia?

10 Who was not one of the original 12, though he probably labored harder for the gospel than anyone else?

11 Which apostle was traditionally supposed to have been crucified in Egypt?

12 Which apostle, originally a disciple of John the Baptist, was supposed to have been crucified on an X-shaped cross?

13 Which of the apostles were fishermen?

14 Of all the apostles, which is the only one who is supposed to have died a natural death?

15 Who is supposed to have provided the background information for the Gospel of Mark?

16 Who, according to tradition, preached in Phrygia?

17 What hard-working companion of Paul was called an apostle?

(More Apostles on the next page)

The Company of Apostles
1 James (Acts 12:1-2). 2 Matthias (Acts 1:23-26). 3 Matthew. 4 Thomas. 5 Peter. 6 Judas Iscariot. 7 Crucifixion or being sawn in pieces. 8 John. 9 Jude. 10 Paul. 11 James the less. 12 Andrew. 13 Peter, Andrew, James, John. 14 John. 15 Peter. 16 Philip. 17 Barnabas (Acts 13:1-3; 14:4).

18 What was Peter's original name?

19 Who is supposed to have been a missionary to Armenia?

20 Who preached at Pentecost?

21 Who is supposed to have suffered martyrdom in Ethiopia?

22 Who was banished to the island of Patmos?

23 Who is supposed to have been flayed to death?

24 Who is thought to have been pushed from a summit of the Temple, then beaten to death?

25 By what other name was Matthew known?

26 Who is supposed to have been executed by being sawn in pieces?

27 Who doubted the resurrected Jesus?

28 Who were the sons of Zebedee?

29 Unscramble the letters below to spell out the names of the two believers in Romans 16 whom Paul referred to as apostles.

NURDOCNSIA

— — — — — — — — — —

SIJANU

— — — — —

(More Apostles on the next page)

The Company of Apostles

18 Simon. 19 Bartholomew. 20 Peter (Acts 2). 21 Matthias. 22 John. 23 Bartholomew. 24 James, the brother of Jesus. 25 Levi. 26 Simon the Zealot. 27 Thomas (John 21:25). 28 James and John. 29 Andronicus and Junias.

30 Who was the apostle to the Gentiles?

31 What was Paul's original name?

32 Who brought Peter to Jesus?

33 Who had Jesus as a guest at a meal with many tax collectors?

34 Who, according to Catholic tradition, was the first pope?

35 Who criticized the woman who anointed Jesus?

36 Nathaneal of Cana, mentioned in John 1:45, is believed to be the same person as this apostle with a different name. Who is it?

37 Who brought Nathanael to Jesus?

38 Who said to Jesus, "My Lord and my God"?

39 Who asked Jesus to show the disciples the Father?

40 Who were the "sons of thunder"?

41 Who was with Jesus at the Transfiguration?

42 Who was the only apostle we know for sure was married?

43 In which Gospel is John not mentioned by name?

44 Who spoke for all the apostles at Caesarea Philippi?

45 Who, in John's Gospel, is the "son of perdition"?

46 Who requested special places for themselves in Jesus' kingdom?

(More Apostles on the next page)

The Company of Apostles
30 Paul. **31** Saul. **32** Andrew. **33** Matthew (Luke 5:29). **34** Peter. **35** Judas Iscariot (John 12:3-5). **36** Bartholomew. **37** Philip (John 1:43-46). **38** Thomas (John 20:28). **39** Philip (John 14:8). **40** James and John (Mark 3:17). **41** Peter, James, and John (Mark 9:2). **42** Peter (Mark 1:30). **43** John. **44** Peter (Mark 8:27-33). **45** Judas Iscariot (John 17:12). **46** James and John (Mark 10:39).

THE COMPANY OF APOSTLES (CONTINUED)

47 Who was absent when the risen Jesus appeared to the apostles?

48 Who brought Greeks to Jesus?

49 Who had Silas as a traveling companion on his second journey?

50 Which apostles were present at the raising of Jairus's daughter?

51 Who was a Roman citizen?

52 Who healed the crippled man at the Beautiful Gate?

53 Who healed a paralytic named Aeneas in Lydda?

54 Who was baptized by a man named Ananias?

55 What was Barnabas's original name?

56 Whom did the Sanhedrin put in jail for disturbing the peace?

57 Who raised a young man named Eutychus from the dead?

58 Whom did Paul oppose when he met him in Antioch?

59 Who asked Jesus why he intended to show himself to the disciples but not to the world?

60 To whom did Jesus say, "Feed my lambs"?

61 Who preached to the intellectuals of Athens?

62 Who had a vision of a sheet filled with unclean animals?

(More Apostles on the next page)

The Company of Apostles
47 Thomas (John 20:24). **48** Philip and Andrew (John 12:20-28). **49** Paul (Acts 15-18). **50** Peter, John, and James (Mark 5:37). **51** Paul (Acts 23:27). **52** Peter and John (Acts 3:1-10). **53** Peter (Acts 9:32-35). **54** Paul (Acts 9:10-18). **55** Joseph (Acts 4:36). **56** Peter and John (Acts 4:1-4). **57** Paul (Acts 20:7-12). **58** Peter (Galatians 2:11-21). **59** Jude (John 14:22). **60** Peter (John 21:15-19). **61** Paul (Acts 17:16-34). **62** Peter (Acts 10:9-16).

63 From the choices listed, whom did Jesus say he would make into fishers of men?

A James and John   B Peter and Andrew

C Everyone who believes in him

64 Who told Jesus he had seen a man driving out demons in Jesus' name?

65 Whom did Jesus take with him to Gethsemane?

66 Who expressed dismay over how to feed the five thousand?

67 Who had a beef against a Greek silversmith named Demetrius?

68 Who brought to Jesus the boy with loaves and fishes?

69 Who was reluctant to have Jesus wash his feet?

70 Who was bitten by a viper on the island of Malta?

71 What brother of Jesus does Paul call an apostle?

72 What young friend of Paul, a coauthor of 1 Thessalonians, was an apostle?

73 What apostle, a traveling companion of Paul, was sometimes called Silvanus?

74 According to tradition, what apostle lived to a ripe old age after miraculously living through being boiled in oil?

The Company of Apostles

63 B: Peter and Andrew (Mark 1:17).   64 John (Mark 9:38).   65 Peter, James, and John (Mark 14:33).
66 Philip (John 6:7).   67 Paul (Acts 19:23-41).   68 Andrew (John 6:8-9).   69 Peter (John 13:6-9).
70 Paul (Acts 28:1-6).   71 James (Galatians 1:19).   72 Timothy (1 Thessalonians 1:1; 2:7).   73 Silas
(1 Thessalonians 1:1; 2:7).   74 John.

SPEAKING OF CHURCHES

1 What church was neither hot nor cold?

2 What church began in the home of Lydia, the seller of purple?

3 At what church was Paul accused of turning the world upside down?

4 What church had two bickering women named Euodia and Syntyche?

5 In what church did Paul raise up Eutychus, who had fallen to his death out of a window?

6 Who founded the church at Colossae?

The answers to the next two questions can be found by unscrambling the letters given after each one.

7 What church was the scene of a burning of wicked books?

SEEPSUH

— — — — — — —

8 At what church were believers first called Christians?

TINCOAH

— — — — — — —

(More Churches on the next page)

Speaking of Churches

1 Laodicea (Revelation 3:15-16).   2 Philippi (Acts 16:15, 40).   3 Thessalonica (Acts 17:6).   4 Philippi (Philippians 4:1-3).   5 Troas (Acts 20:7-12).   6 Epaphras (Colossians 1:7).   7 Ephesus (Acts 19:19). 8 Antioch (Acts 11:26).

SPEAKING OF CHURCHES (CONTINUED)

9 What church had a false prophetess named Jezebel as a member?

10 Who visited the church at Babylon?

11 What church suffered because of the "synagogue of Satan"?

12 What member of the Colossian church received a letter from Paul?

13 What church received epistles from two different apostles?

14 At what church did Paul preach his first recorded sermon?

15 What church had a former demon-possessed girl as a member?

16 What was the first church to appoint deacons?

17 Who helped Paul establish the church in Corinth?

18 What church tolerated the heresy of the Nicolaitans?

19 What church had fallen prey to the legalistic Judaizers?

20 What is the most commended church in Revelation?

21 What church received from Paul an epistle that has never been found?

22 What church took up a large love offering for the needy believers in Jerusalem?

23 At what church did the Egyptian-born Apollos first serve?

24 What church saw the martyrdom of faithful Antipas?

25 What was the first church to send forth missionaries?

(More Churches on the next page)

Speaking of Churches

9 Thyatira (Revelation 2:18-29). **10** Peter (1 Peter 5:13). **11** Smyrna (Revelation 2:8-11).
12 Philemon. **13** Ephesus (the Letter to the Ephesians from Paul and Revelation 2:1-7 from John).
14 Antioch of Pisidia (Acts 13:16). **15** Philippi (Acts 16:18). **16** Jerusalem (Acts 6:1-7). **17** Priscilla
and Aquila (Acts 18:2). **18** Pergamum (Revelation 2:12-17). **19** Galatia (Galatians 1:6-9).
20 Philadelphia (Revelation 3:7-13). **21** Laodicea (Colossians 4:16). **22** Antioch (Acts 11:30).
23 Ephesus (Acts 18:24-28). **24** Pergamum (Revelation 2:13). **25** Jerusalem (Acts 8:5, 14).

26 What church was Silas from?

27 In what church were Christians guilty of taking other Christians to court?

28 What church was noted for hating the Nicolaitan heresy?

29 To what church did Jesus say, "Look! I stand at the door and knock"?

30 At what church did believers hold their property in common?

31 Who was sent by the Jerusalem church to oversee the church at Antioch?

32 To what church did Paul send Epaphroditus as a minister?

33 What church began at Pentecost?

34 What church had Crispus, a synagogue leader, as a member?

35 Where did Paul have a vision asking him to found churches in Europe?

36 At what church were Paul and Barnabas set apart by the Holy Spirit to do missionary work?

37 Who reported his vision of unclean animals to the church at Jerusalem?

38 At what church did Paul have a loyal "partner"?

39 At what church did some people follow the teachings of Balaam?

40 What church was told by John to buy white clothing to hide its nakedness?

41 Who established the church at Ephesus?

(More Churches on the next page)

Speaking of Churches

26 Antioch (Acts 15:34).   **27** Corinth (1 Corinthians 6:1-4).   **28** Ephesus (Revelation 2:6).
29 Laodicea (Revelation 3:20).   **30** Jerusalem (Acts 2:44-45).   **31** Barnabas (Acts 11:22).   **32** Philippi
(Philippians 2:25).   **33** Jerusalem (Acts 2:47).   **34** Corinth (Acts 18:8).   **35** Troas (Acts 16:9).
36 Antioch (Acts 13:2).   **37** Peter (Acts 11:1-18).   **38** Philippi (Philippians 4:3).   **39** Pergamum
(Revelation 2:14).   **40** Laodicea (Revelation 3:18).   **41** Paul (Acts 18:19; 19:1-10).

SPEAKING OF CHURCHES (CONTINUED)

41 What church was overseen by James?

42 From what Asian church was Paul driven out by unbelieving Jews?

The answers to the next five questions are hidden in the puzzle following the questions. Can you find them?

43 What church did Timothy grow up in?

44 What apostle was supposed to be the rock on which the church was built?

45 Who founded the church at Antioch of Pisidia?

46 What love-filled church sent members to accompany Paul all the way to Athens?

47 On what Greek island did Titus supervise the churches?

D	A	A	G	R
L	E	R	E	E
U	R	T	T	N
A	E	S	E	B
P	B	Y	R	A
M	O	L	C	I

Speaking of Churches
41 Jerusalem (Acts 15:13). 42 Iconium (Acts 14:5). 43 Lystra (Acts 16:1). 44 Peter (Matthew 16:18). 45 Paul (Acts 13:14). 46 Berea (Acts 17:10-15). 47 Crete (Titus 1:5).

CURSES, CURSES

1 What was the only animal to be cursed by God?

2 Who was sent by the king of Moab to put a curse on Israel?

3 What grandson of Noah was cursed for his father's sins?

4 Who cursed a fig tree for not bearing fruit?

5 Who put a curse on Cain and made him a wanderer?

6 What son of Josiah was cursed by God?

7 In what story did Jesus place a curse on the unrighteous?

8 According to Paul, what was put under a curse because of man's sin?

9 What nation did God say would have its towns and fields cursed because of disobedience?

10 What happened to the ground as a result of God's curse?

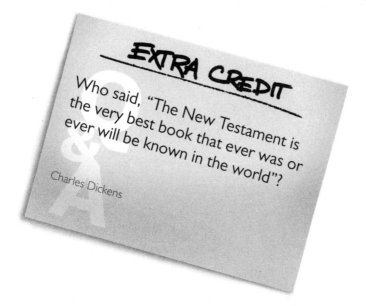

(More Curses on the next page)

EXTRA CREDIT

Who said, "The New Testament is the very best book that ever was or ever will be known in the world"?

Charles Dickens

Curses, Curses

1 The serpent (Genesis 3:14-15). 2 Balaam (Numbers 22:1-6). 3 Canaan (Genesis 4:11). 4 Jesus (Mark 11:21). 5 God (Genesis 4:11). 6 Jehoiakim (Jeremiah 22:18; 36:30). 7 The story of the sheep and the goats (Matthew 25:31-41). 8 Nature (Romans 8:19-22). 9 Israel (Deuteronomy 28:15-16). 10 It brought forth thorns and weeds (Genesis 3:17-18).

RELIGIOUS MATTERS   113

11 Who received a promise from God that all persons who cursed him would be cursed themselves?

12 According to Galatians, what people remain under a curse?

13 Who said that people who taught a false gospel would be cursed?

14 According to Paul, who was made a curse for our sins?

15 From the choices listed, what sort of handicapped people should we not curse, according to the law?

A The blind and the mute   B Lepers

C The blind and the deaf

16 Who was told by his wife to curse God and die?

17 What prophet ended his book with God's threat to come and strike the land with a curse?

18 What epistle says that blessing and cursing should not come out of the same mouth?

19 Who had enemies that bound themselves under a curse because they were so determined to kill him?

20 Who told God that Job would curse him to his face?

21 What book says that kings should not be cursed, for little birds will tell on the cursing person?

Curses, Curses

11 Abraham (Genesis 12:3).   12 Those who attempt to remain under the law (Galatians 3:10).
13 Paul (Galatians 1:8).   14 Christ (Galatians 3:13).   15 C: The blind and the deaf (Leviticus 19:14).
16 Job (2:9).   17 Malachi (4:6).   18 James (3:10).   19 Paul (Acts 23:12).   20 Satan (Job 1:11;
2:5).   21 Ecclesiastes (10:20).

HEALTHY CONFESSIONS

1 What wicked king of Judah confessed his sins when he was taken captive in Assyria?

2 Who confessed to God that he had done wrong in taking a census of Israel?

3 Who confessed his denial of Jesus?

4 What sneaky Israelite confessed that he had stolen goods from fallen Jericho?

5 Who confessed his own sin and Israel's after seeing a vision of God on his throne?

6 What king confessed his adulterous affair after being confronted by the prophet Nathan?

7 What scribe bowed in front of the Temple and confessed the sins of Israel while the people around him wept bitterly?

8 What young man confessed his riotous living to his forgiving father?

9 Who confessed the building of the golden calf to God?

10 Who confessed his sexual immorality with his daughter-in-law, Tamar?

11 Who made a false confession to Aaron and Moses?

12 Who confessed his remorse over betraying his master?

13 Who confessed Israel's sins after he heard the walls of Jerusalem were in ruins?

14 Who was visited by the angel Gabriel while he was confessing his sins?

15 Who confessed that he had been self-righteous?

16 Who confessed his sin to an angel that only his donkey had seen?

17 Who was pardoned by David after confessing his sin and begging for mercy?

18 Who confessed to Samuel that he had disobeyed God by not destroying all the spoils of war?

Healthy Confessions

1 Manasseh (2 Chronicles 33:11-13). 2 David (2 Samuel 24:10). 3 Peter (Matthew 26:75). 4 Achan (Joshua 7:20). 5 Isaiah (6:5). 6 David (2 Samuel 12:13). 7 Ezra (10:1). 8 The Prodigal Son (Luke 15:18). 9 Moses (Exodus 32:31). 10 Judah (Genesis 38:26). 11 Pharaoh (Exodus 10:16). 12 Judas (Matthew 27:4). 13 Nehemiah (1:6). 14 Daniel (9:20). 15 Job (42:6). 16 Balaam (Numbers 22:34). 17 Shimei (2 Samuel 19:20). 18 Saul (1 Samuel 15:24).

EXTRA CREDIT

What year was the first
American Bible printed?

1752, in Boston

EXTRA CREDIT

What is the oldest known
manuscript of the New
Testament, written in Greek?

Codex Sinaiticus

PART FIVE

ENCOUNTERS WITH THE DIVINE

SUPERNATURAL FIRE

1 What two sinful cities were destroyed by fire and brimstone from heaven?

2 When the Israelites were wandering in the wilderness, what did they follow by night?

3 According to Daniel, this astonishing person had a throne like a fire of flame. Who was he?

4 What did the seraph touch the trembling Isaiah's tongue with?

5 According to Revelation, where is the place reserved for those whose names are not in the Book of Life?

6 What did the cherubim use to guard the entrance to Eden?

7 How did God first appear to Moses?

8 What strange phenomenon accompanied the plague of hail in Egypt?

9 What mountain did the Lord descend upon in fire?

10 What two sons of Aaron were devoured by fire for making an improper offering to the Lord?

11 How did God deal with the Israelites who were complaining about their misfortunes in the wilderness?

12 What judge of Israel was visited by an angel, whose staff caused meat and bread to be consumed by fire?

13 How did Elijah respond to an army captain's summons to present himself to King Ahaziah?

14 What two men saw a chariot of fire drawn by horses of fire?

15 Where, in answer to Elijah's prayer, did fire from the Lord consume both the sacrifice and the altar?

Supernatural Fire

1 Sodom and Gomorrah (Genesis 19:24). 2 A pillar of fire (Exodus 13:21). 3 The Ancient of Days (Daniel 7:9). 4 A live coal from the altar (Isaiah 6:6). 5 A lake of fire and brimstone (Revelation 20). 6 A flaming sword (Genesis 3:24). 7 In a burning bush that was not consumed (Exodus 3:2). 8 Fire that ran along the ground (Exodus 9:23). 9 Sinai (Exodus 19:18). 10 Nadab and Abihu (Leviticus 10:1-2). 11 His fire devoured them (Numbers 11:1-3). 12 Gideon (Judges 6:21). 13 He called down fire from heaven on the captain and his men (2 Kings 1:9-12). 14 Elijah and Elisha (2 Kings 2:11). 15 Mount Carmel (1 Kings 18:16-40).

WHO ASKED GOD THE QUESTION?

1 Must I forever see these evil deeds? Why must I watch all this misery? (Hint: a prophet)

2 Why then does my suffering continue? Why is my wound so incurable? (Hint: a prophet)

3 Should I go and attack them? (Hint: a king referring to the Philistines)

4 Am I my brother's keeper? (KJV) (Hint: an angry sibling)

5 LORD, will you destroy an innocent nation? (Hint: a king)

6 Should not the Judge of all the earth do what is right? (Hint: a patriarch)

7 Who am I to appear before Pharaoh? (Hint: this should be obvious)

8 O Sovereign LORD, are you going to kill everyone in Israel? (Hint: a prophet)

9 I am nothing—how could I ever find the answers? (Hint: a righteous man)

10 O Sovereign LORD, how can I be sure that I will actually possess it? (Hint: a patriarch asking about a promise of God)

(More Questioners on the next page)

Who Asked God the Question?
1 Habakkuk (1:3). 2 Jeremiah (15:18). 3 David (1 Samuel 23:2). 4 Cain (Genesis 4:9). 5 Abimelech (Genesis 20:4). 6 Abraham (Genesis 18:25). 7 Moses (Exodus 3:10-11). 8 Ezekiel (11:13). 9 Job (40:4). 10 Abram (Genesis 15:8).

11 Why have you brought all this trouble on your own people, Lord? Why did you send me? (Hint: a leader and a miracle worker)

12 O LORD my God, why have you brought tragedy to this widow who has opened her home to me, causing her son to die? (Hint: a prophet)

13 O Sovereign LORD, what good are all your blessings when I don't even have a son? (Hint: a patriarch)

14 Must you be angry with all the people when only one man sins? (Hint: a leader and his brother)

15 Who by himself is able to govern this great people of yours? (Hint: a king)

16 If I go to the people of Israel and tell them, "The God of your ancestors has sent me to you," they will ask me, "What is his name?" Then what should I tell them? (Hint: a leader)

17 I am the one who has sinned and done wrong! But these people are as innocent as sheep—what have they done? (Hint: a king)

18 O LORD, God of Israel, why has this happened in Israel? Now one of our tribes is missing from Israel! (Hint: a nation)

19 What should I do with these people? They are ready to stone me! (Hint: a leader)

20 Oh, Sovereign LORD, why did you bring us across the Jordan River if you are going to let the Amorites kill us? (Hint: a leader)

21 But Lord, how can I rescue Israel? . . . I am the least in my entire family! (Hint: a reluctant soldier)

(More Questioners on the next page)

Who Asked God the Question?
11 Moses (Exodus 5:22). 12 Elijah (1 Kings 17:20). 13 Abram (Genesis 15:2). 14 Moses and Aaron (Numbers 16:22). 15 Solomon (1 Kings 3:9). 16 Moses (Exodus 3:13). 17 David (2 Samuel 24:17). 18 The Israelites (Judges 21:3). 19 Moses (Exodus 17:4). 20 Joshua (7:7). 21 Gideon (Judges 6:15).

WHOM DID GOD ASK . . . ?

1 How long will these people treat me with contempt? Will they never believe me, even after all the miraculous signs I have done among them? (Hint: a leader)

2 Whom should I send as a messenger to this people? Who will go for us? (Hint: a prophet)

3 Do you think that I like to see wicked people die? (Hint: a prophet)

4 Is it right for you to be angry because the plant died? (Hint: a reluctant prophet)

5 Who told you that you were naked? (no hints needed)

6 Why are you so angry? Why do you look so dejected? (Hint: a farmer)

7 How long wilt thou mourn for Saul, seeing I have rejected him from reigning over Israel? (KJV) (Hint: a judge and prophet)

8 I am the LORD, the God of all the peoples of the world. Is anything too hard for me? (Hint: a prophet)

9 Son of man, can these bones become living people again? (Hint: a prophet)

10 Who is this that questions my wisdom with such ignorant words? (Hint: a righteous man)

(More Questions on the next page)

11 Who makes a person's mouth? Who decides whether people speak or do not speak, hear or do not hear, see or do not see? Is it not I, the LORD? (Hint: a leader)

12 What have you done? (Hint: a woman)

13 Does a clay pot argue with its maker? Does the clay dispute with the one who shapes it, saying, "Stop, you're doing it wrong!" Does the pot exclaim, "How clumsy can you be?" (Hint: a foreign king)

14 Will you choose three years of famine throughout your land, three months of fleeing from your enemies, or three days of severe plague throughout your land? (Hint: a king)

15 Shouldn't I feel sorry for such a great city? (Hint: a prophet)

16 Are you as strong as God? Can you thunder with a voice like his? (Hint: a righteous man)

17 Why do these people stay on their self-destructive path? Why do the people of Jerusalem refuse to turn back? (Hint: a prophet)

18 Have I not commanded you? Be strong and courageous. Do not be terrified. (NIV) (Hint: a conqueror)

19 Is anything too hard for the LORD? (Hint: a patriarch)

20 Wasn't it enough that you killed Naboth? Must you rob him, too? (Hint: a king)

21 Why are you persecuting me? (Hint: a member of the Jewish council)

Whom Did God Ask . . . ?
11 Moses (Exodus 4:11).   12 Eve (Genesis 3:13).   13 Cyrus (Isaiah 45:9).   14 David (2 Samuel 24:13).   15 Jonah (4:11).   16 Job (40:9).   17 Jeremiah (8:5).   18 Joshua (1:1, 9).   19 Abraham (Genesis 18:13).   20 Ahab (1 Kings 21:19).   21 Saul (Acts 9:3).

ENCOUNTERS WITH ANGELS

1 The angel of the Lord appeared to the banished Hagar and told her what to name her child. What was the child's name?

2 Complete the math problem and find out how many angels rescued Lot and his family from the doomed city of Sodom.

$$18 \times 5 \div 9 \times 8 + 6 - 84 = \underline{\quad}$$

3 What apostle was released from prison by an angel who opened the prison's iron gate?

4 The prophet Balaam could not see the Lord's angel, but his talking donkey could. What was it about the angel that made the donkey turn away?

5 Joshua encountered an angel who was captain of the host of the Lord. Fill in the blanks to find out why the angel was appearing to Joshua.

TO GIVE HIM INSTRUCTIONS ON

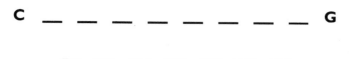

C _ _ _ _ _ _ _ _ G

_ _ _ _ _ _ _

6 The angel of the Lord instructed Philip to go to Gaza. What person did Philip encounter afterward?

7 What was the name of the angel who appeared to Mary and to Zacharias?

(More Angels on the next page)

8 This man's mother was visited by the angel of the Lord, who told her she would have a son who would be dedicated as a Nazarite. Who was he?

9 Elijah was nurtured by an angel after his flight from Israel's evil queen. Who was the queen?

10 Jacob is the only person known to have wrestled with an angel. What kindly act did the angel perform after the wrestling match?

11 What Roman official was visited by an angel who told him God had heard his prayers?

12 Who was commissioned by an angel to save Israel from the Midianites?

13 What kind of angelic beings guarded the entrance to Eden?

14 Who had his lips touched by a live coal held by a seraph?

15 What foreign army had 185,000 men killed by the angel of the Lord?

16 What person did an angel prevent from the act of child sacrifice?

17 What two guides did the angel of the Lord provide for the Israelites in the wilderness?

18 What ungodly ruler in New Testament times was struck down by an angel?

19 Who was carried by angels to Abraham's bosom?

20 What angel helped Daniel understand the future?

21 Who was told by an angel that the angel's name was a secret?

22 According to Revelation, what angel fights against Satan?

23 What kind of angels did Isaiah see in the Temple praising God?

24 Who had a dream about an angel and goats?

(More Angels on the next page)

Encounters with Angels

8 Samson (Judges 13:1-20). **9** Jezebel (1 Kings 19:1-8). **10** He blessed Jacob (Genesis 32:24-29). **11** Cornelius (Acts 10:1-8). **12** Gideon (Judges 6:11-23). **13** Cherubim (Genesis 3:24). **14** Isaiah (6:5-7). **15** The Assyrians (2 Kings 19:35). **16** Abraham (Genesis 22:11-18). **17** A pillar of fire and a pillar of cloud (Exodus 14:19-20). **18** Herod (Acts 12:23). **19** Lazarus (Luke 16:22). **20** Gabriel (Daniel 8:15-26; 9:21-27). **21** Samson's parents (Judges 13:17-18). **22** Michael (Revelation 12:7). **23** Seraphim (Isaiah 6:1-6). **24** Jacob (Genesis 31:11-12).

25 What person saw the angel of the Lord in the form of a flame?

26 What prophet was fed two meals by an angel?

27 According to Jude, who fought with Satan over the body of Moses?

28 Where was Jesus when an angel came and strengthened him?

29 Where was Paul when an angel assured him that he would be brought before Caesar?

30 How many angels will be at the gates of the new Jerusalem?

31 According to Jesus, what causes the angels to rejoice?

32 Who had a vision of four angels holding the four winds of the earth?

33 Which Gospel says that an angel rolled away the stone from Jesus' tomb?

34 At the end times, what will an angel bind Satan with?

35 Complete the math problem and find out how many angels pour out the bowls of wrath on the earth.

$$14 \times 9 \div 2 - 8 + 1 - 49 = \underline{\qquad}$$

36 What prophet saw the Lord's angel riding on a red horse?

37 What is the name of the evil angel of the abyss in Revelation?

Encounters with Angels

25 Moses (Exodus 3:1-22). **26** Elijah (1 Kings 19:5-8). **27** The archangel Michael (Jude 9). **28** Gethsemane (Luke 22:43). **29** On board ship during a storm (Acts 27:23-24). **30** Twelve (Revelation 21:12). **31** A repentant sinner (Luke 15:10). **32** John (Revelation 7:1). **33** Matthew (28:2). **34** A chain (Revelation 20:2). **35** Seven (Revelation 16:1-21). **36** Zechariah (1:8). **37** Abaddon or Apollyon (Revelation 9:11).

VISIONS OF GOD

1 Who had a vision of the Ancient of Days seated upon a throne?

2 Who looked up steadfastly into heaven and saw Jesus on the right hand of God?

3 Who humbly mentions that he had been caught up into the "third heaven"?

4 What seer described himself as "in the Spirit" when he received his visions?

5 What did Isaiah see filling the Temple when he beheld God sitting on his throne?

6 Who saw the back of God, since he could not bear to see him face-to-face?

7 Who, besides Isaiah, saw the Lord sitting upon his throne?

8 What seer of weird visions beheld a throne like a sapphire?

9 Who saw a heavenly ladder with the Lord standing above it?

10 Who, along with Moses, saw God during the wilderness wanderings?

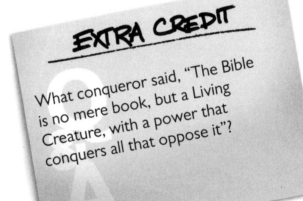

EXTRA CREDIT

What conqueror said, "The Bible is no mere book, but a Living Creature, with a power that conquers all that oppose it"?

Napoleon

Visions of God

1 Daniel (7:9). 2 Stephen (Acts 7:55). 3 Paul (2 Corinthians 12:2). 4 John, author of Revelation (Revelation 4:2). 5 The train of God's robe (Isaiah 6:1). 6 Moses (Exodus 33:23). 7 The prophet Micaiah (2 Chronicles 18:18). 8 Ezekiel (1:26). 9 Jacob (Genesis 28:12-13). 10 Aaron, Nadab, Abihu, and 70 of the Israelite elders (Exodus 24:9-10).

126   THE GOOD BOOK BIBLE TRIVIA

ORDAINED BEFORE BIRTH BY GOD

1   What strongman was ordained before birth to deliver Israel from the Philistines?

2   What child, who later ministered with the priest Eli, was ordained before birth to serve God?

3   What apostle was foreordained to minister to the Gentiles?

4   What kinsman of Christ was ordained to be his forerunner?

5   Fill in the blanks to reveal the Greek ruler whose reign is usually considered to be predicted in the book of Daniel.

    __ __ __ __ __ __ __ __ __

    __ __ __ __ __ __

6   What prophet was ordained before birth to be God's messenger?

7   What king of Judah had his birth and reign foretold to King Jeroboam?

8   Fill in the blanks to reveal who foretold Jesus' birth and ministry to Mary.

    __ __ __ __ __ __ __

9   What psalm, usually assumed to have been written by David, talks about God knowing him before his birth?

Ordained before Birth by God

1 Samson (Judges 13:2-5). 2 Samuel (1 Samuel 1:11-20). 3 Paul (Galatians 1:15). 4 John the Baptist (Luke 1:13-17). 5 Alexander the Great (Daniel 11:2-4). 6 Jeremiah (1:5). 7 Josiah (1 Kings 13:2). 8 Gabriel (Luke 1:26-38). 9 Psalm 139.

ENCOUNTERS WITH THE DIVINE   127

SUPERNATURAL JOURNEYS

1 What prophet was able to travel for 40 days on just the strength from a cake and water?

2 Elijah and Elisha walked across the Jordan River on dry ground after Elijah struck the waters with what?

3 Elijah outran a king's chariot, running all the way from Mount Carmel to Jezreel, almost 10 miles. Who was the king?

4 How was Elijah taken up into heaven?

5 Israel crossed the Red Sea on dry ground and also crossed a river on dry ground. Which river?

6 What carried Philip from Gaza to Azotus?

7 What two people walked on water in the midst of a storm?

8 Who took Jesus to a pinnacle of the Temple in Jerusalem?

9 Ezekiel was lifted up by a spirit, which held him between earth and heaven. What was the spirit holding on to?

10 Who was taken up into heaven in the sight of his followers?

11 In Paul's description of being caught up to the third heaven, he uses the same Greek verb that he has in another verse describing Christians who will be caught up in the clouds to meet the Lord. What verse is it?

Supernatural Journeys

1 Elijah (1 Kings 19:5-8). 2 His mantle (2 Kings 2:8). 3 Ahab (1 Kings 18:41-46). 4 In a whirlwind (2 Kings 2:11). 5 The Jordan (Joshua 3). 6 The Spirit of the Lord (Acts 8:39-40). 7 Jesus and Peter (Matthew 14:22-32). 8 The devil (Matthew 4:5-7). 9 A lock of Ezekiel's hair (Ezekiel 8:1-3). 10 Jesus (Acts 1:9). 11 1 Thessalonians 4:17.

MOSES AND MIRACLES

1   What did Moses mount on a pole as a way for healing the ailing Israelites?

2   What bird served as miracle food for the Israelites?

3   What did Moses do to bring forth water from the rock at Kadesh?

4   What animal came forth out of the Nile in droves?

5   What miraculous thing happened to Moses' hand?

6   What was the unique feature of the hailstorm that God sent upon the Egyptians?

7   What did Moses' staff turn into?

8   What everyday substance was changed into a plague of lice?

9   What caused the boils on the Egyptians?

10   What did the Nile waters turn into?

11   What disease was sent upon the Egyptians' livestock (KJV)?

12   Who appeared on the Mount of Transfiguration with Moses and Jesus?

13   What did Moses cast into the bitter water at Marah to make it sweet?

14   What happened to Aaron's staff when placed in the Tent of Meeting?

15   What was done to stop the plague that killed 14,700 of the Israelites?

16   What voracious insect was a plague on the Egyptian flora?

17   What happened to the rebellious Korah and his men?

(More Miracles on the next page)

Moses and Miracles

1 A brass serpent (Numbers 21:5-9).   2 Quail (Exodus 16:11-13).   3 He struck it twice (Numbers 20:1-11).   4 Frogs (Exodus 8:5-7).   5 It became leprous, then became normal again (Exodus 4:7).   6 It was accompanied by fire that ran along the ground (Exodus 9:22-26).   7 A serpent (Exodus 4:2-4).   8 Dust (Exodus 8:16-17).   9 Ashes that were turned into dust (Exodus 9:8-12).   10 Blood (Exodus 7:19-25).   11 Murrain (Exodus 9:1-7).   12 Elijah (Luke 9:28-36).   13 A tree (Exodus 15:23-25).   14 It sprouted and blossomed and bore almonds (Numbers 17).   15 An offering of incense was made (Numbers 16:46-50).   16 Locusts (Exodus 10:12-15).   17 They were swallowed up by the earth (Numbers 16:28-33).

ENCOUNTERS WITH THE DIVINE   129

18 What happened to 250 men who offered incense?

19 For how long did the thick darkness hang over the Egyptians?

20 What substance, called bread from heaven, fed the Israelites in the wilderness?

21 What hid the departing Israelites?

22 Who was made leprous and then healed after her rebellious acts?

23 What did the Israelites put on their doorposts so the angel of death would pass over?

24 What did the Lord use to part the Red Sea?

25 What means did the Lord use to halt the Egyptian chariots?

26 What happened to the manna the Israelites tried to hoard?

27 Who was slain by the angel of death?

28 What was Moses supposed to do to the rock at Horeb to bring water from it?

29 What consumed the offering on the altar?

30 What did Moses do at Taberah when the fire of the Lord destroyed many Israelites?

31 What brought the locust plague to a halt?

32 When the plague of hail came, where was the one place it did not fall?

33 Whose rod was turned into a serpent that swallowed the Egyptian sorcerers' serpents?

34 What bit the Israelites, causing Moses to fix a brass figure on a pole?

Moses and Miracles

18 They were consumed by fire from the Lord (Numbers 16:16-18). 19 Three days (Exodus 10:21-23). 20 Manna (Exodus 16:14-15). 21 A cloud (Exodus 14:19-20). 22 Miriam (Numbers 12). 23 Lambs' blood (Exodus 12:21-30). 24 A strong east wind (Exodus 14:21). 25 He made their wheels come off (Exodus 14:23-25). 26 It was filled with maggots (Exodus 16:20). 27 The firstborn among the Egyptians (Exodus 12:29-30). 28 Strike it (Exodus 17:1-6). 29 Fire from the Lord (Leviticus 9:22-24). 30 He prayed and the fire died down (Numbers 11:1-3). 31 The Lord blew them away with a strong west wind (Exodus 10:16-20). 32 In Goshen, where the Israelites dwelled (Exodus 9:26). 33 Aaron's (Exodus 7:10-12). 34 Venomous snakes (Numbers 21:5-9).

WONDERS OF ELIJAH AND ELISHA

1 What happened to the children who made fun of Elisha's bald head?

2 Whom did Elijah supply meal and oil to through miraculous means?

3 What did the bones of Elisha do to a dead man?

4 What did Elisha supply the poor widow with?

5 Who was healed of leprosy when he followed Elisha's instructions?

6 Who appeared with Jesus and Elijah on the Mount of Transfiguration?

7 Who fed Elijah after he prayed to the Lord to take his life?

8 What river did Elijah part by striking it with his mantle?

9 What did Elisha do to make the poisoned stew edible?

10 What did Elisha's servant see after Elisha prayed that his eyes would be opened?

11 How long was rain withheld after Elijah's prayer?

12 Who conceived a son after Elisha predicted she would?

13 What did Elijah call on to destroy the soldiers sent to arrest him?

14 Who was Elijah up against when fire from the Lord burned up a sacrifice and the water around the altar?

15 How many men did Elisha feed with 20 loaves of barley and some ears of corn?

16 How did Elisha raise the Shunammite woman's son from the dead?

(More Wonders on the next page)

WONDERS OF ELIJAH AND ELISHA (CONTINUED)

17 For whom did Elisha supply water miraculously?

18 What took Elijah into heaven?

The answers to the next five questions are hidden in the puzzle that follows the questions. Can you find them?

19 What birds fed Elijah in the wilderness?

20 Elisha performed a miraculous healing for some Syrian soldiers after leading them to Samaria. What was wrong with them?

21 What did Elisha throw into the water to make an ax head float to the surface?

22 What did Elisha throw into the bitter water to purify it?

23 Whom did Elijah miraculously outrun on the way to Jezreel?

R	T	L	A	S
A	V	D	E	K
V	U	N	C	B
E	L	I	S	A
N	T	L	O	H
S	A	B	M	A

MIRACLES OF JESUS

1 How was the woman with the issue of blood healed by Jesus?

2 What woman got up and started doing household chores after Jesus healed her of a fever?

3 What unproductive tree did Jesus wither by cursing it?

4 Where did Jesus work his first miracle?

5 From the choices listed, who appeared with Jesus at his miraculous transfiguration?

    A Abraham   **B** God   **C** Elijah   **D** Moses

6 Which apostle did Jesus enable to walk (briefly) on water?

7 What disciples did Jesus call after blessing them with an enormous catch of fish?

8 Whom did Jesus send to catch a fish that had a coin in its mouth?

9 When Jesus healed the blind man of Bethsaida, what did the man say people looked like?

10 What widow had her dead son brought to life by Jesus?

11 Where was Jesus when he healed the son of an official from Capernaum?

12 What was the affliction of the man Jesus healed by sending him to the pool of Siloam?

13 Why did the people complain when Jesus healed a woman who had been stooped for 18 years?

14 Where was Jesus when he miraculously escaped from a crowd that was going to push him off a cliff?

15 What was the other affliction of the deaf man Jesus healed in the Decapolis?

(More Miracles on the next page)

Miracles of Jesus

1 She touched the hem of his garment (Matthew 9:20-22). 2 Peter's mother-in-law (Matthew 8:14-15). 3 A fig tree (Matthew 21:17-20). 4 Cana (John 2:1-11). 5 C: Elijah and D: Moses (Matthew 17:1-9). 6 Peter (Matthew 14:28-31). 7 Peter, James, and John (Luke 5:4-11). 8 Peter (Matthew 17:24-27). 9 Like trees walking (Mark 8:22-26). 10 The widow of Nain (Luke 7:11-15). 11 Cana (John 4:46-54). 12 Blindness (John 9:1-7). 13 He healed her on the Sabbath (Luke 13:11-13). 14 His hometown, Nazareth (Luke 4:29-30). 15 Almost mute (Mark 7:31-35).

ENCOUNTERS WITH THE DIVINE   **133**

MIRACLES OF JESUS (CONTINUED)

16 How many loaves of bread were used to feed the five thousand?

17 How was Joseph told about Jesus' miraculous conception?

18 Who announced Jesus' conception to Mary?

19 What was the affliction of the man Jesus healed after his famous Sermon on the Mount?

20 What little girl did Jesus raise from the dead after telling people she was only asleep?

21 Fill in the blanks to reveal what Jesus said to calm the storm on the lake.

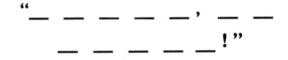

22 When Jesus healed a man of dumbness, what did the Pharisees accuse him of?

23 When Jesus healed a paralyzed man, what did the man pick up and carry home?

24 When Jesus healed 10 lepers, how many came back to thank him?

25 How many loaves did Jesus use to feed the four thousand?

26 What woman had her daughter healed, even after Jesus told her that he had been sent to the Jews, not to foreigners?

27 Which Gospel records the miraculous catch of fish after Jesus' resurrection?

28 Which apostle cut off a man's ear at Jesus' arrest and then watched Jesus heal the ear?

(More Miracles on the next page)

MIRACLES OF JESUS (CONTINUED)

29 In what town did Jesus heal a demon-possessed man in the synagogue?

30 What man of Bethany did Jesus bring back to life?

31 Which Gospel records Jesus walking through locked doors?

32 What was the affliction of the man Jesus healed on the Sabbath at the home of a Pharisee?

33 What Roman of Capernaum asked that Jesus heal his servant?

34 When Jesus was healing people, whose prophecy did he claim to be fulfilling?

35 Where did Jesus send the demons he drove out of the Gadarene demoniacs?

36 According to Matthew's Gospel, what Sabbath healing caused the Pharisees to plot to kill Jesus?

37 What did Jesus tell the two blind men not to do after he healed them?

38 What future disciple did Jesus see, through miraculous means, sitting under a fig tree?

39 When Jesus healed a man who was both blind and dumb, what demon did the Pharisees accuse him of consorting with?

40 When the disciples saw Jesus walking on the water, what did they think he was?

41 What afflicted the boy who was throwing himself into the fire?

42 How did Jesus heal the two blind men who asked for his help?

43 Where was Jesus doing his healing work when he caused the chief priests and the scribes to be angry?

44 What miracle in Jesus' life is mentioned most in the New Testament?

45 Where did Jesus heal a man who had been sick for 38 years?

Miracles of Jesus
29 Capernaum (Luke 4:31-37). **30** Lazarus (John 11). **31** John (20:19-21). **32** Dropsy (Luke 14:1-4). **33** The centurion (Matthew 8:5-13). **34** Isaiah's (Matthew 8:17). **35** Into a herd of pigs (Matthew 8:28-34). **36** The healing of the man with the withered hand (Matthew 12:10-14). **37** Not to tell any-one else (Matthew 9:27-31). **38** Nathanael (John 1:48). **39** Beelzebub (Matthew 12:24). **40** A ghost (Mark 6:45-50). **41** He was demon possessed (Matthew 17:14-18). **42** He touched their eyes (Matthew 20:30-34). **43** In the Temple (Matthew 21:14-16). **44** His resurrection. **45** The pool at Bethesda (John 5:1-15).

MIRACLES OF PETER AND PAUL

1   What dead man at Troas was raised up by Paul after falling out of a window?

2   Whom did Peter heal of long-term palsy?

3   Where did Paul exorcise a spirit from a possessed slave girl, whose owners then became furious?

4   What woman did Peter raise from the dead?

5   Where did Paul heal a crippled man?

6   Who, with Peter, healed a crippled man at the Beautiful Gate?

7   What sorcerer was blinded at Paul's command?

8   What, placed on Paul's body, brought about healings and exorcisms?

9   On what island did Paul heal the governor's family and many other people?

10 What miraculous occurrence delivered Paul and Silas from prison in Philippi?

11 What happened when Peter and John placed their hands on the believers at Samaria?

12 What part of Peter was supposed to produce healings?

13 What happened when Paul placed his hands on the believers at Ephesus?

14 What dangerous creature did not affect Paul when it bit him?

15 How many times was Peter delivered from prison by an angel?

WORKING WONDERS WITH WATER

1 Who made an ax head float on the water?

2 Who walked on the Sea of Galilee?

3 What did Moses do to heal the bitter waters of Marah?

4 Who was healed of leprosy after dipping seven times in the Jordan?

5 What judge wrung out a bowlful of water from a fleece in answer to prayer?

6 From the choices listed, what river was turned into blood?

     A Euphrates   **B** Jordan   **C** Nile

7 Who healed Jericho's water supply by throwing salt into it?

8 Who turned water into wine?

9 Who died when the parted Red Sea became unparted?

10 When the Israelites in the wilderness complained about lack of water, where did the water come from?

11 How did God water the thirsty army of Israel?

12 Who calmed the sea by speaking to it?

13 Who parted the Jordan by striking it with his mantle?

14 What were the Israelite priests carrying when they crossed the Jordan on dry ground?

Working Wonders with Water

1 Elisha (2 Kings 2:19-22). 2 Jesus and Peter (Matthew 14:25-31). 3 He cast a tree into the waters (Exodus 15:23-25). 4 Naaman the Syrian (2 Kings 5:14). 5 Gideon (Judges 6:38). 6 C: Nile (Exodus 7:20). 7 Elisha (2 Kings 2:19-22). 8 Jesus (John 2:1-10). 9 The Egyptians (Exodus 14:21-29). 10 A rock (Exodus 17:1-6; 20:1-11). 11 He ordered them to dig trenches, and in the morning they were filled with water (2 Kings 3:14-22). 12 Jesus (Mark 4:39). 13 Elijah (2 Kings 2:8-14). 14 The Ark of the Covenant (Joshua 3:7-17).

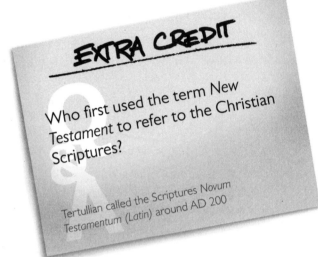

EXTRA CREDIT

Who first used the term New Testament to refer to the Christian Scriptures?

Tertullian called the Scriptures Novum Testamentum (Latin) around AD 200

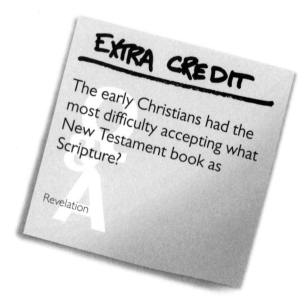

EXTRA CREDIT

The early Christians had the most difficulty accepting what New Testament book as Scripture?

Revelation

PART SIX

DABBLING WITH THE DEMONIC

THE VERY DEVIL

1 According to Jude's epistle, who disputed with Satan over the body of Moses?

2 What animal does 1 Peter compare Satan to?

3 In what epistle does Paul refer to Satan as "the god of this world"?

4 What, according to the New Testament, is the final place for Satan?

5 In what Gospel does Jesus call Satan "the ruler of this world"?

6 What is Satan the father of?

7 What prophet spoke of the fallen Lucifer (Satan) as a fallen angel?

8 According to the parable of the sower, what happens when someone hears the word of the Kingdom and does not understand it?

9 Fill in the blanks to reveal what, according to John's Gospel, Satan was from the very beginning.

A _ _ _ _ _ _ _

AND A _ _ _ _ .

10 In what epistle does Paul call Satan the "commander of the powers in the unseen world"?

11 What Gospel uses the name Beelzebub?

12 What book of the Bible speaks of the demonic fiend Abaddon and Apollyon, both names for Satan?

13 What apostle spoke of the contrast between Christ and Belial (presumably another name for the devil)?

14 What prophet spoke of a "funeral song for the king of Tyre" in a passage that has traditionally been interpreted as referring to Satan instead of a human king?

(More Devil on the next page)

15 In Luke's Gospel, Jesus refers to seeing the fall of Satan. What does he compare the fall to?

16 Whom did Satan provoke to do a census in Israel?

17 What disciple did Satan enter into?

18 What disciple was told by Jesus that Satan wanted to sift him like wheat?

19 What New Testament man did Satan provoke to lie to the Holy Spirit?

20 Who had seven sons that were overcome by an evil spirit they were trying to cast out of a man?

21 What king of Israel was tormented by an evil spirit?

22 In the story of the demon-possessed boy healed by Jesus, what had the evil spirit been doing to the poor child?

23 What did the evil spirit do when Jesus cast him out of the man at Capernaum?

24 What possessed man ran around naked?

25 What was the affliction of the woman who had had an evil spirit for 18 years?

26 What king had court prophets who had been the agents of a lying spirit?

27 What woman had Jesus driven seven demons out of?

28 In Revelation, for what reason do the demons perform miracles?

29 According to Jesus, when an evil spirit returns to a person, how many companions does it bring with it?

30 What does Satan masquerade as in the present world?

The Very Devil
15 Lightning (Luke 10:18).   16 David (1 Chronicles 21:1).   17 Judas Iscariot (Luke 22:3-4).   18 Peter (Luke 22:31).   19 Ananias (Acts 5:3).   20 Sceva (Acts 19:16).   21 Saul (1 Samuel 16:14-23).   22 Throwing him into the fire or water and making him foam at the mouth and grind his teeth (Mark 9:17-29).   23 Gave a loud scream (Mark 1:23-26).   24 The Gerasene demoniac (Luke 8:27).   25 She was bent and could not straighten up (Luke 13:11-16).   26 Ahab (1 Kings 22:2-22).   27 Mary Magdalene (Luke 8:2).   28 To bring the nations to war (Revelation 16:13-14).   29 Seven (Matthew 12:45).   30 An angel of light (2 Corinthians 11:14).

SORCERERS, WITCHES, AND SO FORTH

1 What emperor had a bevy of magicians and psychics who could not interpret his strange dreams?

2 What prophet called the city of Nineveh the mistress of witchcraft?

3 In what city did Paul find many believers who had formerly dabbled in witchcraft?

4 What queen of Israel practiced witchcraft?

5 What prophet claimed that Edom, Moab, Ammon, and Tyre all had sorcerers?

6 From the choices listed, who called on magicians to duplicate the miracles of Moses?

    A Nebuchadnezzar   **B** Pharaoh   **c** Herod   **D** Ahab

7 Who was the sorcerer Paul encountered on the isle of Paphos?

8 What medium was consulted by a king who had outlawed all mediums?

A GALLERY OF GODS

1 What fish-shaped god of the Philistines was disgraced when his statue was broken by the presence of the Ark of the Covenant?

2 The Ammonites' bloodthirsty god was widely known in Israel because of the horrible practice of children being sacrificed to him. What was the name of this god?

3 The god of the Moabites also had child sacrifice as part of his worship. Solomon erected an altar for him, but Josiah tore it down. What was he called?

4 The people of Lystra were so dazzled by Paul and Barnabas that they called them by the name of two Greek gods. What were the names?

5 This fertility god of Canaan is mentioned more than any other foreign deity in the Bible. The prophet Elijah and, later, King Jehu of Israel, worked hard to stamp out his cult. What was his name?

6 This goddess of Canaan was associated with depraved worship practices. After Saul's death, his armor was placed in her temple by the Philistines. What was her name?

7 This Babylonian god is mentioned by Jeremiah as being filled with terror after the downfall of Babylon. What was his name?

8 This goddess of Asia had a magnificent temple in Ephesus, a city where Paul ran into trouble with some of her followers. Who was she?

9 In Paul's speech to the men of Athens, he mentions the altar of a god. Fill in the blanks to reveal what was inscribed on the altar.

__ __ __

__ __ __ __ __

__ __ __

(More gods on the next page)

A Gallery of Gods

1 Dagon (Judges 16:23; 1 Samuel 5:1–5; 1 Chronicles 10:10).   2 Molech (Leviticus 18:21; 1 Kings 11:7; 2 Kings 23:10; Amos 5:26).   3 Chemosh (Numbers 21:29; 1 Kings 11:7; 2 Kings 23:13).   4 Zeus and Hermes (also called Jupiter and Mercury in some Bible translations) (Acts 14:12).   5 Baal (Judges 2:11; 1 Kings 16:32; 18:19; 19:18; 2 Kings 10:18).   6 Astaroth, or Ashtoreth (Judges 2:13; 1 Samuel 7:3; 31:10; 1 Kings 11:33; 2 Kings 23:13).   7 Marduk (Jeremiah 50:2).   8 Artemis (called Diana in some translations) (Acts 19:23–20:1).   9 "To an Unknown God" (Acts 17:22-23).

DABBLING WITH THE DEMONIC   143

A GALLERY OF GODS (CONTINUED)

10 After Gideon's death, what Canaanite god did the Israelites turn to?

11 Ezekiel saw a woman weeping for what god?

12 Who worshiped Succoth-benoth?

13 What gods did the Avites worship?

14 What was the god of Ekron, consulted by King Ahaziah?

15 What was Nehushtan?

16 What god did the Sepharvites sacrifice their children to?

17 What nation was Milcom the god of?

18 While in the wilderness, what Moabite god did the Israelites begin to worship?

19 What god did Naaman the Syrian apologize to Elisha for worshiping?

20 What was the god of the men of Hamath?

21 What god did Amos say was symbolized by a star?

22 Who was King Sennacherib worshiping when his sons murdered him?

23 Whose ship had figures of the gods Castor and Pollux?

24 Who was the god of the men of Cuth?

25 What nation was Bel a god of?

26 What prophet mentions Nebo as one of the gods of Babylon?

OFFERINGS TO IDOLS

1 When Elijah challenged the priests of Baal, what were they sacrificing to their god?

2 What king of Israel offered sacrifices to the two golden calves he had made?

3 Fill in the blanks to reveal the idol, associated with Moses, that was offered sacrifices by later generations.

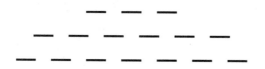

— — —

— — — — —

— — — — —

4 What wicked king, a dabbler in sorcery, sacrificed his son in the fire?

5 What goddess did Jeremiah accuse the people of Judah of making sacrifices to?

6 Fill in the blanks to reveal the idol that the Israelites in the wilderness brought offerings to while Moses was gone.

— — —

— — — — —

— — — —

7 What people burnt their children as an offering to the gods Adramelech and Anammelech?

8 What king despaired in the face of battle and offered his oldest son, the heir to the throne, as a sacrifice?

9 What wicked king of Judah built a Syrian-style altar and offered up his son as a sacrifice?

10 What was the name of the foreign god that many Israelites had sacrificed their children to?

EXTRA CREDIT

Who printed the first Bible, and in what year?

Johann Gutenberg in 1456

EXTRA CREDIT

What U. S. president said of the Bible, "That book is the rock on which our republic rests"?

Andrew Jackson

PART SEVEN

GETTING IT IN WRITING

SCRIPTURE TRANSLATES ITSELF

In several places Scripture explains the meaning of phrases or the names of certain people and places. For the meanings listed below, pick the proper name or phrase from the choices given. These are from the King James Version though many of them are in other Bible versions too.

1	Sons of thunder	Zoar
2	The place of the skull	Talitha
3	Teacher	King of Salem
4	Sorcerer	Lo-Ammi
5	Be opened	Babel
6	King of righteousness	Boanerges
7	My God, my God, why have you forsaken me?	Siloam
		Rabboni or Rabbi
8	Red	Edom
9	Shelters	Emmanuel
10	Not my people	Taberah
11	God with us	Golgotha
12	King of peace	Barnabas
13	Son of encouragement	Ephphatha
14	Little girl	Eloi, eloi, lama sabachthani
15	Sent	
16	Bitter	Elymas
17	Confused	Lo-Ruhamah
18	Small	Marah
19	Burning	Succoth
20	Not loved	Melchizedek

WHO SAID THAT? (I)

1 I am the one who needs to be baptized by you, so why are you coming to me?

2 I will not let you go unless you bless me.

3 We are all brothers—members of the same family. We are honest men, sir! We are not spies!

4 What crime has he committed? I have found no reason to sentence him to death. So I will have him flogged, and then I will release him.

5 Let the day of my birth be erased, and the night I was conceived.

6 I am going where everyone on earth must someday go. Take courage and be a man.

7 Speak, your servant is listening.

8 Has the LORD spoken only through Moses? Hasn't he spoken through us, too?

9 One night I had a dream that frightened me; I saw visions that terrified me as I lay in my bed.

10 Let us search the empire to find beautiful young virgins for the king.

11 Men of Athens, I notice that you are very religious in every way.

12 I will give half my wealth to the poor, Lord, and if I have cheated people on their taxes, I will give them back four times as much!

13 Set your affairs in order, for you are going to die.

14 May Canaan be cursed! May he be the lowest of servants to his relatives.

15 Who am I to appear before Pharaoh?

16 Remember what Moses, the servant of the LORD, commanded you: "The LORD your God is giving you a place of rest. He has given you this land."

17 I am like a little child who doesn't know his way around.

(More Sayings on the next page)

Who Said That? (I)

1 John the Baptist (Matthew 3:14). 2 Jacob (Genesis 32:26). 3 Joseph's brothers (Genesis 42:11). 4 Pilate (Luke 23:22). 5 Job (3:3). 6 David (1 Kings 2:2). 7 Samuel (1 Samuel 3:10). 8 Miriam and Aaron (Numbers 12:2). 9 Nebuchadnezzar (Daniel 4:5). 10 Ahasuerus's servants (Esther 2:2). 11 Paul (Acts 17:22). 12 Zacchaeus (Luke 19:8). 13 Isaiah (2 Kings 20:1). 14 Noah (Genesis 9:25). 15 Moses (Exodus 3:11). 16 Joshua (1:13). 17 Solomon (1 Kings 3:7).

18 If my misery could be weighed and my troubles be put on the scales, they would outweigh all the sands of the sea.

19 O Sovereign LORD, I can't speak for you! I'm too young!

20 This must be John the Baptist raised from the dead! That is why he can do such miracles.

21 Ananias, why have you let Satan fill your heart? You lied to the Holy Spirit, and you kept some of the money for yourself.

22 I correct and discipline everyone I love. So be diligent and turn from your indifference.

23 Who is the LORD? Why should I listen to him and let Israel go?

24 Israel's leaders took charge, and the people gladly followed. Praise the LORD!

25 Treason! Treason!

26 How can there be peace as long as the idolatry and witchcraft of your mother, Jezebel, are all around us?

27 O my son Absalom! O Absalom, my son, my son!

28 It's all over! I am doomed, for I am a sinful man.

29 I'm not a professional prophet, and I was never trained to be one. I'm just a shepherd, and I take care of sycamore-fig trees.

30 Oh, Lord, please leave me—I'm too much of a sinner to be around you.

31 Rabbi, we all know that God has sent you to teach us. Your miraculous signs are evidence that God is with you.

32 Don't be afraid, Mary, for you have found favor with God!

33 You stubborn people! You are heathen at heart and deaf to the truth. Must you forever resist the Holy Spirit?

(More Sayings on the next page)

Who Said That? (I)

18 Job (6:2-3). **19** Jeremiah (1:6). **20** Herod (Matthew 14:2). **21** Peter (Acts 5:3). **22** Jesus (Revelation 3:19). **23** Pharaoh (Exodus 5:2). **24** Deborah and Barak (Judges 5:2). **25** Athaliah (2 Kings 11:14). **26** Jehu (2 Kings 9:22). **27** David (2 Samuel 19:4). **28** Isaiah (6:5). **29** Amos (7:14). **30** Peter (Luke 5:8). **31** Nicodemus (John 3:2). **32** The angel, Gabriel (Luke 1:30). **33** Stephen (Acts 7:51).

34 Tell me, was the prophet talking about himself or someone else?

35 You've been making fun of me and telling me lies! Now please tell me how you can be tied up securely.

36 Why are you all coming out to fight? I am the Philistine champion, but you are only the servants of Saul.

37 I have found the Book of the Law in the LORD's Temple!

38 Skin for skin! A man will give up everything he has to save his life.

39 Your Majesty, you are the greatest of kings. The God of heaven has given you sovereignty, power, strength, and honor.

40 Where is the newborn king of the Jews?

41 Why does it seem incredible to any of you that God can raise the dead?

42 The LORD is my rock, my fortress, and my savior.

43 If I am a man of God, let fire come down from heaven and destroy you and your fifty men!

44 Are you still trying to maintain your integrity? Curse God and die.

45 Everything I heard in my country about your achievements and wisdom is true!

46 Why are you looking so sad? You don't look sick to me. You must be deeply troubled.

47 Get out of here, you prophet! Go on back to the land of Judah, and earn your living by prophesying there! Don't bother us with your prophecies here in Bethel.

48 Teacher, we saw someone using your name to cast out demons, but we told him to stop because he wasn't in our group.

49 That perfume was worth a year's wages. It should have been sold and the money given to the poor.

(More Sayings on the next page)

Who Said That? (I)
34 The Ethiopian eunuch (Acts 8:34). **35** Delilah (Judges 16:10). **36** Goliath (1 Samuel 17:8).
37 Hilkiah (2 Kings 22:8). **38** Satan (Job 2:4). **39** Daniel (2:37). **40** The wise men (Matthew 2:2).
41 Paul (Acts 26:8). **42** David (2 Samuel 22:2). **43** Elijah (2 Kings 1:10). **44** Job's wife (Job 2:9).
45 The queen of Sheba (1 Kings 10:6). **46** Artaxerxes (Nehemiah 2:2). **47** Amaziah (Amos 7:12-13).
48 John (Mark 9:38). **49** Judas Iscariot (John 12:5).

50 What should I do with these people? They are ready to stone me!

51 The scepter will not depart from Judah, nor the ruler's staff from his descendants, until the coming of the one to whom it belongs, the one whom all nations will honor.

52 The serpent deceived me. That's why I ate it.

53 Why should you go on with me? Can I still give birth to other sons who could grow up to be your husbands?

54 Have you come in peace, you murderer? You're just like Zimri, who murdered his master!

55 So take this seriously. The LORD has chosen you to build a Temple as his sanctuary. Be strong, and do the work.

56 Look! The virgin will conceive a child! She will give birth to a son and will call him Immanuel (which means "God is with us").

57 I heard you walking in the garden, so I hid. I was afraid because I was naked.

58 I'm warning you. Never come back to see me again! The day you see my face, you will die!.

59 My punishment is too great for me to bear!

60 How much longer will you waver, hobbling between two opinions? If the LORD is God, follow him! But if Baal is God, then follow him!

61 Out of the one who eats came something to eat; out of the strong came something sweet.

62 The king will take your daughters from you and force them to cook and bake and make perfumes for him.

63 What do you know about peace? Fall in behind me!

64 He must become greater and greater, and I must become less and less.

65 Let everyone in Israel know for certain that God has made this Jesus, whom you crucified, to be both Lord and Messiah!

(More Sayings on the next page)

Who Said That? (I)
50 Moses (Exodus 17:4). **51** Jacob (Genesis 49:10). **52** Eve (Genesis 3:13). **53** Naomi (Ruth 1:11). **54** Jezebel (2 Kings 9:31). **55** David (1 Chronicles 28:10). **56** Isaiah (7:14). **57** Adam (Genesis 3:10). **58** Pharaoh (Exodus 10:28). **59** Cain (Genesis 4:13). **60** Elijah (1 Kings 18:21). **61** Samson (Judges 14:14). **62** Samuel (1 Samuel 8:13). **63** Jehu (2 Kings 9:19). **64** John the Baptist (John 3:30). **65** Peter (Acts 2:36).

WHO SAID THAT? (I) (CONTINUED)

66 O Sovereign LORD, what good are all your blessings when I don't even have a son?

67 Should I go and find one of the Hebrew women to nurse the baby for you?

68 What have I done to you that deserves your beating me three times?

69 Look, Rabbi! The fig tree you cursed has withered and died!

70 Each of you must repent of your sins and turn to God, and be baptized in the name of Jesus Christ for the forgiveness of your sins.

71 Look, I see the heavens opened and the Son of Man standing in the place of honor at God's right hand!

72 What sign will the LORD give to prove that he will heal me and that I will go to the Temple of the LORD three days from now?

73 O LORD, God of Abraham, Isaac, and Jacob, prove today that you are God in Israel . . .

74 The LORD has prevented me from having children. Go and sleep with my servant. Perhaps I can have children through her.

75 A star will rise from Jacob; a scepter will emerge from Israel.

76 Let me die with the Philistines.

77 I know Nabal is a wicked and ill-tempered man; please don't pay any attention to him. He is a fool, just as his name suggests.

78 My father laid heavy burdens on you, but I'm going to make them even heavier!

79 How could a worn-out woman like me enjoy such pleasure, especially when my master—my husband—is also so old?

80 I know the LORD has given you this land. We are all afraid of you. Everyone in the land is living in terror.

(More Sayings on the next page)

(More Sayings on the next page)

Who Said That? (I)

66 Abraham (Genesis 15:2). **67** Miriam (Exodus 2:7). **68** Balaam's donkey (Numbers 22:28). **69** Peter (Mark 11:21). **70** Peter (Acts 2:38). **71** Stephen (Acts 7:56). **72** Hezekiah (2 Kings 20:8). **73** Elijah (1 Kings 18:36). **74** Sarah (Genesis 16:2). **75** Balaam (Numbers 24:17). **76** Samson (Judges 16:30). **77** Abigail (1 Samuel 25:25). **78** Rehoboam (1 Kings 12:14). **79** Sarah (Genesis 18:12). **80** Rahab (Joshua 2:9).

81 Can one blind person lead another? Won't they both fall into a ditch?

82 Get rid of that slave woman and her son. He is not going to share the inheritance with my son, Isaac.

83 Don't ask me to leave you and turn back. Wherever you go, I will go; wherever you live, I will live.

84 My father beat you with whips, but I will beat you with scorpions!

85 I know that you can do anything, and no one can stop you.

86 If it please the king, let the king and Haman come today to a banquet I have prepared for the king.

87 I am the Lord's servant.

88 I see very clearly that God shows no favoritism.

89 I am . . . the one you are persecuting!

90 This must be one of the Hebrew children.

91 Saul has killed his thousands, and David his ten thousands!

92 Am I a dog that you come at me with a stick?

93 The time is coming when everything in your palace—all the treasures stored up by your ancestors until now—will be carried off to Babylon.

94 Will you sweep away both the righteous and the wicked?

95 I find nothing wrong with this man!

WHAT GETS QUOTED MOST?

1 What book, one of the prophets, gets quoted in the New Testament more than any Old Testament book (419 times)?

2 Fill in the blanks to reveal the longest book in the Old Testament, which has 414 references in the New, ranking it second.

    __ __ __ __ __ __

3 What book, part of the Torah, ranks third, with 260 references?

4 What book, part narrative and part law, ranks fourth, with 250 references?

5 What book, more law than history, ranks fifth, with 208 references?

6 Fill in the blanks to reveal this long book of prophecy, which ranks sixth in being quoted, with 141 references.

    __ __ __ __ __ __ __

7 What book, with many visions in it, ranks seventh, with 133 references?

8 Fill in the blanks to reveal the book, by one of the later prophets, that is the eighth most quoted, with 125 references.

    __ __ __ __ __ __

9 What book, probably one of the least read of Old Testament books, ranks ninth, with 107 references?

10 What book, mostly history and part law, ranks tenth, with 73 references?

What Gets Quoted Most?
1 Isaiah. 2 Psalms. 3 Genesis. 4 Exodus. 5 Deuteronomy. 6 Ezekiel. 7 Daniel. 8 Jeremiah. 9 Leviticus. 10 Numbers.

GETTING IT IN WRITING   155

EVERYDAY PHRASES FROM THE BIBLE

Fill in the missing word, then identify the book and, if possible, the chapter and verse where these commonly used phrases originated. These are all found in the King James Version.

1 The __SKIN__ of my teeth

2 Wolf in __SHeeps__ clothing

3 Salt of the __EARth__

4 Holier __ThAN__ thou

5 Woe is __Me__ !

6 Can a leopard change his __Spots__ ?

7 A __PROP__ in a bucket

8 Eat, __DRiNK__ , and be merry.

9 Pride goeth __BeFORe__ a fall.

10 Give __UP__ the ghost

11 Spare the rod and __Spoil__ the child.

12 My __BROther__ 's keeper

13 __FAT__ of the land

14 A lamb for the __SLAUgHTeR__

15 The blind __LeADiNg__ the blind

THE OLD TESTAMENT IN THE NEW (I)

Each of these passages from the New Testament is a quotation from the Old Testament. Name the Old Testament book (and, if you're sharp, chapter and verse) where the passage appears.

1 Look! The virgin will conceive a child! She will give birth to a son and will call him Immanuel (which means "God is with us"). (Matthew 1:23)

2 Prepare the way for the LORD's coming! Clear the road for him! (Matthew 3:3)

3 The people who sat in darkness have seen a great light. And for those who lived in the land where death casts its shadow, a light has shined. (Matthew 4:16)

4 People do not live by bread alone, but by every word that comes from the mouth of God. (Matthew 4:4)

5 You must not test the LORD your God. (Matthew 4:7)

6 You must worship the LORD your God and serve only him. (Matthew 4:10)

7 An eye for an eye, and a tooth for a tooth. (Matthew 5:38)

8 Love your neighbor and hate your enemy. (Matthew 5:43)

9 He took our sicknesses and removed our diseases. (Matthew 8:17)

10 I want you to show mercy, not offer sacrifices. (Matthew 9:13)

11 Look, I am sending my messenger ahead of you, and he will prepare your way before you. (Matthew 11:10)

(More OT in the NT on the next page)

12 Look at my Servant, whom I have chosen. He is my Beloved, who pleases me. I will put my Spirit upon him, and he will proclaim justice to the nations. (Matthew 12:18)

13 He will not fight or shout or raise his voice in public. (Matthew 12:19)

14 He will not crush the weakest reed or put out a flickering candle. Finally he will cause justice to be victorious. (Matthew 12:20)

15 And his name will be the hope of all the world. (Matthew 12:21)

16 When you hear what I say, you will not understand. When you see what I do, you will not comprehend. (Matthew 13:14)

17 For the hearts of these people are hardened, and their ears cannot hear, and they have closed their eyes. (Matthew 13:15)

18 I will speak to you in parables. I will explain things hidden since the creation of the world. (Matthew 13:35)

19 These people honor me with their lips, but their hearts are far from me. (Matthew 15:8)

20 My Temple will be called a house of prayer. (Matthew 21:13)

21 You have taught children and infants to give you praise. (Matthew 21:16)

22 The stone that the builders rejected has now become the cornerstone. (Matthew 21:42)

23 I am the God of Abraham, the God of Isaac, and the God of Jacob (Matthew 22:32)

24 You must love the LORD your God with all your heart, all your soul, and all your mind. (Matthew 22:37)

25 Love your neighbor as yourself. (Matthew 22:39)

26 The LORD said to my Lord, Sit in the place of honor at my right hand until I humble your enemies beneath your feet. (Matthew 22:44)

27 After they had nailed him to the cross, the soldiers gambled for his clothes by throwing dice. (Matthew 27:35)

(More OT in the NT on the next page)

28 He trusted God, so let God rescue him now if he wants him! (Matthew 27:43)

29 My God, my God, why hast thou forsaken me? (Matthew 27:46, KJV)

30 He is a voice shouting in the wilderness, "Prepare the way for the LORD's coming!" (Mark 1:3)

31 When they see what I do, they will learn nothing. When they hear what I say, they will not understand. Otherwise, they will turn to me and be forgiven. (Mark 4:12)

32 These people honor me with their lips, but their hearts are far from me. (Mark 7:6)

33 But "God made them male and female" from the beginning of creation. "This explains why a man leaves his father and mother and is joined to his wife." (Mark 10:6-7)

34 Where the maggots never die and the fire never goes out. (Mark 9:48)

35 For everyone will be tested with fire. (Mark 9:49)

36 Listen, O Israel! The LORD our God is the one and only LORD. (Mark 12:29)

37 God will strike the Shepherd, and the sheep will be scattered. (Mark 14:27)

38 If a woman's first child is a boy, he must be dedicated to the LORD. (Luke 2:23)

39 Every valley shall be filled, and every mountain and hill shall be brought low. (Luke 3:5, KJV)

40 Then all people will see the salvation sent from God. (Luke 3:6)

41 He will order his angels to protect and guard you. (Luke 4:10)

42 And they will hold you up with their hands so you won't even hurt your foot on a stone. (Luke 4:11)

(More OT in the NT on the next page)

The Old Testament in the New (1)

28 Psalm 22:8. **29** Psalm 22:1. **30** Isaiah 40:3. **31** Isaiah 6:9. **32** Isaiah 29:13. **33** Genesis 2:24. **34** Isaiah 66:24. **35** Leviticus 2:13. **36** Deuteronomy 6:4. **37** Zechariah 13:7. **38** Exodus 13:2. **39** Isaiah 40:3-4. **40** Isaiah 40:5. **41** Psalm 91:11. **42** Psalm 91:12.

43 The Spirit of the LORD is upon me, for he has anointed me to bring Good News to the poor. (Luke 4:18)

44 When they look, they won't really see. When they hear, they won't understand. (Luke 8:10)

45 My house is the house of prayer. (Luke 19:46, KJV)

46 Clear the way for the LORD's coming! (John 1:23)

47 Passion for God's house will consume me. (John 2:17)

48 I say, you are gods! (John 10:34)

49 Look, your King is coming, riding on a donkey's colt. (John 12:15)

50 LORD, who has believed our message? To whom has the LORD revealed his powerful arm? (John 12:38)

51 The Lord has blinded their eyes and hardened their hearts (John 12:40)

52 The one who eats my food has turned against me. (John 13:18)

53 They hated me without cause. (John 15:25)

54 They will look on the one they pierced. (John 19:37)

55 Not one of his bones will be broken. (John 19:36)

56 Let his home become desolate, with no one living in it. (Acts 1:20)

57 In the last days, God says, I will pour out my Spirit upon all people. Your sons and daughters will prophesy. Your young men will see visions, and your old men will dream dreams. (Acts 2:17)

58 The sun will become dark, and the moon will turn blood red before that great and glorious day of the LORD arrives. (Acts 2:20)

59 I see that the LORD is always with me. I will not be shaken, for he is right beside me. (Acts 2:25)

60 For you will not leave my soul among the dead or allow your Holy One to rot in the grave. (Acts 2:27)

(More OT in the NT on the next page)

The Old Testament in the New (I)
43 Isaiah 61:1.   **44** Isaiah 6:9.   **45** Isaiah 56:7.   **46** Isaiah 40:3.   **47** Psalm 69:9.   **48** Psalm 82:6.
49 Zechariah 9:9.   **50** Isaiah 53:1.   **51** Isaiah 6:9.   **52** Psalm 41:9.   **53** Psalm 35:19.   **54** Zechariah
12:10.   **55** Exodus 12:46.   **56** Psalm 69:25.   **57** Joel 2:28.   **58** Joel 2:31.   **59** Psalm 16:8.
60 Psalm 16:10.

61 The LORD said to my Lord, Sit in the place of honor at my right hand until I humble your enemies, making them a footstool under your feet. (Acts 2:34-35)

62 The LORD your God will raise up for you a Prophet like me from among your own people. Listen carefully to everything he tells you. (Acts 3:22)

63 The stone that you builders rejected has now become the cornerstone. (Acts 4:11)

64 Why were the nations so angry? Why did they waste their time with futile plans? (Acts 4:25)

65 Take off your sandals, for you are standing on holy ground. (Acts 7:33)

66 I have certainly seen the oppression of my people in Egypt. I have heard their groans and have come down to rescue them. (Acts 7:34)

67 Make us some gods who can lead us, for we don't know what has become of this Moses, who brought us out of Egypt. (Acts 7:40)

68 Was it to me you were bringing sacrifices and offerings during those forty years in the wilderness, Israel? (Acts 7:42)

69 He was led like a sheep to the slaughter. And as a lamb is silent before the shearers, he did not open his mouth. (Acts 8:32)

70 He was humiliated and received no justice. Who can speak of his descendants? For his life was taken from the earth. (Acts 8:33)

The Old Testament in the New (I)
61 Psalm 110:1. **62** Deuteronomy 18:15. **63** Psalm 118:22. **64** Psalm 2:1. **65** Exodus 3:5. **66** Exodus 3:7. **67** Exodus 32:1. **68** Amos 5:25. **69** Isaiah 53:7. **70** Isaiah 53:8.

GETTING IT IN WRITING   161

BOOKS WITHIN THE BOOK

1 Who ate a book and found it sweet as honey (though it later gave him a sour stomach)?

2 What book of the Bible mentions the Lamb's Book of Life?

3 Which king's acts are said to be recorded in *The Record of Jehu Son of Hanani*?

4 Fill in the blanks to reveal whose acts are recorded in *The Record of Shemaiah the Prophet*.

 — — — — — — — —

5 What book of the Bible makes reference to *The Book of the History of the Kings of Media and Persia*?

6 *The Record of Gad the Seer* records which king's deeds?

7 Fill in the blanks to reveal the name of the court prophet in whose book the acts of King David are said to be recorded.

 — — — — — —

8 Whose acts are recorded in *The Record of Iddo the Seer*?

9 Fill in the blanks to reveal the Persian king who received a letter, asking him to search through his ancestors' records to remind himself how rebellious the Jews had been.

 — — — — — — — — —

(More Books on the next page)

10 What Old Testament prophet mentions the Lord's "scroll of remembrance"?

11 According to Revelation, who will open the book with seven seals?

12 What king cut up Jeremiah's scroll and tossed it piece by piece into a fireplace?

13 In what city in Asia did people burn their valuable books on sorcery?

14 What Old Testament book mentions *The Book of the Acts of Solomon*?

15 Who described to the people of Israel what life would be like under a king and then wrote down his statements in a book?

16 Who instructed the men of Israel to go through Canaan and write down descriptions of the area?

17 What phenomenal event, described in Joshua, is also said to be described in *The Book of Jashar*?

18 What Old Testament book makes reference to *The Book of the Wars of the Lord*?

19 According to tradition, the "book of the law" found in the Temple during Josiah's reign was a form of which Old Testament book?

Books within the Book
10 Malachi 3:16-17. **11** The lion of the tribe of Judah (Revelation 5:5). **12** Jehoiakim (Jeremiah 36:23). **13** Ephesus (Acts 19:18-19). **14** 1 Kings 11:41. **15** Samuel (1 Samuel 10:25). **16** Joshua 18:9. **17** The sun standing still (Joshua 10:13). **18** Numbers 21:14-15. **19** Deuteronomy.

WHO SAID THAT? (II)

1 Lord, don't charge them with this sin!

2 Look! There's some water! Why can't I be baptized?

3 Soon I will die, but God will surely come to help you and lead you out of this land of Egypt. He will bring you back to the land he solemnly promised to give to Abraham, to Isaac, and to Jacob.

— — — — —

4 You are Peter (which means "rock"), and upon this rock I will build my church.

5 This child is destined to cause many in Israel to fall, but he will be a joy to many others.

6 Put my personal silver cup at the top of the youngest brother's sack, along with the money for his grain.

7 This time I cannot be blamed for everything I am going to do to you Philistines.

8 I am a Hebrew, and I worship the LORD, the God of heaven, who made the sea and the land.

— — — — —

9 Someone is coming soon who is greater than I am—so much greater that I'm not even worthy to stoop down like a slave and untie the straps of his sandals.

10 The God of our ancestors raised Jesus from the dead after you killed him by hanging him on a cross.

11 As surely as the LORD lives, any man who would do such a thing deserves to die!

12 Come and sleep with me.

(More Sayings on the next page)

WHO SAID THAT? (II) (CONTINUED)

13 Take your sword and kill me before these pagan Philistines come to run me through and taunt and torture me.

14 This time I have sinned. The LORD is the righteous one, and my people and I are wrong.

15 I have told you all this so that you may have peace in me.

16 I have given Esther the property of Haman, and he has been impaled on a pole because he tried to destroy the Jews.

17 Whoever can read this writing and tell me what it means will be dressed in purple robes of royal honor and will have a gold chain placed around his neck. He will become the third highest ruler in the kingdom!

18 My soul doth magnify the Lord. (KJV)

19 I will give it all to you, if you will kneel down and worship me.

20 Repent of your sins and turn to God, for the Kingdom of Heaven is near.

21 Brothers, I am a Pharisee, as were my ancestors! And I am on trial because my hope is in the resurrection of the dead!

22 I don't have any silver or gold for you. But I'll give you what I have. In the name of Jesus Christ the Nazarene, get up and walk!.

23 The voice is Jacob's, but the hands are Esau's.

24 Oh, how the mighty heroes have fallen! Stripped of their weapons, they lie dead.

25 If you are truly going to help me, show me a sign to prove that it is really the LORD speaking to me.

26 You brought this man to me, accusing him of leading a revolt. I have examined him thoroughly on this point in your presence and find him innocent.

27 Are you the king of Israel or not? Get up and eat something, and don't worry about it. I'll get you Naboth's vineyard!

(More Sayings on the next page)

Who Said That? (II)

13 Saul (1 Samuel 31:4). 14 Pharaoh (Exodus 9:27). 15 Jesus (John 16:33). 16 Xerxes or Ahasuerus (Esther 8:7). 17 Belshazzar (Daniel 5:7). 18 Mary (Luke 1:46). 19 The devil (Matthew 4:9). 20 John the Baptist (Matthew 3:2). 21 Paul (Acts 23:6). 22 Peter (Acts 3:6). 23 Isaac (Genesis 27:22). 24 David (2 Samuel 1:27). 25 Gideon (Judges 6:17). 26 Pilate (Luke 23:14). 27 Jezebel (1 Kings 21:7).

WHO SAID THAT? (II) (CONTINUED)

28 Truly, your God is the greatest of gods, the Lord over kings, a revealer of mysteries, for you have been able to reveal this secret.

29 My Lord and my God!

30 My husband has brought this Hebrew slave here to make fools of us! He came into my room to rape me, but I screamed.

31 Plead with the LORD to take the frogs away from me and my people.

32 Samson! The Philistines have come to capture you!

33 But will God really live on earth? Why, even the highest heavens cannot contain you. How much less this Temple I have built!

34 Leave that innocent man alone. I suffered through a terrible nightmare about him last night.

35 I am the living one. I died, but look—I am alive forever and ever!

36 Go and worship the LORD. But leave your flocks and herds here. You may even take your little ones with you.

37 Listen! Obedience is better than sacrifice, and submission is better than offering the fat of rams.

38 I was dedicated to God as a Nazirite from birth. If my head were shaved, my strength would leave me.

39 I have heard all this before. What miserable comforters you are!

40 Oh no, sir! I haven't been drinking wine or anything stronger. But I am very discouraged, and I was pouring out my heart to the LORD.

41 Your brother was here, and he tricked me. He has taken away your blessing.

42 Would you like me to release to you this King of the Jews?

43 Surely this man was innocent.

(More Sayings on the next page)

Who Said That? (II)
28 Nebuchadnezzar (Daniel 2:47). **29** Thomas (John 20:28). **30** Potiphar's wife (Genesis 39:14).
31 Pharaoh (Exodus 8:8). **32** Delilah (Judges 16:20). **33** Solomon (1 Kings 8:27). **34** Pilate's wife
(Matthew 27:19). **35** Jesus (Revelation 1:18). **36** Pharaoh (Exodus 10:24). **37** Samuel (1 Samuel
15:22). **38** Samson (Judges 16:17). **39** Job (16:2). **40** Hannah (1 Samuel 1:15). **41** Isaac (Genesis
27:35). **42** Pilate (Mark 15:9). **43** The centurion at the Crucifixion (Luke 23:47).

THE GOOD BOOK BIBLE TRIVIA

WHO SAID THAT? (II) (CONTINUED)

The answers to all of the questions are hidden in the puzzle following the questions. Can you find them?

44 Listen, my daughter. Stay right here with us when you gather grain; don't go to any other fields. Stay right behind the young women working in my field.

45 You are that man!

46 Brothers, I have always lived before God with a clear conscience!

47 Forty days from now Nineveh will be destroyed!

48 Your people will be my people, and your God will be my God.

49 I had only heard about you before, but now I have seen you with my own eyes.

50 Since your vineyard is so convenient to my palace, I would like to buy it to use as a vegetable garden. I will give you a better vineyard in exchange, or if you prefer, I will pay you for it.

J	A	N	A	I
O	Z	A	O	B
B	A	H	A	R
L	O	T	M	U
L	U	A	P	T
J	O	N	A	H

(More Sayings on the next page)

Who Said That? (II)
44 Boaz (Ruth 2:8). 45 Nathan (2 Samuel 12:7). 46 Paul (Acts 23:1). 47 Jonah (3:4). 48 Ruth (1:16). 49 Job (42:5). 50 Ahab (1 Kings 21:2).

GETTING IT IN WRITING   167

51 May the LORD keep watch between us to make sure that we keep this covenant when we are out of each other's sight.

52 Just kill me now, LORD! I'd rather be dead than alive.

53 Go to Bethlehem and search carefully for the child. And when you find him, come back and tell me so that I can go and worship him, too!

54 The LORD forbid that I should kill the one he has anointed!

55 I came naked from my mother's womb, and I will be naked when I leave. The LORD gave me what I had, and the LORD has taken it away. Praise the name of the LORD!

56 Here I am. Send me.

57 Please test us for ten days on a diet of vegetables and water.

58 We have a father who is an old man, and his youngest son is a child of his old age.

59 Am I my brother's keeper? (KJV)

60 He is the God who made the world and everything in it. Since he is Lord of heaven and earth, he doesn't live in man-made temples.

61 Lord, it's wonderful for us to be here! If you want, I'll make three shelters as memorials—one for you, one for Moses, and one for Elijah.

62 Leave these men alone. Let them go. If they are planning and doing these things merely on their own, it will soon be overthrown.

63 Sovereign Lord, now let your servant die in peace, as you have promised. I have seen your salvation.

64 Praise to the God of Shadrach, Meshach, and Abednego! He sent his angel to rescue his servants who trusted in him.

65 The Scripture you've just heard has been fulfilled this very day!

(More Sayings on the next page)

WHO SAID THAT? (II) (CONTINUED)

66 Do you think you can persuade me to become a Christian so quickly?

67 Now we are all here, waiting before God to hear the message the Lord has given you.

68 Look, the people of Israel now outnumber us and are stronger than we are.

69 How could I become a father at the age of 100?

70 This is how a king will reign over you. The king will draft your sons and assign them to his chariots and his charioteers, making them run before his chariots.

71 Give me an understanding heart so that I can govern your people well and know the difference between right and wrong.

72 There is a certain race of people scattered through all the provinces of your empire who keep themselves separate from everyone else. . . . They refuse to obey the laws of the king.

73 For before the child is that old, the lands of the two kings you fear so much will both be deserted.

74 You skillfully sidestep God's law in order to hold on to your own tradition.

75 Great is Artemis of the Ephesians!

76 What is truth?

77 Can anything good come from Nazareth?

78 You'll have to shout louder for surely he is a god! Perhaps he is daydreaming. . . . Or maybe he is away on a trip, or is asleep and needs to be wakened!

79 First let me go and kiss my father and mother good-bye, and then I will go with you!

80 Wherever you go, stay in the same house until you leave town.

81 How can an old man go back into his mother's womb and be born again?

(More Sayings on the next page)

(More Sayings on the next page)

Who Said That? (II)
66 Agrippa (Acts 26:28). 67 Cornelius (Acts 10:33). 68 Pharaoh (Exodus 1:9). 69 Abraham (Genesis 17:17). 70 Samuel (1 Samuel 8:11). 71 Solomon (1 Kings 3:9). 72 Haman (Esther 3:8). 73 Isaiah (7:16). 74 Jesus (Mark 7:9). 75 The people of Ephesus (Acts 19:34). 76 Pilate (John 18:38). 77 Nathanael (John 1:46). 78 Elijah (1 Kings 18:27). 79 Elisha (1 Kings 19:20). 80 Jesus (Mark 6:10). 81 Nicodemus (John 3:4).

82 Someone go and bury this cursed woman, for she is the daughter of a king.

83 God Almighty appeared to me at Luz in the land of Canaan and blessed me.

84 It was the woman you gave me who gave me the fruit, and I ate it.

85 Is it true, Shadrach, Meshach, and Abednego, that you refuse to serve my gods or to worship the gold statue I have set up?

86 No, Lord. I have never eaten anything that our Jewish laws have declared impure and unclean.

87 For he took notice of his lowly servant girl, and from now on all generations will call me blessed.

88 I am doing this because the LORD has appointed you to be the ruler over Israel, his special possession.

89 Now don't worry about a thing, my daughter. I will do what is necessary, for everyone in town knows you are a virtuous woman.

90 Listen carefully, all of you, fellow Jews and residents of Jerusalem! Make no mistake about this. These people are not drunk. . . . Nine o'clock in the morning is much too early for that.

91 This is what the king says: Don't let Hezekiah deceive you. He will never be able to rescue you from my power.

92 I want the head of John the Baptist on a tray!

93 That's true, Lord, but even dogs are allowed to eat the scraps that fall beneath their masters' table.

94 What therefore God hath joined together, let not man put asunder. (KJV)

95 A host always serves the best wine first. Then, when everyone has had a lot to drink, he brings out the less expensive wine. But you have kept the best until now!

Who Said That? (II)
82 Jehu (2 Kings 9:34). 83 Jacob (Genesis 48:3). 84 Adam (Genesis 3:12). 85 Nebuchadnezzar (Daniel 3:14). 86 Peter (Acts 10:14). 87 Mary (Luke 1:48). 88 Samuel (1 Samuel 10:1). 89 Boaz (Ruth 3:11). 90 Peter (Acts 2:14-15). 91 Rabshakeh (2 Kings 18:29). 92 The daughter of Herodias (Matthew 14:8). 93 The Canaanite woman (Matthew 15:27). 94 Jesus (Mark 10:9). 95 The ruler of the marriage feast at Cana (John 2:10).

CHAPTER 1, VERSE 1

Each of the following is the first complete verse (or portion thereof) of a book of the Bible. Can you name the books?

1 This is the Good News about Jesus the Messiah, the Son of God.

2 Oh, the joys of those who do not follow the advice of the wicked, or stand around with sinners, or join in with mockers.

3 There once was a man . . . who lived in the land of Uz.

4 In my first book I told you, Theophilus, about everything Jesus began to do and teach.

5 I am writing to Gaius, my dear friend, whom I love in the truth.

6 During the third year of King Jehoiakim's reign in Judah, King Nebuchadnezzar of Babylon came to Jerusalem and besieged it.

7 These are the names of the sons of Israel (that is, Jacob) who moved to Egypt with their father, each with his family.

8 These are the words of the Teacher, King David's son, who ruled in Jerusalem.

9 Long ago God spoke many times and in many ways to our ancestors through the prophets.

10 We proclaim to you the one who existed from the beginning, whom we have heard and seen. We saw him with our own eyes and touched him with our own hands. He is the Word of life.

11 The LORD called to Moses from the Tabernacle and said to him.

12 The descendants of Adam were Seth, Enosh.

13 This is a record of the ancestors of Jesus the Messiah, a descendant of David and of Abraham.

14 This letter is from Paul, an apostle of Christ Jesus, appointed by the command of God our Savior and Christ Jesus, who gives us hope.

15 These events happened in the days of King Xerxes, who reigned over 127 provinces stretching from India to Ethiopia.

(More First Verses on the next page)

Chapter 1, Verse 1
1 Mark. 2 Psalms. 3 Job. 4 Acts. 5 3 John. 6 Daniel. 7 Exodus. 8 Ecclesiastes. 9 Hebrews. 10 1 John. 11 Leviticus. 12 1 Chronicles. 13 Matthew. 14 1 Timothy. 15 Esther.

16 Jerusalem, once so full of people, is now deserted. She who was once great among the nations now sits alone like a widow. Once the queen of all the earth, she is now a slave.

17 In the beginning the Word already existed. The Word was with God, and the Word was God.

18 In the beginning God created the heaven and the earth.

19 This letter is from Paul, an apostle. I was not appointed by any group of people or any human authority, but by Jesus Christ himself and by God the Father, who raised Jesus from the dead.

20 On July 31 of my thirtieth year, while I was with the Judean exiles beside the Kebar River in Babylon, the heavens were opened and I saw visions of God.

21 A year after Israel's departure from Egypt, the LORD spoke to Moses in the Tabernacle in the wilderness of Sinai.

— — — — — — —

22 Solomon son of David took firm control of his kingdom, for the LORD his God was with him and made him very powerful.

23 I am writing to the chosen lady and to her children, whom I love in the truth—as does everyone else who knows the truth.

24 This letter is from Paul, a slave of Christ Jesus, chosen by God to be an apostle and sent out to preach his Good News.

— — — — — — —

25 There was a man named Elkanah who lived in Ramah in the region of Zuph in the hill country of Ephraim. He was the son of Jeroham, son of Elihu, son of Tohu, son of Zuph, of Ephraim.

(More First Verses on the next page)

Chapter 1, Verse 1
16 Lamentations. **17** John. **18** Genesis. **19** Galatians. **20** Ezekiel. **21** Numbers.
22 2 Chronicles. **23** 2 John. **24** Romans. **25** 1 Samuel.

172   THE GOOD BOOK BIBLE TRIVIA

26 In the first year of King Cyrus of Persia, the LORD fulfilled the prophecy he had given through Jeremiah. He stirred the heart of Cyrus to put this proclamation in writing and to send it throughout his kingdom.

27 After King Ahab's death, the land of Moab rebelled against Israel.

— — — — — —

28 This letter is from Paul, a slave of God and an apostle of Jesus Christ. I have been sent to proclaim faith to those God has chosen and to teach them to know the truth that shows them how to live godly lives.

29 These are the words that Moses spoke to all the people of Israel while they were in the wilderness east of the Jordan River. They were camped in the Jordan Valley near Suph, between Paran on one side and Tophel, Laban, Hazeroth, and Di-zahab on the other.

30 This letter is from Paul, chosen by the will of God to be an apostle of Christ Jesus, and from our brother Sosthenes.

31 Many people have set out to write accounts about the events that have been fulfilled among us.

— — — —

32 After the death of Saul, David returned from his victory over the Amalekites and spent two days in Ziklag.

33 King David was now very old, and no matter how many blankets covered him, he could not keep warm.

34 After the death of Joshua, the Israelites asked the LORD, "Which tribe should go first to attack the Canaanites?"

33 1 Kings. 34 Judges.
26 Ezra. 27 2 Kings. 28 Titus. 29 Deuteronomy. 30 1 Corinthians. 31 Luke. 32 2 Samuel.
Chapter 1, Verse 1

GETTING IT IN WRITING   173

BEGINNING AT THE END

Each of the following is the last verse (or portion thereof) of a book of the Bible. Can you name the book?

1 Remember this in my favor, O my God.

2 Or have you utterly rejected us? Are you angry with us still?

3 HERE IS MY GREETING IN MY OWN HANDWRITING—PAUL.

4 He served Baal and worshiped him, provoking the anger of the LORD, the God of Israel, just as his father had done.

5 Eleazar son of Aaron also died. He was buried in the hill country of Ephraim, in the town of Gibeah . . .

6 So the Babylonian king gave him a regular food allowance as long as he lived. This continued until the day of his death.

7 May the grace of the Lord Jesus Christ be with your spirit.

8 May the grace of the Lord Jesus be with God's holy people.

9 So Joseph died at the age of 110. The Egyptians embalmed him, and his body was placed in a coffin in Egypt..

10 David built an altar there to the LORD and sacrificed burnt offerings and peace offerings. And the LORD answered his prayer for the land, and the plague on Israel was stopped.

11 Let everything that breathes sing praises to the LORD! Praise the LORD!

12 I will give you a good name, a name of distinction, among all the nations of the earth, as I restore your fortunes before their very eyes. I, the LORD, have spoken!

13 God will judge us for everything we do, including every secret thing, whether good or bad.

14 All glory to the only wise God, through Jesus Christ, forever. Amen.

15 For the worms that devour them will never die, and the fire that burns them will never go out. All who pass by will view them with utter horror.

(More Endings on the next page)

Beginning at the End

1 Nehemiah. 2 Lamentations. 3 Colossians. 4 1 Kings. 5 Joshua. 6 Jeremiah. 7 Philippians. 8 Revelation. Other manuscripts read *be with all*; still others read *be with all of God's holy people*. Some manuscripts add *Amen*. 9 Genesis. 10 2 Samuel. 11 Psalms. 12 Zephaniah. 13 Ecclesiastes. 14 Romans. 15 Isaiah.

16 Reward her for all she has done. Let her deeds publicly declare her praise.

17 As for you, go your way until the end. You will rest, and then at the end of the days, you will rise again to receive the inheritance set aside for you.

The answers to the next six questions are hidden in the puzzle that follows the questions. Can you find them?

18 Afterward Jesus himself sent them out from east to west with the sacred and unfailing message of salvation that gives eternal life.

19 I will pardon my people's crimes, which I have not yet pardoned; and I, the LORD, will make my home in Jerusalem with my people.

20 You can be sure that whoever brings the sinner back will save that person from death and bring about the forgiveness of many sins.

21 And they spent all of their time in the Temple, praising God.

22 You will show us your faithfulness and unfailing love as you promised to our ancestors Abraham and Jacob long ago.

23 Each of these men had a pagan wife, and some even had children by these wives.

M	J	O	E	L
I	A	N	Z	U
C	M	A	R	K
A	E	H	A	E
H	O	S	E	A
S	E	M	A	J

(More Endings on the next page)

Beginning at the End
16 Proverbs. 17 Daniel. 18 Mark (This is probably the real ending of Mark. Many Bibles include verses 9–20, the longer ending.) 19 Joel. 20 James. 21 Luke. 22 Micah. 23 Ezra.

24 Peace be with you. Your friends here send you their greetings. Please give my personal greetings to each of our friends there.

25 These accounts include the mighty deeds of his reign and everything that happened to him and to Israel and to all the surrounding kingdoms.

26 My love to all of you in Christ Jesus.

27 The cloud of the LORD hovered over the Tabernacle during the day, and at night fire glowed inside the cloud so the whole family of Israel could see it. This continued throughout all their journeys.

28 Then they took their bones and buried them beneath the tamarisk tree at Jabesh, and they fasted for seven days.

29 The distance around the entire city will be 6 miles. And from that day the name of the city will be The LORD Is There.

30 All glory to him who alone is God, our Savior through Jesus Christ our Lord. All glory, majesty, power, and authority are his before all time, and in the present, and beyond all time! Amen.

31 His preaching will turn the hearts of fathers to their children, and the hearts of children to their fathers. Otherwise I will come and strike the land with a curse.

32 Greet each other with Christian love. Peace be with all of you who are in Christ.

33 These are the commands and regulations that the LORD gave to the people of Israel through Moses while they were camped on the plains of Moab beside the Jordan River across from Jericho.

34 Come away, my love! Be like a gazelle or a young stag on the mountains of spices.

35 Mordecai the Jew became the prime minister, with authority next to that of King Xerxes himself. He was very great among the Jews, who held him in high esteem, because he continued to work for the good of his people and to speak up for the welfare of all their descendants.

(More Endings on the next page)

Beginning at the End
24 3 John. **25** 1 Chronicles. **26** 1 Corinthians. **27** Exodus. **28** 1 Samuel. **29** Ezekiel. **30** Jude.
31 Malachi. **32** 1 Peter. **33** Numbers. **34** Song of Songs (Song of Solomon). **35** Esther.

36 May the Lord be with your spirit. And may his grace be with all of you.

37 Teach these new disciples to obey all the commands I have given you. And be sure of this: I am with you always, even to the end of the age.

38 May the grace of the Lord Jesus Christ, the love of God, and the fellowship of the Holy Spirit be with you all.

39 May God's grace be eternally upon all who love our Lord Jesus Christ.

40 Those who have been rescued will go up to Mount Zion in Jerusalem to rule over the mountains of Edom. And the LORD himself will be king!

41 So the Babylonian king gave him a regular food allowance as long as he lived.

42 And on that day there will no longer be traders [Canaanite] in the Temple of the LORD of Heaven's Armies.

43 In those days Israel had no king; all the people did whatever seemed right in their own eyes.

44 Rather, you must grow in the grace and knowledge of our Lord and Savior Jesus Christ. All glory to him, both now and forever! Amen.

45 Obed was the father of Jesse. Jesse was the father of David.

46 These are the commands that the LORD gave through Moses on Mount Sinai for the Israelites.

47 Jesus also did many other things. If they were all written down, I suppose the whole world could not contain the books that would be written.

48 There is no healing for your wound; your injury is fatal. All who hear of your destruction will clap their hands for joy. Where can anyone be found who has not suffered from your continual cruelty?

(More Endings on the next page)

Beginning at the End
36 2 Timothy. **37** Matthew. **38** 2 Corinthians. **39** Ephesians. **40** Obadiah. **41** 2 Kings.
42 Zechariah. **43** Judges. **44** 2 Peter. **45** Ruth. **46** Leviticus. **47** John. **48** Nahum.

BEGINNING AT THE END (CONTINUED)

49 Any of you who are the LORD's people may go there for this task. And may the LORD your God be with you!

50 Dear children, keep away from anything that might take God's place in your hearts.

51 Dear brothers and sisters, may the grace of our Lord Jesus Christ be with your spirit. Amen.

52 Some people have wandered from the faith by following such foolishness. May God's grace be with you all.

53 I will firmly plant them there in their own land. They will never again be uprooted from the land I have given them, says the LORD your God.

54 Then he died, an old man who had lived a long, full life.

55 Let those who are wise understand these things. Let those with discernment listen carefully. The paths of the LORD are true and right, and righteous people live by walking in them. But in those paths sinners stumble and fall.

56 With mighty power, Moses performed terrifying acts in the sight of all Israel.

57 But Nineveh has more than 120,000 people living in spiritual darkness, not to mention all the animals. Shouldn't I feel sorry for such a great city?

58 Boldly proclaiming the Kingdom of God and teaching about the Lord Jesus Christ. And no one tried to stop him.

59 The Sovereign LORD is my strength! He makes me as surefooted as a deer, able to tread upon the heights.

60 Greetings from the children of your sister, chosen by God.

61 But when this happens, says the LORD of Heaven's Armies, I will honor you, Zerubbabel son of Shealtiel, my servant. I will make you like a signet ring on my finger, says the LORD, for I have chosen you.

Beginning at the End

49 2 Chronicles. 50 1 John. 51 Galatians. 52 1 Timothy. 53 Amos. 54 Job. 55 Hosea. 56 Deuteronomy. 57 Jonah. 58 Acts. 59 Habakkuk. 60 2 John. 61 Haggai.

THE OLD TESTAMENT IN THE NEW (II)

Here are more verses (or portions thereof) from the New Testament, each of them a quotation from the Old Testament. Name the Old Testament book (and, if you're sharp, chapter and verse) where the passage appears.

1 You are my Son. Today I have become your Father. (Acts 13:33)

2 You will not allow your Holy One to rot in the grave. (Acts 13:35)

3 Afterward I will return and restore the fallen house of David. I will rebuild its ruins and restore it. (Acts 15:16)

4 Go and say to this people: When you hear what I say, you will not understand. When you see what I do, you will not comprehend. (Acts 28:26)

5 No wonder the Scriptures say, "The Gentiles blaspheme the name of God because of you." (Romans 2:24)

6 You will be proved right in what you say, and you will win your case in court. (Romans 3:4)

7 All have turned away; all have become useless. No one does good, not a single one. (Romans 3:12)

8 Their talk is foul, like the stench from an open grave. Their tongues are filled with lies. Snake venom drips from their lips. (Romans 3:13)

9 Their mouths are full of cursing and bitterness. (Romans 3:14)

10 They rush to commit murder. (Romans 3:15)

11 For your sake we are killed every day; we are being slaughtered like sheep. (Romans 8:36)

12 I loved Jacob, but I rejected Esau. (Romans 9:13)

13 I will show mercy to anyone I choose, and I will show compassion to anyone I choose. (Romans 9:15)

(More OT in the NT on the next page)

The Old Testament in the New (II)

1 Psalm 2:7. 2 Psalm 16:10. 3 Amos 9:11. 4 Isaiah 6:9. 5 Isaiah 52:5. 6 Psalm 51:4. 7 Psalm 14:3. 8 Psalm 5:9. 9 Psalm 10:7. 10 Isaiah 59:7. 11 Psalm 44:22. 12 Malachi 1:2-3. 13 Exodus 33:19.

GETTING IT IN WRITING 179

14 I have appointed you for the very purpose of displaying my power in you and to spread my fame throughout the earth. (Romans 9:17)

15 Should the thing that was created say to the one who created it, "Why have you made me like this?" (Romans 9:20)

16 Those who were not my people, I will now call my people. And I will love those whom I did not love before. (Romans 9:25)

17 Though the people of Israel are as numerous as the sand of the seashore, only a remnant will be saved. (Romans 9:27)

18 If the LORD of Heaven's Armies had not spared a few of our children, we would have been wiped out like Sodom, destroyed like Gomorrah. (Romans 9:29)

19 I am placing a stone in Jerusalem that makes people stumble, a rock that makes them fall. (Romans 9:33)

20 Anyone who trusts in him will never be disgraced. (Romans 10:11)

21 LORD, who has believed our message? (Romans 10:16)

22 I will rouse your jealousy through people who are not even a nation. I will provoke your anger through the foolish Gentiles. (Romans 10:19)

23 I was found by people who were not looking for me. I showed myself to those who were not asking for me. (Romans 10:20)

24 All day long I opened my arms to them, but they were disobedient and rebellious. (Romans 10:21)

25 I ask, then, has God rejected his own people, the nation of Israel? (Romans 11:1)

26 LORD, they have killed your prophets and torn down your altars. I am the only one left, and now they are trying to kill me, too. (Romans 11:3)

27 No, I have 7,000 others who have never bowed down to Baal! (Romans 11:4)

(More OT in the NT on the next page)

The Old Testament in the New (II)
14 Exodus 9:16.   **15** Isaiah 29:16.   **16** Hosea 2:23.   **17** Isaiah 10:22.   **18** Isaiah 13:19.   **19** Isaiah 28:16.   **20** Isaiah 28:16.   **21** Isaiah 53:1.   **22** Deuteronomy 32:21.   **23** Isaiah 65:1.   **24** Isaiah 65:2.   **25** Psalm 94:4.   **26** 1 Kings 19:10, 14.   **27** 1 Kings 19:18.

180   THE GOOD BOOK BIBLE TRIVIA

28 God has put them into a deep sleep. To this day he has shut their eyes so they do not see, and closed their ears so they do not hear. (Romans 11:8)

29 Let their bountiful table become a snare, a trap that makes them think all is well. Let their blessings cause them to stumble, and let them get what they deserve. Let their eyes go blind so they cannot see, and let their backs be bent forever. (Romans 11:9-10)

30 The one who rescues will come from Jerusalem, and he will turn Israel away from ungodliness. And this is my covenant with them, that I will take away their sins. (Romans 11:26-27)

31 For who can know the LORD's thoughts? Who knows enough to give him advice? (Romans 11:34)

32 And who has given him so much that he needs to pay it back? (Romans 11:35)

33 I will take revenge; I will pay them back. (Romans 12:19)

34 If your enemies are hungry, feed them. If they are thirsty, give them something to drink. In doing this, you will heap burning coals of shame on their heads. (Romans 12:20)

35 As surely as I live, every knee will bend to me, and every tongue will confess and give praise to God. (Romans 14:11)

36 The insults of those who insult you, O God, have fallen on me. (Romans 15:3)

37 For this, I will praise you among the Gentiles; I will sing praises to your name. (Romans 15:9)

38 Rejoice with his people, you Gentiles. (Romans 15:10)

39 Praise the LORD, all you Gentiles. Praise him, all you people of the earth. (Romans 15:11)

40 The heir to David's throne will come, and he will rule over the Gentiles. They will place their hope on him. (Romans 15:12)

(More OT in the NT on the next page)

The Old Testament in the New (II)

28 Isaiah 29:10. **29** Psalm 69:22-23. **30** Isaiah 27:9. **31** Isaiah 40:13. **32** Job 41:11. **33** Deuteronomy 32:35. **34** Proverbs 25:21-22. **35** Isaiah 45:23. **36** Psalm 69:9. **37** Psalm 18:50. **38** Deuteronomy 32:43. **39** Psalm 117:1. **40** Isaiah 11:10.

GETTING IT IN WRITING 181

41 Those who have never been told about him will see, and those who have never heard of him will understand. (Romans 15:21)

42 I will destroy the wisdom of the wise and discard the intelligence of the intelligent. (1 Corinthians 1:19)

43 So where does this leave the philosophers, the scholars, and the world's brilliant debaters? God has made the wisdom of this world look foolish. (1 Corinthians 1:20)

44 If you want to boast, boast only about the LORD. (1 Corinthians 1:31)

45 No eye has seen, no ear has heard, and no mind has imagined what God has prepared for those who love him. (1 Corinthians 2:9)

46 Who can know the LORD's thoughts? Who knows enough to teach him? (1 Corinthians 2:16)

47 He traps the wise in the snare of their own cleverness. (1 Corinthians 3:19)

48 The LORD knows the thoughts of the wise; he knows they are worthless. (1 Corinthians 3:20)

49 You must remove the evil person from among you. (1 Corinthians 5:13)

50 You must not muzzle an ox to keep it from eating as it treads out the grain. (1 Corinthians 9:9)

51 The people celebrated with feasting and drinking, and they indulged in pagan revelry. (1 Corinthians 10:7)

52 For the earth is the LORD's, and everything in it. (1 Corinthians 10:26)

53 I will speak to my own people through strange languages and through the lips of foreigners. But even then, they will not listen to me, says the LORD. (1 Corinthians 14:21)

54 Let's feast and drink, for tomorrow we die! (1 Corinthians 15:32)

(More OT in the NT on the next page)

The Old Testament in the New (II)

41 Isaiah 52:15. **42** Isaiah 29:14. **43** Isaiah 33:18. **44** Jeremiah 9:22-23. **45** Isaiah 64:4.
46 Isaiah 40:13. **47** Job 5:13. **48** Psalm 94:11. **49** Deuteronomy 13:6. **50** Deuteronomy 25:4.
51 Exodus 32:6. **52** Psalm 24:1. **53** Isaiah 28:11-12. **54** Isaiah 22:13.

55 The first man, Adam, became a living person. (1 Corinthians 15:45)

56 O death, where is your victory? O death, where is your sting? (1 Corinthians 15:55)

57 I believed in God, so I spoke. (2 Corinthians 4:13)

58 At just the right time, I heard you. On the day of salvation, I helped you. (2 Corinthians 6:2)

59 I will live in them and walk among them. I will be their God, and they will be my people. (2 Corinthians 6:16)

60 Therefore, come out from among unbelievers, and separate yourselves from them, says the LORD. Don't touch their filthy things, and I will welcome you. (2 Corinthians 6:17)

61 And I will be your Father, and you will be my sons and daughters, says the LORD Almighty. (2 Corinthians 6:18)

62 Those who gathered a lot had nothing left over, and those who gathered only a little had enough. (2 Corinthians 8:15)

63 God loveth a cheerful giver. (2 Corinthians 9:7, KJV)

64 They share freely and give generously to the poor. Their good deeds will be remembered forever. (2 Corinthians 9:9)

65 If you want to boast, boast only about the LORD. (2 Corinthians 10:17)

66 The facts of every case must be established by the testimony of two or three witnesses. (2 Corinthians 13:1)

67 Abraham believed God, and God counted him as righteous because of his faith. (Galatians 3:6)

68 All nations will be blessed through you. (Galatians 3:8)

69 Cursed is everyone who does not observe and obey all the commands that are written in God's Book of the Law. (Galatians 3:10)

70 It is through faith that a righteous person has life. (Galatians 3:11)

The Old Testament in the New (II)

55 Genesis 2:7. **56** Hosea 13:14. **57** Psalm 116:10. **58** Isaiah 49:8. **59** Leviticus 26:12; Jeremiah 32:38. **60** Isaiah 52:11. **61** Isaiah 43:6. **62** Exodus 22:8. **63** Proverbs 22:8. **64** Psalm 112:9. **65** Jeremiah 9:23. **66** Deuteronomy 19:15. **67** Genesis 15:6. **68** Genesis 12:3. **69** Deuteronomy 27:26. **70** Habakkuk 2:4.

AUTHOR, AUTHOR

According to tradition, who wrote the following books of the Bible?

1 Exodus

2 Revelation

3 Hebrews

4 Esther

5 Proverbs

6 Ruth

7 1 and 2 Chronicles

8 Lamentations

9 Song of Songs

10 Numbers

11 Nehemiah

12 Judges

13 Psalms

14 Ecclesiastes

15 Ezra

16 Deuteronomy

17 Job

18 1 and 2 Kings

19 Leviticus

20 Joshua

21 Acts

22 Jude

23 Genesis

24 1 and 2 Samuel

25 James

EXTRA CREDIT

What 1963 film title is from Jesus' reference to "Solomon in all his glory"?

Lilies of the Field

Author, Author

1 Moses. 2 The apostle John. 3 Not known, though often attributed to Paul, Apollos, and many others. 4 Attributed to Ezra, Mordecai, and others. 5 Solomon, although the book itself names other contributors. 6 Samuel. 7 Ezra. 8 Jeremiah. 9 Solomon. 10 Moses. 11 Nehemiah. 12 Samuel. 13 David, Asaph, and many others. 14 Solomon. 15 Ezra. 16 Moses. 17 Moses. 18 Jeremiah. 19 Moses. 20 Joshua. 21 Luke. 22 Jude, the brother of Jesus. 23 Moses. 24 Samuel and, possibly, the prophet Nathan. 25 James, the brother of Jesus.

CURIOUS QUOTATIONS

For each of the strange quotations listed, name the book of the Bible where it is found. (If you're really good, name the chapter and verse.) All of these verses are from the King James Version.

1 At Parbar westward, four at the causeway, and two at Parbar.
2 Therefore will I discover thy skirts upon thy face.
3 The mountains skipped like rams, and the little hills like lambs.
4 All faces shall gather blackness.
5 The ships of Tarshish did sing of thee in thy market.
6 The herds of cattle are perplexed.
7 The voice of the turtle is heard in our land.
8 And they made two ouches of gold.
9 A bell and a pomegranate, a bell and a pomegranate, round about the hem of the robe to minister in.
10 I have put on my coat; how shall I put it on?
11 Dead flies cause the ointment of the apothecary to send forth a stinking savor.
12 Every man shall kiss his lips that giveth a right answer.
13 And kings shall be thy nursing fathers.
14 This thy stature is like to a palm tree, and thy breasts to clusters of grapes.
15 Destruction and death say, We have heard the fame thereof with our ears.
16 Associate yourselves, O ye people, and ye shall be broken in pieces.
17 And the rest of the tree of his forest shall be few, that a child may write them.

(More Curious Quotes on the next page)

Curious Quotations

1 I Chronicles (26:18). 2 Jeremiah (13:26). 3 Psalms (114:4). 4 Daniel (8:10). 5 Ezekiel (27:25). 6 Joel (1:18). 7 Song of Songs (39:16). 8 Exodus (39:26). 9 Exodus (1:18). 10 Song of Songs (Song of Solomon) (10:1). 11 Ecclesiastes (10:1). 12 Proverbs (24:26). 13 Isaiah (49:23). 14 Song of Songs (Song of Solomon) (7:7). 15 Job (28:22). 16 Isaiah (8:9). 17 Isaiah (10:19).

CURIOUS QUOTATIONS (CONTINUED)

18 And on the eighth she shall take unto her two turtles.

19 Thou shalt not seethe a kid in his mother's milk.

20 Thy lips, O my spouse, drop as the honeycomb; honey and milk are under thy tongue; and the smell of thy garments is like the smell of Lebanon.

21 And it came to pass in the first month in the second year, on the first day of the month, that the tabernacle was reared up.

22 Behold, he formed grasshoppers in the beginning of the shooting.

23 So two or three cities wandered unto one city to drink water.

24 Let the floods clap their hands; let the hills be joyful together.

25 Every head was made bald, and every shoulder was peeled.

26 Her king is cut off as the foam upon the water.

27 And the sea coast shall be dwellings and cottages for shepherds, and folds for flocks.

28 And it waxed great, even to the host of heaven.

29 Then the king's countenance was changed, and his thoughts troubled him, so that the joints of his loins were loosed, and his knees smote one against the other.

30 He maketh them to skip like a calf; Lebanon and Sirion like a young unicorn.

31 And the wild asses did stand in the high places, they snuffed up the wind like dragons.

32 I have compared thee, O my love, to a company of horses in Pharaoh's chariots.

33 Thy bow was made quite naked.

34 The LORD will smite thee with the botch of Egypt, and with the emerods, and with the scab, and with the itch.

(More Curious Quotes on the next page)

Curious Quotations
18 Leviticus (15:29).　19 Deuteronomy (14:21).　20 Song of Songs (Song of Solomon) (4:11).
21 Exodus (40:17).　22 Amos (7:1).　23 Amos (4:8).　24 Joel (2:6).　25 Ezekiel (29:18).
26 Hosea (10:7).　27 Zephaniah (2:6).　28 Daniel (5:6).　29 Daniel (5:6).　30 Psalms (29:6).
31 Jeremiah (14:6).　32 Song of Songs (Song of Solomon) (1:9).　33 Habakkuk (3:9).
34 Deuteronomy (28:27).

186　THE GOOD BOOK BIBLE TRIVIA

35 Cease ye from man, whose breath is in his nostrils.

36 Behold, I will corrupt your seed, and spread dung upon your faces, even the dung of your solemn feasts.

37 They are all adulterers, as an oven heated by the baker.

38 Feed thy people with thy rod.

39 And the man whose hair is fallen off his head, he is bald; yet is he clean.

— — — — — — — —

40 Ye shall not eat one day, nor two days, nor five days, neither ten days, nor twenty days, but even a whole month, until it come out at your nostrils.

41 I am gone like the shadow when it declineth; I am tossed up and down as the locust.

42 And the unicorns shall come down with them, and the bullocks with the bull; and their land shall be soaked with blood, and their dust made fat with fatness.

— — — — — —

43 Thy teeth are like a flock of sheep that are even shorn, which came up from the washing.

44 The words of a man's mouth are as deep waters.

(More Curious Quotes on the next page)

CURIOUS QUOTATIONS (CONTINUED)

45 Lift up your heads, O ye gates.

46 Will I eat the flesh of bulls, or drink the blood of goats?

47 When she saw Isaac, she lighted off her camel.

48 Thy neck is like the tower of David builded for an armory, whereon there hang a thousand bucklers.

49 Thou shalt not respect persons, neither take a gift.

50 So and more also do God unto the enemies of David, if I leave of all that pertain to him by the morning light any that pisseth against the wall.

51 Moab is my washpot; over Edom will I cast out my shoe.

52 The watchman said, The morning cometh, and also the night; if ye will inquire, inquire ye; return, come.

53 And he will take your menservants, and your maidservants, and your goodliest young men, and your asses, and put them to his work.

54 Their feet are swift to shed blood.

55 Now therefore go, and I will be with thy mouth.

EXTRA CREDIT

Where is the oldest complete Bible in existence preserved?

The Codex Sinaiticus is in the British Museum

Curious Quotations
45 Psalms (24:7). **46** Psalms (50:13). **47** Genesis (25:64). **48** Song of Songs (Song of Solomon) (4:4). **49** Deuteronomy (16:19). **50** 1 Samuel (25:22). **51** Psalms (60:8). **52** Isaiah (21:12). **53** 1 Samuel (8:16). **54** Romans (3:15). **55** Exodus (4:12).

PROPHECIES OF THE MESSIAH

Many passages in the Old Testament are prophecies which were fulfilled by events in Jesus' life. For each event listed here, name the Old Testament book that contains the prophecy of the event.

1   Throwing dice for Jesus' robe
2   Jesus' crucifixion with two thieves
3   The thirty pieces of silver

—   —   —   —   —   —   —

4   The virgin birth
5   Jesus' birth in Bethlehem
6   Jesus' resurrection
7   The piercing of Jesus' side with a spear
8   Not breaking the bones of the crucified Jesus
9   Betrayal by a close companion

—   —   —   —   —   —

10   Jesus' entry into Jerusalem on a donkey
11   Giving vinegar to the crucified Jesus
12   Jesus, Mary, and Joseph leaving Egypt and returning to Galilee
13   Speaking in parables

BETWEEN THE TESTAMENTS

Name the books described below. Some are part of the Apocrypha and are regarded as Scripture by Catholics and others. Some are considered Pseudipigrapha and are not accepted as genuine Scripture by either Jews or Christians. Some are translations or commentaries made (or begun) after the close of the Old Testament.

1 A book of wise sayings attributed to a king of Israel

2 A romantic story of a pious Jew whose son is aided by the angel Raphael

3 A tale of a brave Jewish woman who saves her city from the army of Nebuchadnezzar by murdering a Babylonian captain

4 A book of wisdom whose author is identified in the text as Sirach of Jerusalem

5 A historical work that recounts the story of the Jewish revolt against the evil ruler Antiochus Epiphanes and his successors

—— —— —— —— —— —— —— ——

6 A book of prayers and confessions, supposedly written by the friend of an Old Testament prophet

7 A tale of a virtuous woman accused of adultery and proved innocent by Daniel

8 An eloquent prayer reputed to be the work of a repentant king of Judah

9 A tale of Babylonian idol worship and some conniving priests

10 A historical work that covers some of the same history chronicled in Ezra, Nehemiah, and 2 Chronicles

(More Testaments on the next page)

Between the Testaments

1 Wisdom of Solomon (Apocrypha) 2 Tobit (Apocrypha) 3 Judith (Apocrypha) 4 Ecclesiasticus (Apocrypha) 5 1 Maccabees (Apocrypha) 6 Baruch (Apocrypha) 7 Susanna (Apocrypha) 8 The Prayer of Manasseh (Apocrypha) 9 Bel and the Dragon (Apocrypha) 10 1 Esdras (Apocrypha).

190   THE GOOD BOOK BIBLE TRIVIA

BETWEEN THE TESTAMENTS (CONTINUED)

11 This book consists of alleged predictions of Moses, given to Joshua just before Moses' death.

12 These are additions, not found in the Hebrew Bible, to an Old Testament book about the Persian period.

13 This addition to the book of Daniel contains an eloquent prayer, a miraculous deliverance, and a hymn of praise.

14 This work is a shortened form of a five-volume historical work by Jason of Cyrene. It contains letters to the Jews in Egypt.

15 This apocalyptic work contains bizarre visions, images of the Messiah, and references to the Roman empire.

16 This collection of laws based on the laws of Moses was not completed until AD 500. It consists of the Mishnah and the Gemara and is still widely studied by Jewish scholars today.

— — — — — — — — — —

17 These 18 poems about the coming Messiah are ascribed to a famous Hebrew poet.

18 This collection of predictions speaks about the downfall of empires and the messianic age.

19 This book of revelations purports to have been written by Enoch and Noah.

20 This book purports to be the dying speeches of Jacob's 12 sons.

21 Written by a Pharisee, this book extols the law and the Hebrew patriarchs and urges Jews not to be influenced by Greek culture.

22 These are loose translations of the Hebrew Scriptures into the Aramaic language, made after Aramaic, not Hebrew, was the common language of Palestine.

23 This book about a famous Judean prophet tells of his martyrdom under wicked King Manasseh.

WHO SAID THAT? (III)

1 I sank beneath the waves, and the waters closed over me. Seaweed wrapped itself around my head.

2 I know that my Redeemer lives, and he will stand upon the earth at last.

3 Then what is all the bleating of sheep and goats and the lowing of cattle I hear?

4 Surely the LORD is in this place.

5 For in him we live and move and exist.

6 Lord Jesus, receive my spirit.

7 I fasted and wept while the child was alive, for I said, "Perhaps the LORD will be gracious to me and let the child live."

8 Wherever you die, I will die, and there I will be buried. May the LORD punish me severely if I allow anything but death to separate us!

9 In three days you will cross the Jordan River and take possession of the land the LORD your God is giving you.

10 This is none other but the house of God, and this is the gate of heaven.

11 It was God who sent me here ahead of you to preserve your lives.

12 You may be sure that your sin will find you out.

13 Should not the Judge of all the earth do what is right?

14 I will certainly not sin against the LORD by ending my prayers for you.

15 Take courage and be a man. Observe the requirements of the LORD your God, and follow all his ways.

16 Listen, O Israel! The LORD is our God, the LORD alone.

17 Show us how to increase our faith.

18 O earth, earth, earth! Listen to this message from the LORD!

(More Sayings on the next page)

Who Said That? (III)

1 Jonah (2:5).   2 Job (19:25).   3 Samuel (1 Samuel 15:14).   4 Jacob (Genesis 28:16).   5 Paul (Acts 17:28).   6 Stephen (Acts 7:59).   7 David (2 Samuel 12:22).   8 Ruth (1:17).   9 Joshua (1:11).   10 Jacob (Genesis 28:17).   11 Joseph (Genesis 45:8).   12 Moses (Numbers 32:23).   13 Abraham (Genesis 18:25).   14 Samuel (1 Samuel 12:23).   15 David (1 Kings 2:2-3).   16 Moses (Deuteronomy 6:4).   17 The disciples (Luke 17:5).   18 Jeremiah (22:29).

19 Can the dead live again?

20 O LORD, no one but you can help the powerless against the mighty! Help us, O LORD our God.

21 Everything we have has come from you, and we give you only what you first gave us!

22 Praise the LORD who has given rest to his people Israel, just as he promised. Not one word has failed of all the wonderful promises he gave through his servant Moses.

23 The LORD your God is a devouring fire; he is a jealous God.

24 You intended to harm me, but God intended it all for good. He brought me to this position so I could save the lives of many people.

25 We are on our way to the place the LORD promised us, for he said, "I will give it to you." Come with us and we will treat you well, for the LORD has promised wonderful blessings for Israel!

26 O our God, won't you stop them? We are powerless against this mighty army that is about to attack us. We do not know what to do, but we are looking to you for help.

27 God might kill me, but I have no other hope. I am going to argue my case with him.

28 Is there no medicine in Gilead? Is there no physician there?

29 What sorrow awaits you who lounge in luxury in Jerusalem.

30 For as the waters fill the sea, the earth will be filled with an awareness of the glory of the LORD.

31 And now I entrust you to God and the message of his grace that is able to build you up and give you an inheritance with all those he has set apart for himself.

32 It is not by force nor by strength, but by my Spirit, says the LORD of Heaven's Armies.

(More Sayings on the next page)

Who Said That? (III)

19 Job (14:14). **20** Asa (2 Chronicles 14:11). **21** David (1 Chronicles 29:14). **22** Solomon (1 Kings 8:56). **23** Moses (Deuteronomy 4:24). **24** Joseph (Genesis 50:20). **25** Moses (Numbers 10:29). **26** Jehoshaphat (2 Chronicles 20:12). **27** Job (13:15). **28** Jeremiah (8:22). **29** Amos (6:1). **30** Habakkuk (2:14). **31** Paul (Acts 20:32). **32** Zechariah (4:6).

GETTING IT IN WRITING   193

33 Then, after doing all those things, I will pour out my Spirit upon all people.

34 O people, the LORD has told you what is good, and this is what he requires of you: to do what is right, to love mercy, and to walk humbly with your God.

35 Believe in the LORD your God, and you will be able to stand firm. Believe in his prophets, and you will succeed.

36 For the LORD sees every heart and knows every plan and thought. If you seek him, you will find him.

37 The grass withers and the flowers fade, but the word of our God stands forever.

38 Look, I am sending you the prophet Elijah before the great and dreadful day of the LORD arrives.

39 The stone that you builders rejected has now become the cornerstone.

40 Instead, I want to see a mighty flood of justice, an endless river of righteous living.

41 Do what is good and run from evil so that you may live! Then the LORD God of Heaven's Armies will be your helper, just as you have claimed.

42 Daughter, be encouraged! Your faith has made you well.

43 I'm only from the tribe of Benjamin, the smallest tribe in Israel.

44 What if they won't believe me or listen to me? What if they say, "The LORD never appeared to you"?

45 Please come a little closer and kiss me, my son.

46 What kind of dream is that? Will your mother and I and your brothers actually come and bow to the ground before you?

(More Sayings on the next page)

Who Said That? (III)
33 Joel (2:28). **34** Micah (6:8). **35** Jehoshaphat (2 Chronicles 20:20). **36** David (1 Chronicles 28:9). **37** Isaiah (40:8). **38** Malachi (4:5). **39** Peter (Acts 4:11). **40** Amos (5:24). **41** Amos (5:14). **42** Jesus (Matthew 9:22). **43** Saul (1 Samuel 9:21). **44** Moses (Exodus 4:1). **45** Isaac (Genesis 27:26). **46** Jacob (Genesis 37:10).

47 In a vision I saw all Israel scattered on the mountains, like sheep without a shepherd. And the LORD said, "Their master has been killed."

48 I will never concede that you are right; I will defend my integrity until I die.

49 We will all go—young and old, our sons and daughters, and our flocks and herds. We must all join together in celebrating a festival to the LORD.

50 If you are the King of the Jews, save yourself!

51 Is anyone thirsty? Come and drink—even if you have no money!

52 For this is what the LORD of Heaven's Armies says: In just a little while I will again shake the heavens and the earth, the oceans and the dry land.

— — — — —

53 Do you think God wants us to obey you rather than him?

54 How beautiful on the mountains are the feet of the messenger who brings good news, the good news of peace and salvation, the news that the God of Israel reigns!

55 Who am I, and what is my family in Israel that I should be the king's son-in-law?

56 Give me children, or I'll die!

— — — — —

57 Then what should I do with this man you call the king of the Jews?

58 Look at my servant, whom I strengthen. He is my chosen one, who pleases me. I have put my Spirit upon him. He will bring justice to the nations.

59 Come, let us return to the LORD. He has torn us to pieces; now he will heal us. He has injured us; now he will bandage our wounds.

Who Said That? (III)
47 Micaiah (2 Chronicles 18:16). **48** Job (27:5). **49** Moses (Exodus 10:9). **50** The soldiers at the Crucifixion (Luke 23:37). **51** Isaiah (55:1). **52** Haggai (2:6). **53** Peter and John (Acts 4:19). **54** Isaiah (52:7). **55** David (1 Samuel 18:18). **56** Rachel (Genesis 30:1). **57** Pilate (Mark 15:12). **58** Isaiah (42:1). **59** Hosea (6:1).

SCRIPTURE ON SCRIPTURE

1 According to Paul, who takes away the "veil" over the Old Testament?

2 What group of Christians examined the Scriptures every day to see if Paul was telling the truth?

3 To what young pastor did Paul address his famous words on the divine inspiration of all Scripture?

4 What apostle claimed that the prophets, in writing of the coming Christ, were writing for later generations?

5 Who told the Jews that the Scriptures had testified about him?

6 Where was Jesus when he taught two people how the prophets had predicted his death?

7 To what church did Paul say the Old Testament was written as a set of examples and warnings for the church?

8 In the parable of Lazarus and the rich man, what does Abraham say to the rich man who wants to keep his relatives out of hell?

9 To whom does the writer of Hebrews attribute Psalm 95?

10 What apostle claimed that no Scripture had come about through the prophet's own efforts, but by God's will?

11 In what epistle does Paul promote the public reading of Scripture?

12 What foreign official did Philip teach the predictions of Jesus contained in the Old Testament?

13 In what Gospel does Jesus say that the Scripture cannot be broken?

14 To whom did Peter and John attribute the words of David (Psalm 2)?

15 To whom did Jesus say "Your mistake is that you don't know the Scriptures" after they had posed a ridiculous riddle to him?

TAKE A LETTER

1. What lost letter of Paul is mentioned in the Letter to the Colossians?

2. What mighty king wrote a letter to Hezekiah concerning surrender?

The answers to the next questions are hidden in the puzzle following the questions. Can you find them?

3. Who wrote to the churches concerning the Jerusalem council's decision on the issue of circumcision?

4. Who, using John as a scribe, wrote to the seven churches in Asia?

5. Who asked the high priest for letters of introduction to the synagogues in Damascus?

6. Who wrote to the people of Samaria regarding the fate of Ahab's 70 sons?

7. Who received a letter from David, telling him to put Uriah in the heat of battle?

S	E	S	O	M
J	E	H	U	B
K	P	M	T	A
C	A	D	A	O
S	U	S	E	J
F	L	O	T	G

(More Letters on the next page)

Take a Letter

1 The Letter to the Laodiceans (Colossians 4:16).   2 Sennacherib (2 Kings 19:14).   3 James (Acts 15:23).   4 Jesus (Revelation 1–3).   5 Paul (Acts 9:2).   6 Jehu (2 Kings 10:1-2).   7 Joab (2 Samuel 11:4, 15).

GETTING IT IN WRITING   197

8 Who wrote a letter recommending Apollos to the Corinthian church?

9 Who wrote a letter to Felix concerning the apostle Paul?

10 Who wrote a letter granting permission to continue construction on the second Temple?

11 What king received a letter from Elijah predicting judgment on his sinful reign?

12 What queen wrote to the leaders of Jezreel concerning Naboth?

13 Who had enemies that wrote smear letters about him to the Persian king?

14 Who sent letters of invitation to the tribes of Ephraim and Manasseh, asking them to join in a Passover celebration?

15 Who sent a letter giving Judah's enemies permission to stop the Jews' work on the Temple?

16 What feast did Mordecai prescribe in his letters to the Jews in Persia?

17 What leper carried a letter from the king of Syria to the king of Israel?

18 Who sent a threatening letter designed to discourage Nehemiah from his plans to rebuild Jerusalem?

19 Who, with Paul, penned the First Letter to the Corinthians?

20 Who wrote to Philemon concerning his runaway slave, Onesimus?

Take a Letter
8 The Ephesian church (Acts 18:27). 9 Claudius Lysias (Acts 23:25). 10 King Darius (Ezra 6:6-12).
11 Jehoram (2 Chronicles 21:12). 12 Jezebel (1 Kings 21:8). 13 Zerubbabel (Ezra 4:6-16).
14 Hezekiah (2 Chronicles 30:1-3). 15 King Artaxerxes (Ezra 4:17-22). 16 Purim (Esther 9:20-21).
17 Naaman (2 Kings 5:5-6). 18 Sanballat (Nehemiah 6:5-7). 19 Sosthenes (1 Corinthians 1:1).
20 Paul (Philemon).

THE OLD TESTAMENT IN THE NEW (III)

Here are more verses from the New Testament, each of them a quotation from the Old Testament. Name the Old Testament book (and, if you're sharp, chapter and verse) where the passage appears.

1 Cursed is everyone who is hung on a tree. (Galatians 3:13)
2 It is through obeying the law that a person has life. (Galatians 3:12)
3 Rejoice, O childless woman, you who have never given birth! Break into a joyful shout, you who have never been in labor! For the desolate woman now has more children than the woman who lives with her husband! (Galatians 4:27)
4 Get rid of the slave and her son, for the son of the slave woman will not share the inheritance with the free woman's son. (Galatians 4:30)

— — — — — — —

5 God has put all things under the authority of Christ and has made him head over all things for the benefit of the church. (Ephesians 1:22)
6 He brought this Good News of peace to you Gentiles who were far away from him, and peace to the Jews who were near. (Ephesians 2:17)
7 When he ascended to the heights, he led a crowd of captives and gave gifts to his people. (Ephesians 4:8)
8 Let us tell our neighbors the truth. (Ephesians 4:25)
9 Don't sin by letting anger control you. (Ephesians 4:26)
10 A man leaves his father and mother and is joined to his wife, and the two are united into one. (Ephesians 5:31)
11 Honor your father and mother. This is the first commandment with a promise: If you honor your father and mother, things will go well for you, and you will have a long life on the earth. (Ephesians 6:2-3)

(More OT in the NT on the next page)

12 The LORD knows those who are his. (2 Timothy 2:19)

— — — — — —

13 You are my Son. Today I have become your Father. (Hebrews 1:5)

14 I will be his Father, and he will be my Son. (Hebrews 1:5)

15 Let all of God's angels worship him. (Hebrews 1:6)

16 He sends his angels like the winds, his servants like flames of fire. (Hebrews 1:7)

17 Your throne, O God, endures forever and ever. You rule with a scepter of justice. You love justice and hate evil. Therefore, O God, your God has anointed you, pouring out the oil of joy on you more than on anyone else. (Hebrews 1:8-9)

18 In the beginning, Lord, you laid the foundation of the earth and made the heavens with your hands. (Hebrews 1:10)

19 They will perish, but you remain forever. They will wear out like old clothing. (Hebrews 1:11)

20 But you are always the same; you will live forever. (Hebrews 1:12)

21 What are mere mortals that you should think about them, or a son of man that you should care for him? (Hebrews 2:6)

22 You gave them authority over all things. (Hebrews 2:8)

23 I will proclaim your name to my brothers and sisters. I will praise you among your assembled people. (Hebrews 2:12)

24 I will put my trust in him . . . I and the children God has given me. (Hebrews 2:13)

25 Today when you hear his voice, don't harden your hearts as Israel did when they rebelled, when they tested me in the wilderness. (Hebrews 3:7-8)

26 Their hearts always turn away from me. They refuse to do what I tell them. (Hebrews 3:10)

(More OT in the NT on the next page)

The Old Testament in the New (III)
12 Numbers 16:15. 13 Psalm 2:7. 14 2 Samuel 7:14. 15 Deuteronomy 32:43. 16 Psalm 104:4.
17 Psalm 45:6-7. 18 Psalm 102:25. 19 Psalm 102:26. 20 Psalm 102:27. 21 Psalm 8:4.
22 Psalm 8:6. 23 Psalm 22:22. 24 Isaiah 8:17-18. 25 Psalm 95:7-8. 26 Psalm 95:10.

27 On the seventh day God rested from all his work. (Hebrews 4:4)

28 You are a priest forever in the order of Melchizedek. (Hebrews 5:6)

29 I will certainly bless you, and I will multiply your descendants beyond number. (Hebrews 6:14)

30 I will put my laws in their minds, and I will write them on their hearts. (Hebrews 8:10)

31 And they will not need to teach their neighbors, nor will they need to teach their relatives, saying, "You should know the LORD." (Hebrews 8:11)

32 This blood confirms the covenant God has made with you. (Hebrews 9:20)

33 You did not want animal sacrifices or sin offerings. (Hebrews 10:5-6)

34 Look, I have come to do your will. (Hebrews 10:9)

35 I will take revenge. I will pay them back. (Hebrews 10:30)

36 The LORD will judge his own people. (Hebrews 10:30)

37 Isaac is the son through whom your descendants will be counted. (Hebrews 11:18)

38 My child, don't make light of the LORD's discipline, and don't give up when he corrects you. For the LORD disciplines those he loves, and he punishes each one he accepts as his child. (Hebrews 12:5-6)

39 So take a new grip with your tired hands and strengthen your weak knees. (Hebrews 12:12)

40 Mark out a straight path for your feet so that those who are weak and lame will not fall but become strong. (Hebrews 12:13)

41 Once again I will shake not only the earth but the heavens also. (Hebrews 12:26)

42 I will never fail you. I will never abandon you. (Hebrews 13:5)

43 The LORD is my helper, so I will have no fear. What can mere people do to me? (Hebrews 13:6)

(More OT in the NT on the next page)

The Old Testament in the New (III)
27 Genesis 2:2. **28** Psalm 110:4. **29** Genesis 22:17. **30** Jeremiah 31:33. **31** Jeremiah 31:34.
32 Exodus 24:8. **33** Psalm 40:6. **34** Psalm 40:7-8. **35** Deuteronomy 32:35. **36** Deuteronomy 32:36. **37** Genesis 21:12. **38** Proverbs 3:11-12. **39** Isaiah 35:3. **40** Proverbs 4:26. **41** Haggai 2:6. **42** Deuteronomy 31:6. **43** Psalm 118:6.

44 Abraham believed God, and God counted him as righteous because of his faith. (James 2:23)

45 God opposes the proud but favors the humble. (James 4:6)

46 You must be holy because I am holy. (I Peter 1:16)

47 People are like grass; their beauty is like a flower in the field. The grass withers and the flower fades. But the word of the Lord remains forever. (I Peter 1:24-25)

48 I am placing a cornerstone in Jerusalem, chosen for great honor. (I Peter 2:6)

49 He is the stone that makes people stumble, the rock that makes them fall. (I Peter 2:8)

50 He never sinned, nor ever deceived anyone. (I Peter 2:22)

51 If you want to enjoy life and see many happy days, keep your tongue from speaking evil and your lips from telling lies. (I Peter 3:10)

52 Turn away from evil and do good. Search for peace, and work to maintain it. (I Peter 3:11)

53 The eyes of the Lord watch over those who do right, and his ears are open to their prayers. But the Lord turns his face against those who do evil. (I Peter 3:12)

54 So don't worry or be afraid of their threats. (I Peter 3:14)

55 Christ suffered for our sins once for all time. He never sinned, but he died for sinners to bring you safely home to God. (I Peter 4:18)

56 A dog returns to its vomit. (2 Peter 2:22)

57 A day is like a thousand years to the Lord, and a thousand years is like a day. (2 Peter 3:8)

58 They will rule the nations with an iron rod and smash them like clay pots. (Revelation 2:27)

59 Let anyone who is thirsty come. (Revelation 22:17)

DIFFERENCES OF OPINION

Many readers are puzzled by what seem to be discrepancies in the biblical narratives. Most of these differences can be easily explained by a close reading of the text. Others may be due to errors that occur in centuries of copying manuscripts. None reflect on the inspiration of the Scriptures. I include these questions here, not to cast doubt on the Bible, but merely to test the reader's knowledge of some of these so-called discrepancies.

1 According to Genesis 25:1, Abraham's second wife was Keturah. According to 1 Chronicles 1:32, who was Keturah?

2 In Genesis 29:27, Rachel is given to Jacob seven or eight days after his marriage to Leah. According to Genesis 30:25-32, how long did Jacob have to wait for Rachel?

3 In Exodus 33:20, God tells Moses that no man can see God's face. According to Exodus 33:11, what man saw God face-to-face?

4 The Levites entered the service of the sanctuary at age 30—according to Numbers 4:3. At what age, according to Numbers 8:24, did they enter the service?

5 The mission of the 12 Israelite spies started from Paran—according to Numbers 13:3. In Numbers 20:1, where does the mission start?

6 According to Deuteronomy 10:6, Aaron died at Moserah. Where, according to Numbers 20:28, did he die?

7 Deuteronomy 15:4 says "There should be no poor among you." What does Deuteronomy 15:11 say?

8 According to 1 Samuel 16:10-11, David had seven brothers. How many according to 1 Chronicles 2:13-15?

9 In 1 Samuel 16:19-21, David comes to know Saul by being employed as his harpist. In 1 Samuel 17, how does David come to know Saul?

(More Differences on the next page)

Differences of Opinion

1 His concubine. 2 Fourteen years. 3 Moses. 4 25. 5 Kadesh. 6 Mount Hor. 7 "There will always be some in the land who are poor." 8 Six. 9 Through the killing of Goliath.

10 In 1 Samuel 31:3-4, Saul takes his own life after being wounded. In 2 Samuel 1, who claims he actually killed Saul?

11 Absalom had, according to 2 Samuel 14:27, three sons. How many did he have, according to 2 Samuel 18:8?

12 The Lord moved David to number the people of Israel, according to 2 Samuel 24:1. Who, in the story in 1 Chronicles 21, moved David to do this?

13 According to 2 Kings 24:8, King Jehoiachin was 18 years old when he began to reign. How old was he in the account in 2 Chronicles 36?

14 Samuel was an Ephraimite, according to 1 Samuel 1. What tribe was he from in the account in 1 Chronicles 6?

15 According to 2 Chronicles 33:13-16, evil King Manasseh repented of his sins after being held captive in Babylon. What does the parallel account in 2 Kings 21 say about this repentance?

16 In Matthew's genealogy of the Messiah, Jesus is descended from David's son Solomon. What son of David is, in Luke's account, Jesus' ancestor?

17 In Luke's account of the temptation of Jesus, the last temptation is to jump from the pinnacle of the Temple. What is the last temptation in Matthew's version?

18 According to Matthew 8:5-13, a centurion asks that his servant be healed. In Luke 7:2-11, who does the asking?

19 In Luke 8 and Mark 5, the maniac lives in Gerasa. In Matthew 8, where does he live?

20 Matthew 20:20 states that the mother of James and John requested that her sons be appointed to high office in the coming kingdom. In Mark 10:35, who made the request?

(More Differences on the next page)

Differences of Opinion

10 Saul's Amalekite bodyguard. 11 None. 12 Satan. 13 Eight. 14 Levi. 15 Nothing. 16 Nathan. 17 The temptation to rule the world. 18 The servant. 19 Gadara. 20 James and John.

DIFFERENCES OF OPINION (CONTINUED)

21 In Matthew 26:34, Jesus predicts that Peter will betray him before the rooster crows. In Mark 14:30, how many specific times is the rooster supposed to crow?

22 According to Matthew 27:3-10, Judas hanged himself. How, according to Acts 1:18, did he kill himself?

23 In John 19:19, we are told that the inscription of the cross read "Jesus of Nazareth, the King of the Jews." According to Matthew 27:37, what was the inscription?

24 According to the post-Resurrection account in Luke 24, one disciple ran to Jesus' tomb. John's account says that two disciples ran there. Who were they?

25 In Mark 2:26, Jesus says that Abiathar was priest during David's reign. Who, according to 1 Samuel 21, was priest at that time?

26 Matthew 5:3 (KJV) has Jesus saying, "Blessed are the poor in spirit." What does he say in Luke 6:20?

27 James 1:13 says God does not tempt men. But Genesis 22:1 says God tempted a certain man. Who?

28 Solomon had 40,000 horses, according to 1 Kings 4:26. How many did he have according to 2 Chronicles 9:25?

29 Matthew 27:6-8 says the priests bought the potter's field, but Acts 1:18-19 says someone else bought it. Who?

30 Matthew 27:9-10 attributes the prophecy about the potter's field to Jeremiah. Where is the prophecy found?

31 Mark 15:26 says the inscription on Jesus' cross read "The King of the Jews." What is it in Luke's account (23:38)?

32 Matthew's genealogy of Jesus says that Joseph's father was Jacob (1:16). According to Luke 3:23, who was it?

(More Differences on the next page)

Differences of Opinion

21 Twice. 22 He fell headlong and burst apart. 23 "This is Jesus, the King of the Jews.". 24 Peter and John. 25 Abimelech. 26 "Blessed are the poor." 27 Abraham. 28 Four thousand. 29 Judas Iscariot. 30 Zechariah 11:12-13; neither Jeremiah nor Zechariah quotes the prophecy as it is quoted in Matthew. 31 "This is the King of the Jews." 32 Heli.

33 In what epistle does Paul say "Share each other's burdens" and "We are each responsible for our own conduct"?

34 What book says, in the same chapter, "Don't answer the foolish arguments of fools" and "Be sure to answer the foolish arguments of fools"?

35 David's wife Michal had, according to 2 Samuel 6:23, no children. But according to 2 Samuel 21:8 she had how many children?

36 Solomon stated in Proverbs 18:22, "The man who finds a wife finds a treasure." Who, in the New Testament, stated, "It is good to live a celibate life"?

37 Acts 9:7 says that the people traveling with Paul heard the heavenly voice Paul heard. But, according to Acts 22:9, someone said that the people did not hear the voice. Who said that?

38 Mark 1:12-13 says that Jesus immediately went into the wilderness after his baptism and was there for 40 days. Which Gospel claims that the day after his baptism he called Andrew and Peter to be his disciples?

39 According to 1 Corinthians 15:5, Jesus appeared to the 12 disciples after his resurrection. According to Matthew and Acts, how many apostles were there after his resurrection?

Differences of Opinion

33 Galatians (6:2 and 6:5). **34** Proverbs (26:4 and 26:5). **35** Five (This apparent scribal error is corrected in some translations, where Merab, not Michal, is the mother of the five children.). **36** Paul. The Greek reads *It is good for a man not to touch a woman.* (1 Corinthians 7:1). **37** Paul. **38** John (1:35). **39** Only eleven; Matthew 27:3-5 says that Judas Iscariot hanged himself before Jesus' resurrection, and Acts 1:9-26 says that the new apostle, Matthias, had not yet been chosen at the time of the Resurrection.

THE LAST WORD

Name the persons who said the following as their last words.

1 Lord Jesus, receive my spirit. Lord, don't charge them with this sin!

2 There Abraham and his wife Sarah are buried. There Isaac and his wife, Rebekah, are buried. And there I buried Leah.

3 You should have struck the ground five or six times! Then you would have beaten Aram until it was entirely destroyed. Now you will be victorious only three times.

4 Take your sword and kill me before these pagan Philistines come to run me through and taunt and torture me.

5 When God comes to help you and lead you back, you must take my bones with you.

6 How blessed you are, O Israel! Who else is like you, a people saved by the LORD? He is your protecting shield and your triumphant sword! Your enemies will cringe before you, and you will stomp on their backs!

7 This stone has heard everything the LORD said to us. It will be a witness to testify against you if you go back on your word to God.

8 Sovereign LORD, remember me again. O God, please strengthen me just one more time. With one blow let me pay back the Philistines for the loss of my two eyes.

(More Last Words on the next page)

The Last Word
1 Stephen (Acts 7:59-60). 2 Jacob (Genesis 49:31). 3 Elisha (2 Kings 13:19). 4 Saul (1 Samuel 31:4). 5 Joseph (Genesis 50:25). 6 Moses (Deuteronomy 33:29). 7 Joshua (24:27). 8 Samson (Judges 16:28).

9   Therefore, go and make disciples of all the nations, baptizing them in the name of the Father and the Son and the Holy Spirit. Teach these new disciples to obey all the commands I have given you. And be sure of this: I am with you always, even to the end of the age.

10 Jesus, remember me when you come into your Kingdom.

11 But that oath does not make him innocent. You are a wise man, and you will know how to arrange a bloody death for him.

12 What happened, my son?

13 But you will receive power when the Holy Spirit comes upon you. And you will be my witnesses, telling people about me every-where—in Jerusalem, throughout Judea, in Samaria, and to the ends of the earth.

14 You have asked a difficult thing. If you see me when I am taken from you, then you will get your request. But if not, then you won't.

15 Have you come in peace, you murderer? You're just like Zimri, who murdered his master!

16 Come over here, and I'll give your flesh to the birds and wild animals!

17 Turn the horses and get me out of here! I'm badly wounded!

18 They will be able to handle snakes with safety, and if they drink anything poisonous, it won't hurt them. They will be able to place their hands on the sick, and they will be healed.

WHO SAID THAT? (IV)

1 Jesus Christ heals you! Get up, and roll up your sleeping mat!

2 Why then does my suffering continue? Why is my wound so incurable?

3 But after your kingdom comes to an end, another kingdom, inferior to yours, will rise to take your place. After that kingdom has fallen, yet a third kingdom, represented by bronze, will rise to rule the world.

4 We have found the very person Moses and the prophets wrote about! His name is Jesus, the son of Joseph from Nazareth.

5 Don't extort money or make false accusations. And be content with your pay.

6 In the name of Jesus Christ the Nazarene, get up and walk!

7 What I have written, I have written.

8 No one can receive anything unless God gives it from heaven.

9 God has numbered the days of your reign and has brought it to an end.

10 But the LORD is in his holy Temple. Let all the earth be silent before him.

11 Your guards and officials are also like swarming locusts that crowd together in the hedges on a cold day.

12 Lord, don't trouble yourself by coming to my home, for I am not worthy of such an honor.

13 Should people cheat God?

14 What sorrow awaits you who lie awake at night, thinking up evil plans.

15 My mother and my brothers are all those who hear God's word and obey it.

16 Someday Saul is going to get me.

(More Sayings on the next page)

Who Said That? (IV)

1 Peter (Acts 9:34). 2 Jeremiah (15:18). 3 Daniel (2:39). 4 Philip (John 1:45). 5 John the Baptist (Luke 3:14). 6 Peter (Acts 3:6). 7 Pilate (John 19:22). 8 John the Baptist (John 3:27). 9 Daniel (5:26). 10 Habakkuk (2:20). 11 Nahum (3:17). 12 The centurion of Capernaum (Luke 7:6). 13 Malachi (3:8). 14 Micah (2:1). 15 Jesus (Luke 8:21). 16 David (1 Samuel 27:1).

GETTING IT IN WRITING 209

17 So, my enemy, you have found me!

18 Can two people walk together without agreeing on the direction?

19 Sir, you must be a prophet.

20 Son, why have you done this to us? Your father and I have been frantic, searching for you everywhere.

21 Let's go to Bethlehem! Let's see this thing that has happened, which the Lord has told us about.

22 Your king will bring peace to the nations. His realm will stretch from sea to sea.

23 What have I done to deserve such kindness? I am only a foreigner.

24 Have mercy on me, my friends, have mercy, for the hand of God has struck me.

25 But you, O Bethlehem Ephrathah, are only a small village among all the people of Judah. Yet a ruler of Israel will come from you.

26 You are the Messiah, the Son of the living God.

27 About noon, Your Majesty, as I was on the road, a light from heaven brighter than the sun shone down on me and my companions.

28 I correct and discipline everyone I love.

29 How blessed you are, O Israel! . . . a people saved by the LORD? He is your protecting shield and your triumphant sword!

30 Sing to the LORD, for he has triumphed gloriously; he has hurled both horse and rider into the sea.

31 Lord, is that illustration just for us or for everyone?

32 Listen! It's the voice of someone shouting, "Clear the way through the wilderness for the LORD! Make a straight highway through the wasteland for our God!"

33 The day is coming when I will greatly increase the human population and the number of animals here in Israel and Judah.

(More Sayings on the next page)

Who Said That? (IV)
17 Ahab (1 Kings 21:20). **18** Amos (3:3). **19** The woman at the well (John 4:19). **20** Mary (Luke 2:48). **21** The shepherds (Luke 2:15). **22** Zechariah (9:10). **23** Ruth (2:10). **24** Job (19:21). **25** Micah (5:2). **26** Peter (Matthew 16:16). **27** Paul (Acts 26:13). **28** Jesus (Revelation 3:19). **29** Moses (Deuteronomy 33:29). **30** Miriam (Exodus 15:21). **31** Peter (Luke 12:41). **32** Isaiah (40:3). **33** Jeremiah (31:27).

34 Do you understand what you are reading?

35 May your money be destroyed with you for thinking God's gift can be bought!

36 Name one prophet your ancestors didn't persecute!

37 Hate evil and love what is good; turn your courts into true halls of justice. Perhaps even yet the LORD God of Heaven's Armies will have mercy on the remnant of his people.

38 There are no men left anywhere in this entire area, so we can't get married like everyone else. And our father will soon be too old to have children.

39 Is it true that Amnon has been with you?

40 Is not all human life a struggle? Our lives are like that of a hired hand.

41 I have sinned, for I have betrayed an innocent man.

42 A prophet is honored everywhere except in his own hometown and among his own family.

43 People of Israel . . . why stare at us as though we had made this man walk by our own power or godliness?

44 Call up Samuel.

45 God knows that your eyes will be opened as soon as you eat it, and you will be like God, knowing both good and evil.

46 What crime has he committed? I have found no reason to sentence him to death. So I will have him flogged, and then I will release him.

47 You will know which one to arrest when I greet him with a kiss.

48 So, is it really you, you troublemaker of Israel?

49 No, for all the nations of the world are but a drop in the bucket. They are nothing more than dust on the scales.

50 Lord, why are you going to reveal yourself only to us and not to the world at large?

Who Said That? (IV)

34 Philip (Acts 8:30). **35** Peter (Acts 8:20). **36** Stephen (Acts 7:52). **37** Amos (5:15). **38** Lot's daughters (Genesis 19:31). **39** Absalom (2 Samuel 13:20). **40** Job (7:1). **41** Judas Iscariot (Matthew 27:4). **42** Jesus (Matthew 13:57). **43** Peter (Acts 3:12). **44** Saul (1 Samuel 28:11). **45** The serpent (Genesis 3:5). **46** Pilate (Luke 23:22). **47** Judas Iscariot (Mark 14:44). **48** Ahab (1 Kings 18:17). **49** Isaiah (40:15). **50** Judas (not Iscariot) (John 14:22).

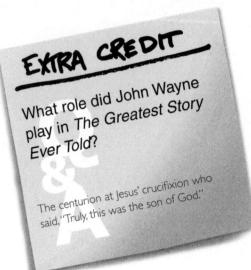

EXTRA CREDIT

What role did John Wayne play in *The Greatest Story Ever Told?*

The centurion at Jesus' crucifixion who said, "Truly, this was the son of God."

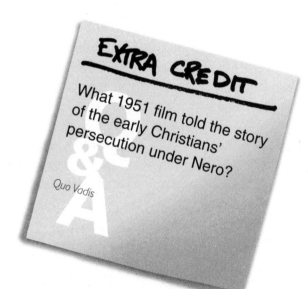

EXTRA CREDIT

What 1951 film told the story of the early Christians' persecution under Nero?

Quo Vadis

PART EIGHT

BACK TO NATURE

SOME AMAZING ANIMALS

1 What four creatures did God send as plagues upon the Egyptians?
2 What venomous creature bit Paul on the hand but did not harm him?
3 What did Jesus use to feed the five thousand?
4 Where did Jesus send the legion of unclean spirits he had cast out of a man?
5 What did Peter find with a coin in its mouth?
6 What did God send to destroy the vine that shaded the sulking prophet Jonah?
7 When children laughed at Elisha for his baldness, what appeared that mauled the children?
8 What croaking birds fed Elijah in his solitude by the brook Cherith?
9 What two animals owned by the Philistines carried the Ark of the Covenant back to Israel?
10 What foreign prophet had a talking donkey to ride on?
11 What bird served as food for the Israelites in the wilderness?
12 What animals, considered rather loathsome in Bible times, ate the carcass of Jezebel?
13 What did God provide as a sacrifice in substitute for Isaac?
14 What miraculous animals parted Elijah and Elisha as Elijah was taken by a whirlwind into heaven?

Some Amazing Animals

1 Frogs, lice, flies, and locusts (Exodus 8; 10). 2 A viper (Acts 28:3-6). 3 Two fish and five barley loaves (John 6:9-12). 4 Into a herd of swine (Mark 5:13). 5 A fish (Matthew 17:27). 6 A worm (Jonah 4:7). 7 Two she-bears (2 Kings 2:24). 8 Ravens (1 Kings 2:11). 9 Two cows (1 Samuel 6:7-12). 10 Balaam of Moab (Numbers 22:28). 11 Quail (Exodus 16:13). 12 Dogs (2 Kings 9:36). 13 A ram (Genesis 22:13). 14 Horses of fire (2 Kings 2:24).

SNAKES AND OTHER CREEPY THINGS

1 Who amazed his comrades by surviving the bite of a viper?

2 According to Proverbs, what substance affects man like the bite of a snake?

3 Who put a bronze snake on a pole in order to heal snakebites?

4 According to Job, what sort of men suck the poison of snakes?

5 What repulsive creatures bit the Israelites in the wilderness?

6 What did the people of Judah call the bronze snake they worshiped in Hezekiah's time?

7 What kind of snake did God promise to Jeremiah as a punishment for Israel's sin?

8 What tribe of Israel was supposed to be like a snake?

9 What animal came out of the Nile in droves as a plague on the Egyptians?

10 In Revelation, what sort of creatures had tails that were like snakes?

11 According to Jesus, what would a loveless father give a child who asked for an egg?

12 What destructive creature did the prophet Joel have a vision of?

13 Who had a rod that God turned into a snake?

14 According to the Law, what hopping insects were edible?

15 What did King Rehoboam say he would use to discipline the people?

16 What book makes the pessimistic statement that whoever breaks through a wall may be bitten by a snake?

(More Creepy Things on the next page)

SNAKES AND OTHER CREEPY THINGS (CONTINUED)

17 Whom did Jesus refer to as sons of vipers?

Complete the crossword to reveal the answers to the next five questions.

18 **(1 Down)** In Revelation, what was the name of the great serpent?

19 **(1 Across)** According to Isaiah, what is the food of the serpent?

20 **(2 Down)** According to Genesis, what part of man is the snake supposed to strike at?

21 **(3 Down)** What tiny insect did David compare himself to when Saul pursued him?

22 **(4 Across)** In Proverbs, what creature is held up as an example of something that can never be satisfied?

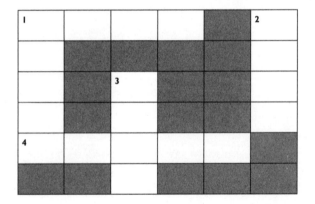

(More Creepy Things on the next page)

Snakes and Other Creepy Things

17 The scribes and Pharisees (Matthew 23:33). **18** Devil (Revelation 12:9). **19** Dust (Isaiah 65:25). **20** Heel (Genesis 3:15). **21** Flea (1 Samuel 24:14). **22** Leech (Proverbs 30:15).

216   THE GOOD BOOK BIBLE TRIVIA

SNAKES AND OTHER CREEPY THINGS (CONTINUED)

23 What was the only animal to lie?

24 According to Psalm 91, what kind of man can tread on a cobra without fear?

25 What did Amos say would happen to a man who rested his hand on the wall of his own house?

26 Who predicted that a child would be able to put his hand over a snake's den?

27 Who told his followers they would have the power to handle deadly snakes?

28 What curse did God put on the lying snake?

29 What creature supposedly melts away as it moves?

30 What kind of tails did the hideous locusts have in Revelation?

31 What did the author of Proverbs admire the snake for?

32 Who had a vision of locusts that were like horses prepared for battle?

33 What voracious insect was a plague on the Egyptians?

34 Who described locusts as stretching across the heavens like a dark curtain?

35 According to Ecclesiastes, what gives perfume a bad smell?

36 What prophet referred to the Sadducees and Pharisees as vipers?

37 Could the Israelites eat lizards?

38 To what loathsome creature did Bildad compare man?

(More Creepy Things on the next page)

Snakes and Other Creepy Things

23 The serpent (Genesis 3:1-13). **24** The man who trusts God (verse 13). **25** A snake would bite him (Amos 5:19). **26** Isaiah (11:8). **27** Jesus (Mark 16:18). **28** It would have to crawl on its belly and eat dust (Genesis 3:14). **29** The slug (Psalm 58:8). **30** Tails like scorpions (Revelation 9:10). **31** Its grace of movement (Proverbs 30:19). **32** John (Revelation 9:7). **33** The locust (Exodus 10:12-19). **34** Isaiah (40:22). **35** Dead flies (Ecclesiastes 10:1). **36** John the Baptist (Matthew 3:7). **37** No (Leviticus 11:29). **38** A worm (Job 25:6).

39 What swarming, pesky insects were sent as a plague on the Egyptians?

40 What ruler was eaten by worms before he died?

41 According to Jesus, what insect devours the treasures we store up on earth?

42 What creature, according to Isaiah, will not die?

43 Who had a fly god named Baal-zebub?

44 Who ate locusts in the wilderness?

45 What stinging creature did God promise to protect Ezekiel from?

46 What prophet had his vine eaten by a worm?

47 What water creature is the Bible probably referring to when it talks about a dragon?

48 When Israel's spies came back from Canaan, what insect did they compare themselves to when describing the giants in the land?

49 In the Law, what mammal is classified as an unclean bird?

50 According to Jesus, what small insects are strained out by the Pharisees?

51 What industrious insect is held up as an example to the lazy man?

52 According to Bildad, what fragile thing is a godless man's trust like?

53 Who imitated Moses' feat of turning a staff into a snake?

Snakes and Other Creepy Things
39 Gnats and flies (Exodus 8:16-32).   **40** Herod (Acts 12:23).   **41** The moth (Luke 12:33).   **42** The worm (Isaiah 66:24).   **43** The people of Ekron (2 Kings 1:2).   **44** John the Baptist (Mark 1:6).
45 The scorpion (Ezekiel 2:6).   **46** Jonah (4:7).   **47** The crocodile.   **48** The grasshopper (Numbers 13:33).   **49** The bat (Leviticus 11:19).   **50** Gnats (Matthew 23:24).   **51** The ant (Proverbs 6:6-8).
52 A spider web (Job 8:14).   **53** The Egyptian court magicians (Exodus 7:11).

THE LIONS' DEN

1 What future king claimed that he had grabbed lions by the throat and beat them to death?

2 Who tore a lion apart with his bare hands?

3 Who saw locusts with lions' teeth?

4 What book speaks of the Lion of the Tribe of Judah?

5 What father and son did David say were stronger than lions?

6 According to 1 Peter, what person is like a ravenous lion?

7 What brave soldier in David's army went into a pit on a snowy day and killed a lion?

8 Who had a throne with lion statues beside it?

9 What prophet foresaw a time when a lion would eat straw instead of meat?

10 Which of his sons did the dying Jacob compare to a vicious lion?

11 What prophet had a vision of a creature that had, on one of its four sides, a lion's face?

12 What devout young man was placed in a lions' den?

13 According to Ecclesiastes, what is better than being a dead lion?

14 Who saw a lionlike creature near the throne of God?

15 What book has a man asking his loved one to come down from the place where lions dwell?

16 Who had a vision of a lion with eagle's wings?

The Lions' Den

1 David (1 Samuel 17:35). 2 Samson (Judges 14:6). 3 Joel (1:6). 4 Revelation (5:5). 5 Saul and Jonathan (2 Samuel 1:23). 6 Satan (1 Peter 5:8). 7 Benaiah (2 Samuel 23:20). 8 Solomon (1 Kings 10:18-20). 9 Isaiah (11:7). 10 Judah (Genesis 49:9). 11 Ezekiel (1:10). 12 Daniel (6:16). 13 A live dog (Ecclesiastes 9:4). 14 John (Revelation 4:7). 15 The Song of Songs (Song of Solomon 4:8). 16 Daniel (7:4).

BACK TO NATURE   219

SHEPHERDS AND SHEEP

1 What wealthy man had 14,000 sheep?

2 Who married the shepherd girl Zipporah?

3 What former shepherd boy is supposed to have written "The LORD is my shepherd"?

4 Whom did Jesus command to shepherd his church?

5 Who was the first shepherd?

6 Who is the good shepherd?

7 Which prophet said, "All we like sheep have gone astray" (KJV)?

8 Which Old Testament book compares a lover's teeth to a flock of newly shorn sheep?

9 In which Gospel does Jesus speak of separating the sheep from the goats?

10 Who had compassion on the people because they seemed like sheep without a shepherd?

11 Who called Saul on the carpet because he had heard the bleating of sheep taken in Saul's battle with the Amalekites?

12 What book warns against sacrificing a defective sheep to God?

13 In what book does God say, "My people have been lost sheep. Their shepherds have led them astray"?

14 To whom did Jesus say, "I am sending you out as sheep among wolves"?

15 In Jesus' parable of the lost sheep, how many sheep were in the field?

(More Shepherds on the next page)

SHEPHERDS AND SHEEP (CONTINUED)

16 Who did God tell Moses would be the new shepherd over Israel?

17 Which psalm says, "We are his people, the sheep of his pasture"?

18 Which epistle says, "You were like sheep who wandered away"?

19 Which psalm says, "We are being slaughtered like sheep"?

20 Who became a shepherd in Midian for his father-in-law?

21 Who paid Jesse a visit when young David was out tending the sheep?

22 What daughter of Laban was a shepherdess?

23 Who was out shearing his sheep when David's servants called on him?

24 What prophet said, "What sorrow awaits this worthless shepherd who abandons the flock"?

25 What prophet said that God would search out his scattered sheep?

26 What prophet told Ahab that Israel was scattered like sheep?

27 What Old Testament book says, "Strike down the shepherd, and the sheep will be scattered"?

28 According to Isaiah, who did God say was his appointed shepherd?

29 Which epistle speaks of the "great shepherd of the sheep"?

30 What prophet talked about a shepherd pulling parts of a sheep from a lion's mouth?

(More Shepherds on the next page)

Shepherds and Sheep
16 Joshua (Numbers 27:16-18). **17** Psalm 100. **18** I Peter (2:25). **19** Psalm 44:22. **20** Moses
(Exodus 3:1). **21** Samuel (1 Samuel 16:11). **22** Rachel (Genesis 29:9). **23** Nabal (1 Samuel
25:2-9). **24** Zechariah (11:17). **25** Ezekiel (34:11). **26** Micaiah (1 Kings 22:17). **27** Zechariah
(13:7). **28** Cyrus (Isaiah 44:28). **29** Hebrews (13:20). **30** Amos (3:12).

BACK TO NATURE   221

31 In what book do we find the words "He will feed his flock like a shepherd"?

32 What almost-slaughtered son asked his father, "Where is the sheep for the burnt offering?"

33 Who said, "Look! The Lamb of God"?

34 What prophet told David a tale about a man with one lamb?

35 What foreign traveler was reading a passage about the Messiah being like a sheep for the slaughter?

36 What book of the Bible describes a lamb with seven horns and seven eyes?

37 What prophet spoke of a wolf dwelling with a lamb?

38 For what festival, instituted during the exodus from Egypt, was a lamb slaughtered?

39 Which epistle refers to Christ as a Passover Lamb?

40 Who found a ram caught in a bramble?

41 Who had a vision of a powerful ram on a destructive rampage?

42 Who used a sheep's horn as a container for oil?

43 In front of what Canaanite city did priests blow trumpets made of rams' horns?

44 What did Samuel tell Saul was more important than sacrificing sheep?

45 What king of Moab was noted as a keeper of sheep?

Shepherds and Sheep
31 Isaiah (40:11). 32 Isaac (Genesis 22:7). 33 John the Baptist (John 1:29). 34 Nathan (2 Samuel 12:1-7). 35 The Ethiopian eunuch (Acts 8:27-35). 36 Revelation (5:6). 37 Isaiah (11:6). 38 Passover (Exodus 12:21). 39 1 Corinthians (5:7). 40 Abraham (Genesis 22:13). 41 Daniel (8:3-4). 42 Samuel (1 Samuel 16:1). 43 Jericho (Joshua 6:4). 44 Obeying God (1 Samuel 15:22). 45 Mesha (2 Kings 3:4).

BIBLICAL BIRD WALK

1 What book says that anyone who scorns his parents will have his eyes pecked out by ravens?

2 In Revelation, what bird went about crying, "Woe! Woe!" (KJV)?

3 What book portrays God as having wings and feathers?

4 What bird does the lover in Song of Songs (Song of Solomon) compare his beloved's eyes to?

5 Unscramble the letters to reveal the king who instructed his people in bird lore.

MOSOLON

— — — — — — —

6 Who compared his days to eagles swooping down on their prey?

7 On what day did God create the birds?

8 Unscramble the letters to reveal who had a dream about birds eating out of a basket on his head.

HORPHASA KEBAR

— — — — — — — , —

— — — — —

9 Who boasted to David that he would give David's body to the birds for food?

10 What king's search for his rival is compared with looking for a partridge in the mountains?

(More Birds on the next page)

Biblical Bird Walk
1 Proverbs (30:17). 2 An eagle (Revelation 8:13). 3 Psalms (91:4). 4 The dove (Song of Songs or Song of Solomon 1:15). 5 Solomon (1 Kings 4:33). 6 Job (9:26). 7 The fifth day (Genesis 1:20). 8 Pharaoh's baker (Genesis 40:16-17). 9 Goliath (1 Samuel 17:44). 10 Saul's search for David (1 Samuel 26:20).

BACK TO NATURE   223

11 What bird in great droves fed the Israelites in the wilderness?

12 On Mount Sinai, God told Moses that he had carried the Israelites from Egypt on the wings of a bird. What bird?

13 What father and son were, according to David, swifter than eagles?

14 According to the law, what must a Nazarite sacrifice if someone dies in his presence during his period of separation?

15 What prophet had a vision of a desolate day when no birds were in the sky?

16 In Ezekiel's vision of the creatures with four faces, what bird's face was on the creatures?

17 What Babylonian king had a dream of a tree where every bird found shelter?

18 Who had a vision of a lion with eagle's wings?

19 What prophet said that Ephraim was as easily deceived as a foolish dove?

20 What nation would, according to Obadiah, be brought down by God even though it had soared like an eagle?

21 Who had a vision of two women with storks' wings?

22 Who prophesied that Assyria would become a roosting place for all sorts of strange night birds?

23 Who had a vision of a sheet filled with all sorts of unclean birds and other animals?

24 What domestic bird signaled Peter's betrayal of Christ?

25 According to Jesus, what inevitably gathers near a dead body?

26 What form did the Holy Spirit assume at Jesus' baptism?

27 In what parable of Jesus do greedy birds play a major role?

(More Birds on the next page)

Biblical Bird Walk
11 Quails (Exodus 16:13).   12 The eagle (Exodus 19:4).   13 Saul and Jonathan (2 Samuel 1:23).
14 Two doves (Numbers 6:10).   15 Jeremiah (4:25).   16 The eagle's (Ezekiel 1:10).
17 Nebuchadnezzar (Daniel 4:12).   18 Daniel (7:4).   19 Hosea (7:11).   20 Edom (Obadiah 4).
21 Zechariah (5:9).   22 Zephaniah (2:14).   23 Peter (Acts 10:9-13).   24 The rooster (John 13:38;
18:27).   25 Vultures (Luke 17:37).   26 A dove (Mark 1:10).   27 The parable of the sower (Mark
4:1-20).

224   THE GOOD BOOK BIBLE TRIVIA

28 Who predicted that desert birds would use a ruined Edom as their home?

29 Who called his lover "my dove, my perfect one"?

30 Who warned people that the birds of the air could be tattletales, telling the king who had said bad things about him?

31 In Revelation, who told the birds to gather together to eat the flesh of warriors?

32 According to Psalm 147, what young birds are fed by God when they call to him?

33 What prophet said that God's protection for Jerusalem was like birds circling overhead?

34 According to Leviticus, what must be done to any bird killed for food?

35 According to the law, what two types of birds comprise the category of unclean fowl?

36 How many of each species of bird was Noah supposed to take into the ark?

37 Who had a vision of a woman with eagle's wings flying to the desert?

38 According to James, what cannot be tamed even though all birds can be tamed?

39 Who said that idolatrous men had exchanged the glory of the true God for images like birds?

40 What bird was being sold in the temple courts when Jesus drove out the salesmen?

41 What bird, according to Jesus, is cared for by God even though it had no barns or storerooms?

42 What kind of bird did Jesus compare to his love for Jerusalem?

(More Birds on the next page)

Biblical Bird Walk
28 Isaiah (34:11-14). **29** The lover in the Song of Songs (Song of Songs 6:9). **30** The author of Ecclesiastes (10:20). **31** An angel standing in the sun (Revelation 19:17). **32** Ravens (verse 9). **33** Isaiah (31:5). **34** The blood must be drained from it (Leviticus 17:13). **35** Mostly scavengers and birds of prey (Deuteronomy 14:12-18). **36** Seven (Genesis 7:3). **37** John (Revelation 12:14). **38** The tongue (James 3:7). **39** Paul (Romans 1:23). **40** Doves (John 2:14). **41** The raven (Luke 12:24). **42** A hen gathering her chicks (Matthew 23:37).

43 What prophet warned of a destruction in which all birds would be swept from the earth?

44 Fill in the blanks to reveal the prophet who warned that he would wail like an owl and walk about barefoot and naked.

— — —

45 Who declared that Nineveh's slave girls would moan like doves when the city was plundered?

46 In what book does God say that he knows all the birds of the air and the beasts of the field?

47 According to Job, what is hidden from the keen-eyed birds of prey?

48 What beautiful bird did Solomon's navy bring to Israel?

49 When the king of Syria besieged Samaria, what unusual substance sold for five shekels in the city?

50 What prophet said that Ahab's people would be eaten by birds?

51 Fill in the blanks to reveal what, according to Psalm 68, the dove's feathers are covered with.

— — — —

52 Who said that he had become a companion of owls?

53 According to Psalm 84, what two small birds have a nesting place near the Temple?

54 Fill in the blanks to reveal what bird's song is, in the Song of Songs (Song of Solomon), a sign of spring.

— — — — — —

(More Birds on the next page)

Biblical Bird Walk
43 Zephaniah (1:3). **44** Micah (1:8). **45** Nahum (2:7). **46** Psalms (50:11). **47** The whereabouts of jewels and precious metal (Job 28:7). **48** The peacock (2 Chronicles 9:21; some modern translations have ape instead of peacock). **49** Dove's dung (2 Kings 6:25). **50** Elijah (1 Kings 21:24). **51** Gold (Psalm 68:13). **52** Job (30:29). **53** The sparrow and the swallow (Psalm 84:3). **54** Turtledove (Song of Songs or Song of Solomon 2:12).

BIBLICAL BIRD WALK (CONTINUED)

55 What bird's youth is, according to Psalms, renewable?

56 What bird does Jeremiah compare to a man who gains riches by unjust means?

57 According to Ezekiel, what will the moaning of the survivors sound like?

58 In what book do you find this: "My enemies, whom I have never harmed, hunted me down like a bird"?

59 What was the first bird released from the ark?

60 In the system of sacrifice, what bird was normally offered?

61 What means did the Lord use to bring quail to the Israelites?

62 What concubine of Saul stood by the unburied bodies of her sons in order to keep the birds away?

63 According to the law, one of the curses of disobedience was the coming of a cruel nation. What bird is that nation compared to?

64 According to the law, what is an Israelite to do if he finds a mother bird with young or with eggs?

65 What was the dove carrying in its beak when it returned to Noah?

66 Who, according to tradition, said, "Oh, that I had wings like a dove"?

67 Who asked Job who provided for the feeding of young ravens?

68 According to the Bible, what foolish bird lays its eggs on the ground in the sun?

(More Birds on the next page)

Biblical Bird Walk

55 The eagle (Psalm 103:5). **56** A partridge that hatches eggs it does not lay (Jeremiah 17:11). **57** Doves (Ezekiel 7:16). **58** Lamentations (3:52). **59** A raven (Genesis 8:7). **60** A dove or pigeon (Leviticus 1:14-17). **61** A wind from the sea (Numbers 11:31). **62** Rizpah (2 Samuel 21:10). **63** An eagle (Deuteronomy 28:49). **64** He may take the young or the eggs but must not kill the mother bird (Deuteronomy 22:6-7). **65** An olive leaf (Genesis 8:11). **66** David (Psalm 55:6). **67** God (Job 38:41). **68** The ostrich (Job 39:13-18; some translations have stork).

69 What psalm speaks of the quail the Israelites ate in the wilderness?

70 What king always had choice poultry in his daily provisions?

71 Who did God tell to have dominion over all the birds?

72 What greedy king does Isaiah compare to a man grabbing eggs from a bird's nest?

73 What black birds fed Elijah when he lived by Kerith Brook?

74 According to Job, what bird feeds blood to its young?

75 What prophet told Baasha, king of Israel, that the birds would feast on those of his household?

76 What bird does Proverbs compare fleeting riches to?

77 What book speaks of the uselessness of spreading out a net in view of the birds it is supposed to catch?

78 According to the Song of Songs (Song of Solomon), what is the male lover's hair like?

79 What nation's women did Isaiah compare to fluttering birds?

80 What book says that the Lord's people have become as heartless as ostriches in the desert?

81 Who told the Moabites to live like doves nesting at the mouth of a cave?

82 According to Isaiah, from what direction does God summon the birds of prey?

83 Who compared Assyria with a cedar of Lebanon that sheltered all the birds in its branches?

84 Who compared Israel with a speckled bird of prey, surrounded and attacked by other birds of prey?

(More Birds on the next page)

Biblical Bird Walk

69 Psalm 78:26-29. **70** Solomon (1 Kings 4:23). **71** Noah (Genesis 9:1-7). **72** The king of Assyria (Isaiah 10:14). **73** Ravens (1 Kings 17:6). **74** The eagle (Job 39:30). **75** Jehu (1 Kings 16:4). **76** An eagle (Proverbs 23:5). **77** Proverbs (1:17). **78** A raven (Song of Songs or Song of Solomon 5:11). **79** Moab's (Isaiah 16:2). **80** Lamentations (4:3). **81** Jeremiah (48:28). **82** The east (Isaiah 46:11). **83** Ezekiel (31:6). **84** Jeremiah (12:9).

85 According to Isaiah, what will those who hope in the Lord fly like?

86 According to Jeremiah, what large bird knows it has appointed seasons?

87 What prophet asked, "Does a bird fall into a trap on the ground where no snare has been set"? (NIV)

88 According to Jesus, what does not sow nor reap?

89 What seed grows a plant so large that the birds can make nests in it?

90 What did Mary and Joseph sacrifice in the Temple when they took the young Jesus there?

91 In John's vision of the four living creatures, what bird does one of the creatures resemble?

92 According to the law, what can be used in place of a lamb as a sin offering?

93 What two birds did Abram sacrifice to God?

94 What prayer of an afflicted man compares him to an owl living among ruins?

95 According to Psalm 104, what bird nests in the pine trees?

96 According to Proverbs, what is an undeserved curse like?

97 What city, according to John, will become a home for every detestable and unclean bird?

98 What book says that in old age the songs of the birds will grow faint?

99 According to Isaiah, what bird honors God for providing streams in the desert?

100 What prophet speaks of God's covenant with the birds of the air?

Biblical Bird Walk
85 Eagles (Isaiah 40:31). **86** The stork (Jeremiah 8:7). **87** Amos (3:5). **88** The birds of the air (Matthew 6:26). **89** The mustard seed (Luke 13:18-19). **90** A pair of doves (Luke 2:24). **91** An eagle (Revelation 4:7). **92** Two doves (Leviticus 5:7). **93** A dove and a pigeon (Genesis 15:9). **94** Psalm 102:6. **95** The stork (v. 17). **96** A fluttering sparrow or swallow (Proverbs 26:2). **97** Babylon (Revelation 18:2). **98** Ecclesiastes (12:4). **99** The owl (Isaiah 43:20). **100** Hosea (2:18).

THE LOWLY DONKEY

1 What prophet of Moab had a talking donkey?

2 What future king was looking for lost donkeys when he ran into Samuel?

3 Who gave his irate brother twenty donkeys as a goodwill gesture?

4 Fill in the blanks to reveal the prince who was riding a mule (that's half donkey, half horse) when he got his head caught in an oak tree.

— — — — — — —

5 Who took his wife and sons and set them on a donkey when he returned to Egypt, his boyhood home?

6 What future wife of David rode out to meet him on a donkey when she was pleading for her husband's life?

7 Who used a donkey to carry the wood he was using to sacrifice his son on?

8 Who sent her servant on a donkey to inform Elisha that her son had died?

9 Fill in the blanks to reveal the prophet who predicted that the Messiah would enter riding on a donkey.

— — — — — — — —

10 What is the only Gospel to mention Jesus riding on a donkey?

The Lowly Donkey
1 Balaam (Numbers 22:21-33). 2 Saul (1 Samuel 9:1-6). 3 Jacob (Genesis 32:13-18). 4 Absalom (2 Samuel 18:9). 5 Moses (Exodus 4:20). 6 Abigail (1 Samuel 25:20). 7 Abraham (Genesis 22:1-3). 8 The Shunemite woman (2 Kings 4:18-32). 9 Zechariah (9:9). 10 Matthew (21:1-9).

HORSES AND HORSEMEN

1 What book of the Old Testament contains a hymn celebrating drowned horses?

2 What New Testament author had a vision of locusts that looked like horses?

3 What evil queen was executed by Jerusalem's Horse Gate?

4 What leader was told by God to cripple his enemies' horses?

5 What king had 12,000 cavalry horses?

6 What king took his household manager out to look for grass for the royal horses?

7 What two prophets were separated by horses of fire?

8 What queen had her blood spattered on King Jehu's horses?

9 Who removed the horse idols that the kings of Judah had dedicated to the worship of the sun?

10 What prophet had a vision of locusts that ran like warhorses?

11 Who had a vision of an angel on a red horse?

12 What king had horses imported from Cilicia and Musri?

13 Who ordered 70 horsemen to accompany Paul out of Jerusalem?

14 Who had a vision of the hills filled with horses and chariots of fire?

15 What prophet saw four chariots pulled by horses that represented the four winds?

16 In Revelation, what horse represents Death?

17 Who had horsemen accompany him as he went to bury his father?

THE BIBLICAL GREENHOUSE

1 What plant sprang up miraculously to give shade to the prophet Jonah?
2 What woman used mandrakes to gain a night in bed with Jacob?
3 Who used rods of poplar, hazel, and chestnut trees to make genetic changes in his sheep?
4 What kind of tree did the weary Elijah sit under?
5 What plant had such a bitter taste that it became a symbol for sorrow and disaster?
6 What, according to the New Testament, produces the smallest seed of any plant?
7 Which book mentions the rose of Sharon and the lily of the valley?
8 What mythical creature eats grass—according to the book of Job?
9 What is the only book of the Bible to mention the apple tree?
10 What kind of tree did Zacchaeus climb in order to see Jesus?
11 What tree was a symbol of grace, elegance, and uprightness?
12 What kind of wood was Noah's ark made of?
13 What miraculous event was the eating of bitter herbs supposed to commemorate?
14 What unusual food was said to have resembled coriander seed?
15 What tree's spice was used in making oil for anointing?
16 What grain did not suffer from the plague of hail in Egypt because it had not grown enough?
17 What did Jacob send as a gift to Joseph in Egypt?

(More Plants on the next page)

The Biblical Greenhouse

1 A gourd (Jonah 4:6). 2 Leah (Genesis 30:14-16). 3 Jacob (Genesis 30:37-39). 4 A broom tree (1 Kings 19:4). 5 Wormwood (Proverbs 5:4; Amos 5:7). 6 Mustard (Matthew 13:31). 7 Song of Songs (Song of Solomon) (2:1). 8 Behemoth (Job 40:15-22). 9 Song of Songs (Song of Solomon) (2:3). 10 A sycamore (Luke 19:1-4). 11 The palm (Psalm 92:12; Jeremiah 10:5). 12 Cypress or gopherwood (Genesis 6:14). 13 The Passover (Exodus 12:8). 14 Manna (Exodus 16:31). 15 The cassia tree (Exodus 30:24). 16 Rye (Exodus 9:32). 17 Almonds (Genesis 43:11).

232   THE GOOD BOOK BIBLE TRIVIA

THE BIBLICAL GREENHOUSE (CONTINUED)

18 What massive trees were brought to make the beams and pillars in the Jerusalem Temple?

19 What expensive wood is mentioned in the book of Revelation?

20 What vine is mentioned in the Old Testament as bearing poisonous berries?

21 What kind of tree does Psalms compare a wicked man to?

22 What prophet complained about the people making sacrifices under spreading oaks, poplars, and elms?

23 Fill in the blanks to reveal the kind of weed Jesus says will be separated from the wheat at the last judgment.

— — — — —

24 What kind of wood was the Ark of the Covenant made of?

25 What prophet took care of sycamore trees?

26 Fill in the blanks to reveal what kind of trees the exiled Jews hung their harps upon.

— — — — — — —

27 What did Delilah use to bind the sleeping Samson?

28 What defeated king was buried with his sons under an oak tree?

29 Which tree does Jesus say can be uprooted and thrown into the sea—if one has enough faith?

30 What city was the "city of palm trees"?

31 What tree's foliage was found in the carvings inside the Temple?

(More Plants on the next page)

32 What king appointed an overseer to watch after the fruits of the olive trees and sycamores?

33 Who was killed after his hair was caught in an oak's branches?

34 What man met the Lord at the oaks of Mamre?

35 Fill in the blanks to reveal the prophet who had a vision of a branch of an almond tree.

— — — — — — — —

36 To what king did Jesus compare the lilies of the field?

37 What plant was used to purify lepers?

38 When Rahab hid the Israelite spies on her rooftop, what did she hide them under?

39 Fill in the blanks to reveal what the dove that Noah released brought back in its beak.

— — — — — —
— — — — —

40 What kind of tree was withered by Jesus because it bore no fruit?

41 What tree's leaves were used to cover the naked Adam and Eve?

42 What tree's fruit was used to make a plaster to heal the diseased King Hezekiah?

43 What furnishings in the Temple were made of olive wood?

44 What epistle uses the grafting of the olive tree as a symbol of God choosing the Gentiles in addition to the Jews?

45 What prophet mentions a gift of ebony wood sent to Tyre?

(More Plants on the next page)

The Biblical Greenhouse:
32 David (1 Chronicles 27:28). **33** Absalom (2 Samuel 18:9-10). **34** Abraham (Genesis 18:1). **35** Jeremiah (1:11). **36** Solomon (Luke 12:27). **37** Hyssop (Leviticus 14:4-6). **38** Stacks of flax (Joshua 2:6). **39** An olive leaf (Genesis 8:11). **40** A fig tree (Mark 11:12-14). **41** The fig's (Genesis 3:7). **42** The fig's (2 Kings 20:7). **43** The cherubim (1 Kings 6:23). **44** Romans (11:17). **45** Ezekiel (27:15).

234   THE GOOD BOOK BIBLE TRIVIA

THE BIBLICAL GREENHOUSE (CONTINUED)

46 In what land did Moses see a burning bush that was not consumed?

47 On what day of Creation did God make the plants?

48 What kind of flowers were supposed to be carved into the sacred lampstands?

49 What were Solomon's chariots made of?

50 What book mentions "apples of gold"?

51 In the parable of the sower, what unwanted plant causes some of the seeds to die?

52 What was Moses' basket made of?

53 What plant was used to lift up a sponge to the dying Jesus?

54 What plant was given to Jesus as a mock scepter by the Roman soldiers?

55 What plant food, given to pigs, was wanted by the Prodigal Son?

56 What flower were the capitals on the Temple columns shaped like?

57 What plant, according to Isaiah, would not be broken by the Messiah?

58 What tree's fruit was symbolically represented on the clothing of Israel's high priest?

59 What leaves were thrown down in front of Jesus on his entry into Jerusalem?

60 What wood was used to make the table in the Tabernacle for holding the sacred bread?

61 What wood was used for building the Temple after the exile in Babylon?

62 What two herbs does Jesus say the Pharisees would tithe?

SOME EARTHQUAKES

1 What famous mountain smoked like a furnace and quaked greatly?

2 An earthquake at Philippi eventually led to the release of two Christians from prison there. Who were they?

3 Which Gospel mentions an earthquake in connection with the Resurrection of Jesus?

4 An earthquake during King Uzziah's reign was so remarkable that one of the Hebrew prophets dates his book "two years before the earthquake." Which prophet?

5 According to Matthew's Gospel, an earthquake occurred when Jesus died on the cross. What other spectacular event occurred at that time in the Temple?

6 From the list of choices, what Hebrew prophet experienced an earthquake, a strong wind, and a supernatural fire all in one day?

    A Elisha   **B** Isaiah   **C** Elijah   **D** Jeremiah

7 During Saul's reign an earthquake occurred during the attack on the Philistines at Michmash. Who led the attack?

8 During a rebellion under Moses, 250 people rebelled and were swallowed up in an earthquake. Who led the rebellion?

Some Earthquakes

1 Sinai (Exodus 19:17-18). 2 Paul and Silas (Acts 16:25-27). 3 Matthew (28:2). 4 Amos (1:1). 5 The Temple veil (curtain) was torn in half from top to bottom (Matthew 27:51). 6 C: Elijah (1 Kings 19:9-12). 7 Jonathan (1 Samuel 14:15). 8 Korah (Numbers 16:31-33).

236   THE GOOD BOOK BIBLE TRIVIA

BLOWING IN THE WIND

1 What Old Testament book speaks of life as "like chasing the wind"?

2 Where were the disciples when they heard a noise that sounded like a mighty wind filling the house they had gathered in?

3 Who had a dream of seven heads of grain being scorched by a hot east wind?

4 What loathsome creatures did God drive into Egypt with an east wind?

5 What prophet was told to cut off his hair and scatter a third of it in the wind?

6 How long did the wind that parted the Red Sea blow?

7 According to James, what sort of person is like a wave tossed by the wind?

8 What prophet experienced a furious wind that split the hills and shattered the rocks?

9 Whose children were destroyed when a strong wind struck the house they were banqueting in?

10 According to the book of Job, what directional wind will inevitably strike down the wicked?

11 What epistle compares false teachers to rainless clouds blown about by the wind?

12 According to Psalms, what sort of people are like chaff that the wind blows away?

13 Whom did God address from a whirlwind?

14 According to Jesus, what sort of man sees his house fall when the winds beat against it?

15 What was blown out of Egypt by a strong west wind?

(More Wind on the next page)

Blowing in the Wind

1 Ecclesiastes (chapters 1 and 2). 2 Jerusalem (Acts 2:2). 3 Pharaoh (Genesis 41:6). 4 Locusts (Exodus 10:13). 5 Ezekiel (5:2). 6 All night (Exodus 14:21). 7 A doubter (James 1:6). 8 Elijah (1 Kings 19:11). 9 Job's (Job 1:19). 10 East (Job 27:21). 11 Jude (12). 12 The wicked (Psalm 1:4). 13 Job (38:1). 14 The foolish man who builds on the sand (Matthew 7:26-27). 15 Locusts (Exodus 10:19).

BACK TO NATURE   237

16 Who had a dream about a statue that crumbled into dust and then was driven away by the wind?

17 What prophet spoke of people who sow a wind and reap a whirlwind?

18 What runaway boarded a ship that the Lord struck with a strong wind?

19 What prophet suffered from a hot east wind after his shade plant was eaten by a worm?

20 Who lost faith and began to flounder when he noticed the strong wind on a lake?

21 Who was saved from being a full-time sailor when God sent a wind to dry up the floodwaters?

22 What food did God bring to the Israelites by using a wind?

23 According to the book of Job, which directional wind punishes the land with its heat?

24 According to Revelation, what sort of creatures held back the winds from blowing on the earth?

25 What prophet had a vision of the four winds lashing the surface of the oceans?

26 In what book does a woman call on the north wind and south wind to blow on her garden?

27 According to Proverbs, what kind of woman is as hard to restrain as the wind itself?

Blowing in the Wind
16 Nebuchadnezzar (Daniel 2:35). 17 Hosea (8:7). 18 Jonah (1:4). 19 Jonah (4:8). 20 Peter (Matthew 14:30). 21 Noah (Genesis 8:1). 22 Quail (Numbers 11:31). 23 South (Job 37:17). 24 Four angels (Revelation 7:1). 25 Daniel (7:2). 26 Song of Songs (Song of Solomon) (4:16). 27 A nagging wife (Proverbs 27:16).

UNDER A CLOUD

1 What two long-dead men were with Jesus when a shining cloud covered them?

2 What sign did God set in the clouds to indicate that he would never again flood the world?

3 Did the pillar of cloud in the wilderness lead the Israelites by day or by night?

4 What prophet saw a little cloud like a man's hand?

5 What epistle talks about a "cloud of witnesses"?

6 At what critical spot did the pillar of cloud separate the Egyptians from the Israelites?

7 What epistle mentions believers being caught up in the clouds to meet the Lord?

8 According to Jesus, what person will appear coming in glory on the clouds of heaven?

9 In Revelation, what two unfortunate men are raised by God and then taken to heaven in a cloud?

10 On what mountain did God appear in the form of a cloud?

11 What object of the Israelites was notable for having the cloud of God's glory upon it?

12 What king, seeing the cloud in the Temple, said that God had chosen to live in clouds and darkness?

13 What portable object did the cloud of God's glory appear over?

14 What epistle compares false teachers to clouds that bring no rain?

15 At what event did a cloud hide Jesus from the apostles' sight?

16 According to Zephaniah, what special day will be a day of clouds and blackness?

RIVERS, BROOKS, LAKES, SEAS

1 What body of water was the first victim of the plague in Egypt?
2 What river did the Israelites cross when they entered Canaan?
3 Unscramble the letters to reveal the four rivers connected with the Garden of Eden.

OHNIG   SINOPH

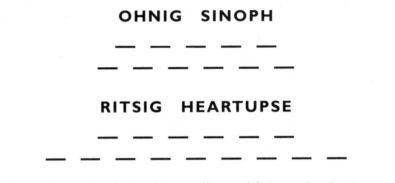

— — — —

— — — —

RITSIG   HEARTUPSE

— — — —

— — — — — — — — —

4 According to the Song of Songs (Song of Solomon), what is so powerful that rivers cannot quench it?
5 Who lived by Kerith Brook?
6 Who proclaimed a fast at the river Ahava?
7 Who had a dream about cows standing by the riverside?
8 Unscramble the letters to reveal who spoke of a brook flowing with honey.

PAZROH

— — — — — —

9 According to God's covenant with Abraham, how far did Abraham's land extend?
10 Who ordered the casting of the Israelite boys into the river?

(More Rivers on the next page)

Rivers, Brooks, Lakes, Seas
1 The Nile (Exodus 7:7-15). 2 The Jordan (Joshua 1:1-2). 3 Gihon, Pishon, Tigris, and Euphrates (Genesis 2:10-14). 4 Love (Song of Solomon) (Song of Solomon 8:7). 5 Elijah (1 Kings 17:1-4). 6 Ezra (8:21). 7 The Pharaoh (Genesis 41:3). 8 Zophar (Job 20:17). 9 From the river of Egypt to the Euphrates (Genesis 15:18). 10 Pharaoh (Exodus 1:22).

240   THE GOOD BOOK BIBLE TRIVIA

RIVERS, BROOKS, LAKES, SEAS (CONTINUED)

11 In John's vision, what caused a third of the rivers on earth to become bitter?

12 What lake is called the Salt Sea in Genesis 14:3?

13 What apostle noted that he had been endangered by the sea and by rivers?

14 Who prophesied to the Jews by the Kebar River?

15 Who had a vision of a river of fire?

16 Who spoke about justice rolling down like a river?

17 Where did John baptize the repentant people?

18 What Christian woman worshiped with a group that met by a river?

19 In John's vision, what happened to the sea when the second angel poured out his bowl on it?

20 Who found a baby while down by the riverside?

21 By what river did Nebuchadnezzar defeat Pharaoh Neco of Egypt?

22 Who had a vision of a deep river that could not be passed over?

23 Who spoke of the Lord being displeased with "ten thousand rivers of olive oil"?

24 In Revelation, what is the fiery lake composed of?

25 Who fled across Kidron Brook to escape from Absalom?

26 Where were Pharaoh and his men drowned?

27 In Revelation, where does the pure river of the water of life flow out from?

(More Rivers on the next page)

11 A star (Revelation 8:10-11). 12 The Dead Sea. 13 Paul (2 Corinthians 11:26). 14 Ezekiel (1:1). 15 Daniel (7:10). 16 Amos (5:24). 17 In the Jordan (Mark 1:5). 18 Lydia (Acts 16:13-14). 19 It turned to blood (Revelation 16:3). 20 Pharaoh's daughter (Exodus 2:5). 21 The Euphrates (Jeremiah 46:2). 22 Ezekiel (47:5). 23 Micah (6:7). 24 Burning sulfur (Revelation 19:20). 25 David (2 Samuel 15:13-23). 26 The Red Sea (Exodus 15:4). 27 The throne of God (Revelation 22:1).

RIVERS, BROOKS, LAKES, SEAS (CONTINUED)

28 According to James, what kind of man is like the waves of the sea?

29 Who lodged at the home of a tanner who lived by the sea?

30 What name is the Sea of Galilee called in the Gospel of John?

31 What were the seafaring people east of Israel known as?

32 What was the Mediterranean usually called in Bible times?

33 What was the Sea of Galilee called in Old Testament times?

34 What happens to the sea in the world to come?

35 Who had a vision of a sea of glass?

36 Who asked his shipmates to cast him into the sea?

37 By what lake did Jesus appear to his disciples after the Resurrection?

38 By what other name is the Salt Sea (Dead Sea) known in the Old Testament?

39 What Syrian army man had his leprosy washed away in the Jordan River?

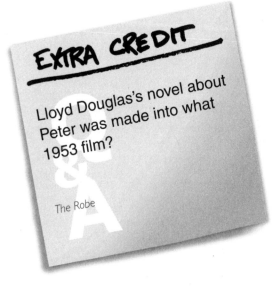

EXTRA CREDIT

Lloyd Douglas's novel about Peter was made into what 1953 film?

The Robe

Rivers, Brooks, Lakes, Seas

28 A doubting man (James 1:6). **29** Peter (Acts 10:6). **30** The Sea of Tiberias (John 6:1). **31** The Philistines. **32** The Great Sea. **33** The Sea of Chinnereth (kjv). **34** It does not exist (Revelation 21:1). **35** John (Revelation 4:6). **36** Jonah (1:12). **37** The Sea of Tiberias (John 21:1). **38** The Sea of the Arabah. **39** Naaman (2 Kings 5:10-14).

242   THE GOOD BOOK BIBLE TRIVIA

CAVE MEN, CAVE WOMEN

1   Who lived in a cave with his daughters after Sodom and Gomorrah were destroyed?
2   Who trapped five Canaanite kings in the cave where they were hiding?
3   What friend of Jesus was buried in a cave?
4   What prophet, fleeing from Jezebel, hid in a cave?
5   In the time of the judges, what tribe did the Israelites hide from in caves?
6   What hero hid in caves to avoid the wrath of Saul?
7   Who hid a hundred prophets in a cave when Jezebel was trying to kill them?
8   In Saul's time, what marauding people drove the Israelites into caves?
9   Who hid in a cave while God passed by?
10 Unscramble the letters to reveal who was buried in the cave of Machpelah.

RASHA   HARMABA

_ _ _ _ _   _ _ _ _ _ _

SAICA   KEERHAB

_ _ _ _ _   _ _ _ _ _ _

HEAL   OJBAC

_ _ _ _   _ _ _ _ _

Cave Men, Cave Women
1 Lot (Genesis 19:30). 2 Joshua (10:16-27). 3 Lazarus (John 11:38). 4 Elijah (1 Kings 19:9).
5 The Midianites (Judges 6:2). 6 David (1 Samuel 22:1-2; 23:14, 29). 7 Obadiah (1 Kings 18:4).
8 The Philistines (1 Samuel 13:5-7). 9 Moses (Exodus 33:21-23). 10 Sarah, Abraham, Isaac,
Rebekah, Leah, and Jacob (Genesis 23:19; 25:9; 35:29; 49:30-31).

FROM THE MOUNTAINS

1 On what mountain did Elijah challenge the priests of Baal?

2 What mountain did Balaam plan to curse Israel from?

3 What mountain did Moses see the Promised Land from?

4 What mountain did Deborah and Barak descend to defeat Sisera?

5 Where did Noah's ark land?

6 Where did Jesus' transfiguration occur?

7 Where did the Samaritans build their temple?

8 Where did Moses see the burning bush?

9 On what mountain did Solomon build the Temple?

10 Where did Jesus weep over Jerusalem?

11 What mountain range did the wood for Solomon's Temple come from?

12 Where were Saul and Jonathan killed by the Philistines?

13 Where was Moses buried?

14 Where did Jacob and Laban make their covenant?

15 Where did Elijah go when he fled from Jezebel?

16 Where did Aaron die?

(More Mountains on the next page)

From the Mountains

1 Carmel (1 Kings 18:19). 2 Pisgah (Numbers 22–24). 3 Nebo (Deuteronomy 34:1-4). 4 Tabor (Judges 4:6-15). 5 Ararat (Genesis 8:4). 6 Harmon (Matthew 17). 7 Gerizim (John 4:20-21). 8 Horeb (Exodus 3:1). 9 Moriah (2 Chronicles 3:1). 10 The Mount of Olives (Luke 19:41). 11 Lebanon (1 Kings 5:6-14). 12 Gilboa (1 Samuel 31:1-6). 13 Pisgah (Deuteronomy 34:5-6). 14 Gilead (Genesis 31:20-49). 15 Horeb (1 Kings 19:8). 16 Mount Hor (Numbers 20:25-29).

244   THE GOOD BOOK BIBLE TRIVIA

17 Where did Abraham take Isaac to be sacrificed?

18 Where did Moses bring water out of the rock?

19 What mountain did David cross on his flight from Absalom?

20 What mountain in Jerusalem is mentioned over 160 times in the Bible?

21 On what smoke-covered mountain did Moses meet God?

22 What leader built an altar on Mount Ebal?

23 What prophet criticized the people who felt secure on Mount Samaria?

24 Where did Jesus deliver his final discourse?

25 In what country is Mount Seir?

26 According to Paul, what country is the site of Mount Sinai?

EXTRA CREDIT

What biblical character appeared in Ben-Hur but did not speak?

Jesus

From the Mountains

17 Moriah (Genesis 22:2). **18** Horeb (Exodus 17:6). **19** The Mount of Olives (2 Samuel 15:30-32). **20** Zion. **21** Sinai (Exodus 31:18). **22** Joshua (8:30). **23** Amos (6:1). **24** The Mount of Olives (Matthew 24-25). **25** Edom (Ezekiel 35:1-7). **26** Arabia (Galatians 4:25).

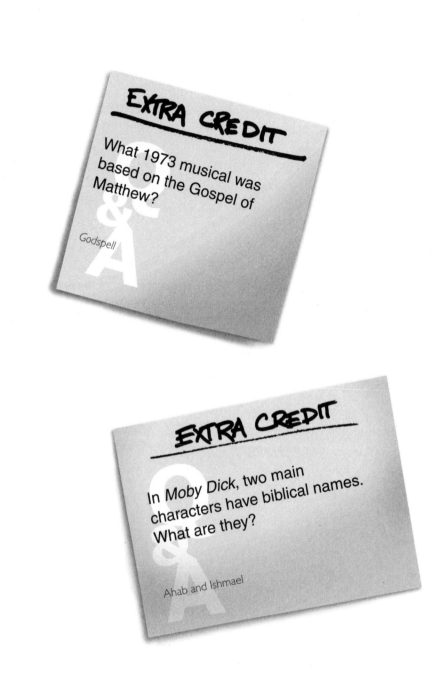

EXTRA CREDIT

What 1973 musical was based on the Gospel of Matthew?

Godspell

EXTRA CREDIT

In *Moby Dick*, two main characters have biblical names. What are they?

Ahab and Ishmael

PART NINE

CITIES AND OTHER CONSTRUCTIONS

BUILDERS OF CITIES

1 Who built ancient Babylon?
2 What king of Judah built up the defenses of Bethlehem?
3 Who built the Egyptian treasure cities of Pithom and Ramses?
4 Who rebuilt Gezer, which had been given as a wedding gift to his Egyptian wife by her father?
5 Who built Nineveh?
6 What king of Israel built Penuel?
7 What man of Bethlehem rebuilt Jericho during Ahab's reign?
8 Who built a city called Enoch east of Eden?
9 What king of Israel built the nation's capital at Samaria?
10 Who rebuilt Ramah in order to keep people from entering or leaving Judah?
11 Who rebuilt Elath and restored it to Judah?
12 Who rebuilt Babylon on a grand scale?

EXTRA CREDIT

What medieval Englishman translated the Latin Bible's New Testament into English?

John Wycliffe

CITIES GREAT AND SMALL

1 What city, a seaport on the western coast of Asia Minor, was the second of the seven churches mentioned by John?

2 What city was Paul's hometown?

3 To what city in Macedonia did Paul send at least two letters?

4 What Asian city was the home of Lydia?

5 What city on the Euphrates did Abram leave?

6 What Canaanite city, destroyed by the Israelites, has a name that means "ruin"?

7 What Pisidian city was visited by Paul and Barnabas on the first missionary journey?

8 In what city were the followers of Jesus first called Christians?

9 In what part of the city was Paul met by Christians from Rome?

10 What city is usually mentioned as the southern limit of Israel?

11 In what Greek city did Silas and Timothy stay while Paul went on to Athens?

12 What city was home to Mary, Martha, and Lazarus?

13 What city was the site of Jacob's famous dream?

14 What city was the birthplace of both David and Jesus?

15 What seaport in Asia did Paul walk to from Troas?

16 In what city did Paul address some of the most brilliant men of his time?

17 What famous city had Nebuchadnezzar as a ruler?

(More Cities on the next page)

18 What Israelite city was built by Omri as his capital?

19 What Asian city was the fifth of the seven churches mentioned by John?

20 In what Canaanite city were Joseph's bones finally laid to rest?

21 What city was the home of Peter, Andrew, and Philip?

22 Where was Cornelius converted?

23 Near what city did Peter profess his faith in Jesus?

24 Where did Jesus perform his first miracle?

25 Where did Jesus stay when John the Baptist was in prison?

26 What city was home to Philemon?

27 What sinful Greek city had a church that received two letters from Paul?

28 In what Syrian city did Paul have his sight restored at the hands of Ananias?

29 What city, usually grouped with Iconium and Lystra, did Paul visit on his first and third missionary journeys?

30 What Asian city did Paul avoid so he could hurry back to Jerusalem?

31 What ancient city is associated with Joshua and the blowing of trumpets?

32 Where did Jonah board a ship bound for Tarshish?

33 What was Solomon's seaport at the head of the Gulf of Elath?

34 What Philistine city was home to Goliath?

(More Cities on the next page)

Cities Great and Small

18 Samaria (1 Kings 16:23-24). **19** Sardis (Revelation 3:1-6). **20** Shechem (Joshua 24:32). **21** Bethsaida (John 1). **22** Caesarea (Acts 10:24-48). **23** Caesarea Philippi (Matthew 16:13-18). **24** Cana (John 2:1-11). **25** Capernaum (Matthew 4:12-13). **26** Colossae (Colossians 4:9). **27** Corinth. **28** Damascus (Acts 9). **29** Derbe (Acts 14:20). **30** Ephesus (Acts 19). **31** Jericho (Joshua 6). **32** Joppa (Jonah 1:3). **33** Ezion-Geber (1 Kings 9:26). **34** Gath (1 Samuel 17:4).

35 What Philistine city did Amos curse for its slave trade with Edom?

36 Where did Solomon have a dream when he asked for wisdom?

37 Where did Abram go after leaving Ur?

38 Unscramble the letters to reveal the city, identified with Mamre, that was the place where Sarah died.

RENHOB

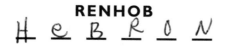

39 In what Asian city did Paul and Barnabas make many converts on the second missionary journey?

40 Where were Paul and Barnabas deserted by Mark?

41 What city was said by John to be where "Satan has his throne"?

42 What city receives most praise of all the seven cities of Asia?

43 Unscramble the letters to reveal where Assyrian king Sennacherib received tribute from Hezekiah.

SHACHIL

L A C H I S H

44 Where was Paul's longest epistle sent?

45 Where did Paul and Silas make their first European converts?

46 What city was said to have Christians that were neither hot nor cold?

(More Cities on the next page)

46 Laodicea (Revelation 3:14-22).
42 Philadelphia (Revelation 3:7-13). **43** Lachish (2 Kings 18:13-16). **44** Rome. **45** Philippi (Acts 16).
23). **39** Iconium (Acts 13-14). **40** Perga (Acts 13:13-14). **41** Pergamum (Revelation 2:12-13).
35 Gaza (Amos 1:6-7). **36** Gibeon (1 Kings 3:5-15). **37** Haran (Genesis 12). **38** Hebron (Genesis
Cities Great and Small

CITIES AND OTHER CONSTRUCTIONS 251

47 Where was Paul mistaken for the god Hermes?

48 Where was King Josiah killed?

49 Where did Paul bid farewell to the elders of Ephesus?

50 What was Jesus' hometown?

51 What port was the site of Paul's first European landing?

52 What city was, according to tradition, founded by Nimrod?

53 What city of Cyprus did Paul and Barnabas visit on their first journey?

54 In what city did Paul, on his way to Jerusalem, board a ship sailing for Phoenicia?

55 What two cities of the plain were destroyed by God for their wickedness?

56 According to the New Testament, in what city will there be no night?

57 What city was Melchizedek king of?

58 Where did tax collector Zacchaeus live?

59 Where did Peter have his vision of a sheet filled with unclean animals?

60 What city is often referred to simply as Zion?

61 What was Jeremiah's hometown?

62 When the captive Paul was taken from Jerusalem to Caesarea, where did his guards stop for the night?

(More Cities on the next page)

63 What city was home to the harlot Rahab?

64 At what town was Saul publicly proclaimed king?

The answers to the next five questions are hidden in the puzzle that follows the questions. Can you find them?

65 What Philistine city worshiped the god Baal-zebub?

66 Where was Paul when he received his famous "Macedonian vision"?

67 What prophet hailed from the town of Tekoa?

68 In what town did Saul massacre 85 priests?

69 What city was Esau's home base?

S	E	I	R	A
D	U	S	B	R
S	A	O	R	T
I	N	M	U	E
C	R	A	M	P
N	O	R	K	E

(More Cities on the next page)

Cities Great and Small
63 Jericho (Joshua 2).   **64** Gilgal (1 Samuel 11:14-15).   **65** Ekron (2 Kings 1:2).   **66** Troas (Acts 16:11).
67 Amos (1:1).   **68** Nob (1 Samuel 22:18-19).   **69** Seir (Genesis 36:8).

CITIES AND OTHER CONSTRUCTIONS   253

CITIES GREAT AND SMALL (CONTINUED)

70 What city of Cyprus was a site of Paul's preaching?

71 What city was the home of Naboth, whose vineyard Ahab wanted?

72 What was King Saul's hometown?

73 What city was punished by Gideon for refusing to feed his hungry troops?

74 In what two cities did King Jeroboam erect his golden calves?

75 What city was home to Philemon and Onesimus?

76 From the choices listed, what city was home to the man who gave Jesus a burial place?

    A Jerusalem   B Samaria   C Nazareth   D Arimathea

77 Where was Moses buried?

78 Where were the bodies of Saul and Jonathan nailed to a wall?

79 Where were a number of men slain for looking into the Ark of the Covenant?

80 Where did Elisha strike Syrian soldiers with blindness?

81 In what Syrian city did Elisha visit a sick king?

82 Where was the witch Saul consulted?

83 What city was home to the most-praised church mentioned in Revelation?

(More Cities on the next page)

Cities Great and Small
70 Salamis (Acts 13:4-5). **71** Jezreel (1 Kings 21:1-29). **72** Gibeah (1 Samuel 10:26). **73** Succoth (Judges 8:5-16). **74** Dan and Bethel (1 Kings 12:29). **75** Colossae (Colossians 4:9). **76** D: Arimathea (Matthew 27:57-60). **77** Beth-peor (Deuteronomy 34:1-6). **78** Beth-shan (1 Samuel 31:8-13). **79** Beth-shemesh (1 Samuel 6:19-21). **80** Dothan (2 Kings 6:13). **81** Damascus (2 Kings 8:7). **82** Endor (1 Samuel 28:7-14). **83** Philadelphia (Revelation 3:7-13).

CITIES GREAT AND SMALL (CONTINUED)

84 Where was Samuel buried?

85 Where did Peter cure Aeneas?

86 What was the site of the Israelites' great victory, led by Jonathan, over the Philistines?

87 What was the place where Jacob and Laban parted company?

88 Where did Jesus raise a widow's son from the dead?

89 What Phoenician city was home to Hiram, who helped construct Solomon's Temple?

90 In what Samaritan town did Jesus meet the woman at the well?

91 What city was home to the Tabernacle after the Israelites conquered Canaan?

92 What Phoenician city was home to evil Jezebel?

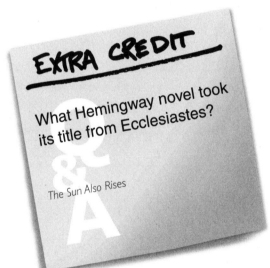

EXTRA CREDIT

What Hemingway novel took its title from Ecclesiastes?

The Sun Also Rises

Cities Great and Small
84 Ramah (1 Samuel 25:1). **85** Lydda (Acts 9:32-35). **86** Michmash (1 Samuel 14:1-23). **87** Mizpah (Genesis 31:49). **88** Nain (Luke 7:11-18). **89** Tyre (1 Kings 5:1-11). **90** Sychar (John 4:5-7). **91** Shiloh (Joshua 18:1). **92** Sidon (1 Kings 16:31-33).

CITIES AND OTHER CONSTRUCTIONS   **255**

PALATIAL LIVING

1 Whose palace had a hand that wrote on the wall?

2 What king of Tyre sent materials for David's palace?

3 Who burned the royal palace of Israel with himself inside?

4 What Babylonian went insane while walking on the roof of his palace?

5 Unscramble the letters to reveal who served as a cupbearer in Persia's royal palace.

MENEHAHI

— — — — — — — —

6 What nation's envoys were taken on a tour of the palace by King Hezekiah?

7 Who had a coveted vineyard close to Israel's royal palace?

8 Who referred to the future Jerusalem Temple as a palace "not for man, but for the LORD God" (KJV)?

9 Who took 13 years to build his palace?

10 Unscramble the letters to reveal who had a palace with marble pillars and beds of gold and silver.

SAUERHAUS

— — — — — — — — —

11 What king was assassinated in his palace by Pekah?

Palatial Living
1 Belshazzar's (Daniel 5:5). 2 Hiram (2 Samuel 5:11). 3 Zimri (1 Kings 16:15-18).
4 Nebuchadnezzar (Daniel 4:28-33). 5 Nehemiah (1:1; 2:1). 6 Babylon's (2 Kings 20:16-18).
7 Naboth (1 Kings 21:1-19). 8 David (1 Chronicles 29:1). 9 Solomon (1 Kings 7:1-12).
10 Ahasuerus (Esther 1:5-6). 11 Pekahiah (2 Kings 15:23-25).

256   THE GOOD BOOK BIBLE TRIVIA

UP ON THE ROOF

1 When Samson pulled the building down, how many people had been sitting on the rooftop?

2 Who had a vision of unclean animals while he prayed on a housetop?

3 Unscramble the letters to reveal what some of the Jews in Ezra's day built on their rooftops to commemorate the Feast of Tabernacles.

TOSHOB

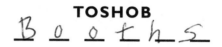

B o o t h s

4 Who prophesied judgment on the people of Jerusalem because they burned incense to idols on their roofs?

5 Cross out the letters that spell the color of the rope hanging from her window and you'll reveal who hid two Israelite spies on her rooftop among stalks of flax.

R S C A A H R L E A T B

R A H A B

6 What king saw his nude neighbor on a rooftop?

7 Who had intercourse on a rooftop with all his father's concubines?

8 What was the ailment of the man who was let down through a roof in Capernaum so he could be healed by Jesus?

9 Who slept on Samuel's roof when he visited with him?

COLLAPSIBLE BUILDINGS

1 Who caused thousands of deaths by toppling the two main pillars in a large building?

2 In Jesus' parable about houses, who had a house that collapsed when the rains came?

3 Whose children perished when the house they were feasting in collapsed in a storm?

4 Fill in the blanks to reveal the judge who tore down the tower of Penuel and slaughtered the people of the city.

— — — — —

5 What building, mentioned by Jesus, killed 18 people when it collapsed?

6 According to Jesus, what building would be so thoroughly destroyed that there would not be one stone left on another?

EXTRA CREDIT

What Old Testament text is considered authoritative for most Bible translators?

The Masoretic text

UP AGAINST THE WALL

1 What perfectly square city is described as having walls made of jasper?

2 What prophet was trapped against a wall by an angel with a drawn sword?

3 Who escaped through the wall of Damascus by being let down in a basket?

4 Whose body was fastened to the wall of Beth-shan by the Philistines?

5 Who sacrificed his son on the city wall when the Moabites were losing the battle to Israel?

6 What city was famous for its fallen walls?

7 What prophet measured the wall of the Temple district?

8 Who built the walls of Jerusalem?

9 What foreign invader tore down the walls of Jerusalem?

10 Fill in the blanks to reveal the besieged city in which the king, walking on the city wall, met a woman who told him she had eaten her son for dinner.

— — — — — — —

11 Who hurled his spear into a wall missing his intended target, David?

12 What warrior, the victim of a king's scheming, was killed when shot by arrows from the wall of Rabbah?

13 What rebel against David was beheaded, with his head thrown over the wall of Abel to Joab?

14 What wine steward sat down and wept when he learned the walls of Jerusalem had not been rebuilt?

Up against the Wall
1 The new Jerusalem (Revelation 21:18). 2 Balaam (Numbers 22:24). 3 Paul (Acts 9:25). 4 Saul's (1 Samuel 31:10). 5 Mesha, king of Moab (2 Kings 3:27). 6 Jericho (Joshua 6:20). 7 Ezekiel (42:20). 8 Solomon (1 Kings 9:15). 9 Nebuchadnezzar (2 Kings 25:10). 10 Samaria (2 Kings 6:26-29). 11 Saul (1 Samuel 19:10). 12 Uriah the Hittite (2 Samuel 11:24). 13 Sheba (2 Samuel 20:22). 14 Nehemiah (1:3-4).

OPENING WINDOWS

1 Who died after falling out of a window during Paul's sermon?

2 What prophet ordered a king to shoot arrows out of a window?

3 What king looked out of his window and saw Isaac and Rebekah wooing?

4 What wicked queen was thrown out of a window by her servants?

5 Who knelt toward Jerusalem and prayed looking out of his eastern window in Babylon?

6 Who let birds fly out of his ship's window?

7 Who let spies escape through a window by using a rope?

8 Who looked out her window and was ashamed to see her husband dancing in the street?

9 In what city did Paul escape a plot by going through a window in the city wall?

10 According to Malachi, what windows would be opened for people that tithed?

11 Who looked out his window and saw a young man being enticed by a prostitute?

12 Whose wife helped him escape from Saul by letting him down through a window?

Opening Windows

1 Eutychus (Acts 20:9). 2 Elisha (2 Kings 13:17). 3 Abimelech (Genesis 26:8). 4 Jezebel (2 Kings 9:30, 32). 5 Daniel (6:10). 6 Noah (Genesis 8:6). 7 Rahab (Joshua 2:15-21). 8 Michal, wife of David (2 Samuel 6:16). 9 Damascus (2 Corinthians 11:33). 10 The windows of heaven (Malachi 3:10). 11 Solomon, or whoever wrote Proverbs (7:6-10). 12 David's (1 Samuel 19:12).

260 THE GOOD BOOK BIBLE TRIVIA

WELLS, CISTERNS, AND OTHER LARGE CONTAINERS

1 Who had a miraculous well opened up for him after he worked up a thirst in battle?

2 What king dug wells in the desert?

3 What king ordered the construction of the Sea, the great basin in the Temple court?

4 Fill in the blanks to reveal the exiled woman who was approached by an angel at a well.

__ __ __ __ __

5 What army man was at the well of Sirah when he was summoned to his death by Joab's men?

6 Who escaped from Absalom's men by hiding in a well?

7 Fill in the blanks to reveal who met his future wife at a well in Midian.

__ __ __ __ __

8 Who found a wife for Isaac at the well of Nahor?

9 Who longed for a drink from the well at Bethlehem?

10 Fill in the blanks to reveal the book that contains laws telling owners of cisterns what to do if a person or animal accidentally falls in.

__ __ __ __ __ __

(More Wells on the next page)

Wells, Cisterns, and Other Large Containers

1 Samson (Judges 15:18-20). 2 Uzziah (2 Chronicles 26:10). 3 Solomon (1 Kings 7:23). 4 Hagar (Genesis 16:7-14). 5 Abner (2 Samuel 3:26-27). 6 Ahimaaz and Jonathan (2 Samuel 17:17-21). 7 Moses (Exodus 2:15-21). 8 Abraham's servant (Genesis 24). 9 David (2 Samuel 23:14-17). 10 Exodus (21:33-34).

CITIES AND OTHER CONSTRUCTIONS   261

11 What prophet was imprisoned in a cistern?

12 Who met his future wife by a well when she came to water her sheep?

13 Fill in the blanks to reveal where God pared down Gideon's troops to three hundred men.

THE __ __ __ __ __ __

OF __ __ __ __ __

14 Who had servants who named their wells Esek, Sitnah, Rehoboth, and Beersheba?

15 What son of Jacob nearly perished in a cistern?

16 Fill in the blanks to reveal who promised the citizens of Jerusalem that they could be free to drink from their own cisterns if they would surrender to Assyria.

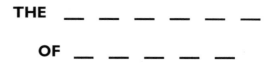

— — — — — — — — —

17 In what country did Jesus talk with an immoral woman beside a well?

18 Who tried to take the well of Beersheba away from Abraham?

Wells, Cisterns, and Other Large Containers

11 Jeremiah (38:6).   12 Jacob (Genesis 29:1-12).   13 The spring of Harod (Judges 7:1-7).   14 Isaac (Genesis 26:17-33).   15 Joseph (Genesis 37:22).   16 Rabshakeh (2 Kings 18:31).   17 Samaria (John 4:5-15).   18 Abimelech (Genesis 21:22-32).

GATES, DOORS, AND OTHER OPENINGS

1 Whom did God speak to about the "gates of death"?

2 What gate of Jerusalem was rebuilt under Nehemiah's leadership?

3 What faithful soldier, home on furlough, chose to sleep in front of the king's palace door instead of going home to his wife?

4 Who removed the massive doors from the gate of Gaza and carried them to a hill at Hebron?

5 According to what Moses told the Israelites, where were the words of God to be written?

6 Who shut up the door of Noah's ark?

7 What king removed the gold from the doors of the Temple and gave it to the king of Assyria?

8 At the first Passover, what did the Israelites put on their doorposts?

9 According to Psalm 24, what is to be lifted up so that the king of glory may enter in?

10 Who rolled back the stone from Jesus' tomb?

11 According to Revelation, which of the seven churches in Asia did the Lord say that he had set before it an open door that no man could shut?

12 Who healed a lame man at the Temple's Beautiful Gate?

13 Solve the math problem below and find out, in John's vision of the new Jerusalem, how many gates the city has.

$$144 \div 12 \times 7 + 16 - 92 + 4 = \underline{}$$

Bonus: From the choices listed, what are these gates made of?

A Gold   B Pearl   C Sapphire   D Amethyst

PORTABLE PLACES TO DWELL

1 Who accepted an invitation to hide in a tent and was then murdered by the woman who invited him?

The answers to the next four questions are hidden in the puzzle following the questions. Can you find them?

2 What famous ship captain lived in a tent?

3 Who was "the first of those who . . . live in tents"?

4 Who took plunder from the fallen Jericho and buried it inside his tent?

5 Who took his wife to his mother's tent on their wedding night?

N	J	T	O	W
C	A	A	S	I
U	B	H	I	P
M	A	A	C	E
F	L	O	R	A
T	E	N	T	S

6 What, in the dream of a Midianite soldier, tumbled into the Midianite camp and flattened a tent?

7 Who stored Goliath's armor in his tent?

(More Portables on the next page)

Portable Places to Dwell
1 Sisera (Judges 4:17-21).   2 Noah (Genesis 9:21).   3 Jabal (Genesis 4:20).   4 Achan (Joshua 7:21).
5 Isaac (Genesis 24:67).   6 A cake of barley (Judges 7:13-14).   7 David (1 Samuel 17:54).

PORTABLE PLACES TO DWELL (CONTINUED)

8 What was the tent that was made according to God's specifications?

9 Who plundered the tents of the Syrians after the army fled their camp?

10 Who commanded his descendants to always live in tents?

11 Who pitched a tent in Jerusalem to house the Ark of the Covenant?

12 Fill in the blanks to reveal who killed an Israelite man and the Midianite woman the man had brought into his tent.

— — — — — — — — —

13 Who lived in tents in the wilderness of Sin?

14 Who did Noah say would dwell in the tents of Shem?

15 What rebel against David said, "Every man to his tents, O Israel"?

16 What prophet said, "The LORD shall save the tents of Judah"?

17 What king were the people of Israel rebelling against when they said, "To your tents, O Israel"?

18 Who compares her skin to the darkness of the "tents of Kedar"?

19 What prophet saw "the tents of Cushan in affliction"?

Portable Places to Dwell

8 The Tabernacle (Exodus 26:1-4). 9 The Samaritans (2 Kings 7:3-16). 10 Jonadab (Jeremiah 35:6-10). 11 David (1 Chronicles 15:1). 12 Phinehas (Numbers 25:6-8). 13 The Israelites (Exodus 33:10). 14 Japheth (Genesis 9:27). 15 Sheba (2 Samuel 20:1, kjv). 16 Zechariah (12:7, kjv). 17 Rehoboam (1 Kings 12:16, kjv). 18 The woman in Song of Songs (Song of Solomon) (1:5). 19 Habakkuk (3:7, kjv).

EXTRA CREDIT

What people from Jesus' early life were characters in *Ben-Hur?*

The three wise men

EXTRA CREDIT

What English Bible translator died as a martyr?

William Tyndale

PART TEN
THE FINER THINGS

MAKERS OF MUSIC

1 What stringed instruments did John hear in his vision of the heavenly throne?

2 Who is mentioned as the father of those who play the harp and organ?

3 What prophetess played a tambourine and led the women of Israel in a victory song after the Red Sea incident?

4 What caused Saul's "evil spirit" to leave him?

5 Who wrote over a thousand songs?

6 What is the only book of the Bible that contains numerous directions for musical accompaniment?

7 At the dedication of Solomon's Temple, 120 priests played what instruments?

8 What king of Israel had four thousand musicians who praised the Lord with instruments the king made?

9 What prophet prophesied while accompanied by a minstrel?

10 When the foundation for the second Temple was laid, the priests played trumpets. What did the Levites play?

11 What king, who was also a poet and musician, embarrassed his wife by dancing in the streets?

12 What prophetic book of the Old Testament contains musical directions?

ARTSY, CRAFTSY TYPES

1 What notorious opponent of Paul was a silversmith in Ephesus?
2 What leader fashioned a brass snake?
3 Who was the first metal craftsman in the Bible?
4 What Israelite, a worker in gold, silver, brass, stone, and wood, had responsibility for furnishing the Tabernacle?
5 Who built a huge ship of gopher wood?
6 What coppersmith had, according to Paul, done him great harm?
7 Unscramble the letters and find both the type of metal this craftsman from Tyre was put in charge of during the construction of the Temple as well as his name.

BANZIRHOREM

— — — — — —

— — — — —

8 What was the trade of Paul, Aquila, and Priscilla?
9 Who fashioned a golden calf?
10 What son of a goldsmith was involved in rebuilding the walls of Jerusalem?
11 What engraver and embroiderer helped construct materials for the Tabernacle?

Artsy, Craftsy Types
1 Demetrius (Acts 19:24). 2 Moses (Numbers 21:9). 3 Tubal-cain (Genesis 4:22). 4 Bezaleel (Exodus 31:1-6). 5 Noah (Genesis 6:13-22). 6 Alexander (2 Timothy 4:14). 7 Bronze; Hiram (1 Kings 7:13-14). 8 Tent making (Acts 18:1-3). 9 Aaron (Exodus 32:4). 10 Uzziel (Nehemiah 3:8). 11 Aholiab (Exodus 38:23).

LOOKING GOOD, SMELLING GOOD

1. Who had a harem with women that were "purified" with perfumes?

2. What evil queen "painted her face" before meeting with the rebel king Jehu?

3. What book mentions a woman using such perfumes as saffron, calamus, cinnamon, frankincense, myrrh, aloes, and many others?

4. What prophet refused to use anointing oils during three weeks of mourning?

5. Who anointed Jesus' head with an expensive perfume?

6. What sweet-smelling substances were brought to the infant Jesus?

7. What Hebrew officials were anointed with holy oil perfumed with aromatic spices?

8. According to Proverbs 27:9, what is as sweet as perfume and incense?

9. What two prophets speak critically of women putting on eye makeup?

10. What woman, portrayed in Proverbs chapter 7, perfumed her bed with myrrh, aloes, and cinnamon?

11. Where was Jesus when a sinful woman poured an alabaster jar of perfume on his feet?

12. What man uses myrrh, frankincense, and other spices as perfumes?

RINGS ON THEIR FINGERS

1 What dreaming ruler gave Joseph his own ring?
2 Fill in the blanks to reveal in which of Jesus' parables a ring plays a part.

         __ __ __

__ __ __ __ __ __ __

         __ __ __

3 Who did King Ahasuerus of Persia give his ring to?
4 When Daniel was sealed up in the lions' den, who placed his signet ring on the stone?
5 For what did the Israelites give up their rings and other jewelry?
6 Fill in the blanks to reveal who, after the death of Haman, received the Persian king's signet ring.

__ __ __ __ __ __ __ __

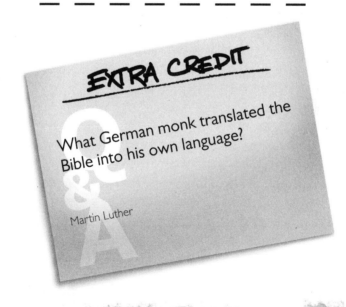

EXTRA CREDIT

Q&A

What German monk translated the Bible into his own language?

Martin Luther

Rings on Their Fingers
1 Pharaoh (Genesis 41:42).   2 The Prodigal Son (the son was given a ring by his father upon returning home) (Luke 15:22).   3 Haman (Esther 3:10-13).   4 The king (Daniel 6:17).   5 As a freewill offering for the Tabernacle (Exodus 35:22).   6 Mordecai (Esther 8:2-13).

GLAD RAGS

1 Who wore a camel's hair tunic?

2 What king of Israel is mentioned as wearing a crown and a gold bracelet?

3 What Egyptian official was given fine linen, the pharaoh's ring, and a gold chain for his neck?

4 What people had such well-made clothes that years of wilderness wandering did not even wear out their shoes?

5 Whose eye-catching cloak caused murderous envy in his brothers?

6 The best-dressed man in Israel wore fine colored linen with embroidered bells and pomegranates, a linen breastplate with gold and precious stones, and a gold-studded hat. Who was he?

7 What down-and-out man is mentioned as having worn a gold earring in his better days?

8 Only one person is mentioned in the Bible as having worn gloves. Who?

9 What warriors were so extravagant that even their camels wore necklaces?

10 What people wore fine Egyptian linen and purple robes?

11 Who was given a gold earring and two gold bracelets as introductory presents from her future husband?

12 Who did Jesus say was "not dressed" as beautifully as this flower? (Name the flower too.)

13 What queen was extremely impressed by this ruler's household, including what his ministers wore?

14 Who, described as being "splendidly clothed in purple and fine linen," was condemned for his treatment of a beggar?

15 What member of the early church was a successful merchant of expensive purple cloth?

Glad Rags:
1 John the Baptist (Matthew 3:4). 2 Saul (2 Samuel 1:10). 3 Joseph (Genesis 42:42). 4 The Israelites (Deuteronomy 29:5). 5 Joseph's (Genesis 37:3). 6 The high priest (Exodus 28). 7 Job (42:11). 8 Jacob (Genesis 27:16). 9 The Midianites (Judges 8:24-26). 10 The "seaport rulers" (Phoenicians) (Ezekiel 27:16). 11 Rebekah, gifts carried by future husband Isaac's servant (Genesis 24:22). 12 Solomon; the lilies of the field (Matthew 6:28-29). 13 The queen of Sheba, a guest of King Solomon (1 Kings 10:4-5). 14 A rich man (Luke 16:19-26). 15 Lydia (Acts 16:14).

PART ELEVEN

THE DOMESTIC SCENE

SO MANY CHILDREN

1 What judge had 70 sons?

2 Who is the first child mentioned in the Bible?

3 Who was Noah's youngest son?

4 What king was the youngest of eight brothers?

5 Who was Joseph's younger son?

6 Who is the youngest son of Adam mentioned by name?

7 Who were the first twins mentioned in the Bible?

8 Which disciple was probably a twin?

9 Who died giving birth to Benjamin?

10 Was the Prodigal Son the older or younger son?

11 What wicked king of Israel had 70 sons?

12 Solve the math problem below and find out how many children David had by his legitimate wives.

$$65 \times 8 \div 10 - 34 + 2 = \underline{}$$

13 Who was older, Moses or Aaron?

14 Who was Jacob's youngest son?

15 Who was born first, Jacob or Esau?

(More Children on the next page)

So Many Children
1 Gideon (Judges 8:30). 2 Cain (Genesis 4:1). 3 Ham (Genesis 9:18-24). 4 David (1 Samuel 17:12-14). 5 Ephraim (Genesis 41:51-52). 6 Seth (Genesis 4:25). 7 Jacob and Esau (Genesis 25:23-26). 8 Thomas (John 11:16). 9 Rachel (Genesis 35:16-18). 10 The younger (Luke 15:11-32). 11 Ahab (2 Kings 10:1). 12 20: nineteen sons and one daughter (1 Chronicles 3:1-9). 13 Aaron (Exodus 7:7). 14 Benjamin (Genesis 35:16-18). 15 Esau (Genesis 25:25-26).

274   THE GOOD BOOK BIBLE TRIVIA

16 What king of Judah had 28 sons and 60 daughters?

17 What court prophet of David's had 14 sons and 3 daughters?

18 What prophet spoke of a time of peace when a little child would lead the wild beasts?

19 Who made sacrifices in case any of his children had sinned?

20 Which epistle advises "Children, obey your parents because you belong to the Lord"?

21 According to Malachi, who will come to turn the hearts of the children to their fathers?

22 What little-known judge of Israel had 30 sons?

23 Whom did Paul advise that a bishop must be able to control his own children?

24 In which Gospel did Jesus predict that children rebelling against their parents would be a sign of the end times?

25 Which of the Ten Commandments states that children will be punished for their parents' sins?

26 Which Gospel does not mention the little children coming to Jesus?

27 Who advised young Christians to stop thinking like children?

28 Which Gospel says that the child Jesus grew up strong?

29 What prophet advised people to tell their children about the locust plague?

30 Which epistle advises fathers not to exasperate their children?

31 What book says that a child raised up in the right way will never depart from it?

(More Children on the next page)

So Many Children

16 Rehoboam (2 Chronicles 11:21). **17** Heman (1 Chronicles 25:5). **18** Isaiah (11:6). **19** Job (1:5).
20 Ephesians (6:1). **21** Elijah (Malachi 4:6). **22** Jair (Judges 10:3-4). **23** Timothy (1 Timothy 3:4).
24 Mark (13:12). **25** The second (against graven images) (Exodus 20:4). **26** John. **27** Paul
(1 Corinthians 14:20). **28** Luke (1:80). **29** Joel (1:3). **30** Ephesians (6:4). **31** Proverbs (22:6).

SO MANY CHILDREN (CONTINUED)

32 What priest was too indulgent toward his spoiled sons?

33 What prophet had dishonest sons who took bribes?

34 Which son was Isaac partial to?

35 What king grieved and wailed over his wayward son?

36 Who was Jacob's favorite son?

37 Who made a little coat for her son every year when she went to offer the annual sacrifice?

38 Which psalm says that children are like arrows in the hands of a warrior?

39 What book mentions how wonderful grandchildren are?

40 What prophet named his sons Maher-shalal-hash-baz and Shear-jashub?

41 According to the law, what is the penalty for anyone who attacks his mother or father?

42 What prophet talks about children dishonoring their parents, so that a man's enemies are in his own household?

43 According to Deuteronomy, what must be done to a rebellious son who will not submit to discipline?

44 What judge of Israel had 40 sons and 30 grandsons?

45 What Old Testament man almost sacrificed his beloved son?

46 What judge of Israel sacrificed his daughter?

47 Who did Paul say had known the Scriptures from his infancy?

(More Children on the next page)

48 Which of Gideon's 70 sons (the youngest) was the only one to escape the plot of his scheming brother Abimelech?

49 Who were Perez and Zerah?

50 Who died after giving birth to a son named Ichabod?

51 Who said that we must change and become like children?

52 Which book says that children will not be put to death for their parents' sins?

53 Who told believers that the promises of God were for their children as well as themselves?

54 Which epistle says that parents are to provide for their children, not vice versa?

55 What prophet said, "I will teach all your children, and they will enjoy great peace"?

56 What prophet said that the son would not share the guilt of the father?

57 What prophet said he was neither a prophet nor a prophet's son?

58 Who envisioned a time when sons and daughters would prophesy?

59 Who asked his childless wife if he was not worth more to her than ten sons?

60 Who was told that she had a daughter-in-law who treated her better than seven sons could?

61 What king made a wise decision about a child claimed by two prostitutes?

62 Who was adopted by Mordecai as his own daughter?

63 What psalm advises dashing the babies of Babylon against stones?

So Many Children

48 Jotham (Judges 9:1-5). **49** Twin sons of Judah and Tamar (Genesis 38:29-30). **50** The wife of Phinehas (1 Samuel 4:19-22). **51** Jesus (Matthew 18:3). **52** Deuteronomy (24:16). **53** Peter (Acts 2:39). **54** 2 Corinthians (12:14). **55** Isaiah (54:13). **56** Ezekiel (18:20). **57** Amos (7:14). **58** Joel (2:28). **59** Elkanah (1 Samuel 1:8). **60** Naomi (Ruth 4:15). **61** Solomon (1 Kings 3:16-28). **62** Esther (2:7). **63** Psalm 137:8-9.

MULTIPLE MARRIAGES

1 What king had 700 wives and 300 concubines?
2 Fill in the blanks to reveal the first man in the Bible mentioned as having more than one wife.

     —   —   —   —   —   —

3 Who married sisters Rachel and Leah?
4 Fill in the blanks to reveal who fathered 70 sons by his many wives.

     —   —   —   —   —   —

5 Whose father had two wives named Hannah and Peninnah?
6 What hairy man had three wives named Judith, Bashemath, and Mahalath?
7 What early king had two wives named Ahinoam and Rizpah?
8 Fill in the blanks to reveal the woman who was married to two of Judah's sons.

     —   —   —   —   —

9 What New Testament woman had had at least five husbands?
10 Who asked Jesus a ridiculous question about a woman who successively married seven brothers?

(More Marriages on the next page)

Multiple Marriages
1 Solomon (1 Kings 11:3).   2 Lamech (Genesis 4:19).   3 Jacob (Genesis 29:15-25).   4 Gideon (Judges 8:30).   5 Samuel's (1 Samuel 1:1-2).   6 Esau (Genesis 26:24; 28:9).   7 Saul (1 Samuel 14:50; 2 Samuel 3:7).   8 Tamar (Genesis 38:6-10).   9 The woman at the well (John 4:6-19).   10 The Sadducees (Mark 12:18-25).

MULTIPLE MARRIAGES (CONTINUED)

11 Who had Mahlon and Boaz for husbands?

12 What woman, given to Phaltiel by her father Saul, was later reclaimed by David?

13 Fill in the blanks to reveal the king of Judah who had 14 wives.

— — — — — — —

14 What Persian king had wives named Vashti and Esther?

15 What son of Solomon had 18 wives and 60 concubines?

16 Fill in the blanks to reveal whose wives included Abigail, Maacah, Haggith, and Eglah.

— — — — —

17 What patriarch took Keturah as his third wife?

18 Who had two wives, one of them named Zipporah?

19 Fill in the blanks to reveal what king, much influenced by his dominating wife, also had other wives.

— — — —

20 What judge of Israel gave up his Philistine wife to his friend?

Multiple Marriages
11 Ruth (Ruth 4:10, 13). **12** Michal (2 Samuel 3:13-16). **13** Abijah (2 Chronicles 13:21).
14 Ahasuerus (Esther 1:10-12; 2:1-17). **15** Rehoboam (2 Chronicles 11:21). **16** David (2 Samuel 12:8). **17** Abraham (Genesis 16:3; 23:19; 25:1). **18** Moses (Exodus 18:2; Numbers 12:1). **19** Ahab (1 Kings 20:7). **20** Samson (Judges 14:20).

WIDOW WOMEN

1 Who probably left more widows than anyone else?

2 What lying woman was a widow for only about three hours?

3 What prophet issued a dire warning against people who took advantage of widows?

4 Who became a widow because of King David's lust?

5 Who did Jesus accuse of "shamelessly cheat[ing] widows out of their property"?

6 Who posed to Jesus a foolish riddle about a woman who was a widow several times over?

7 What commendable deed was done by a poor widow Jesus saw in the Temple?

8 Which church in Greece is mentioned by Paul as having widows in need of care?

9 Which of Paul's protégés had widows under his jurisdiction?

10 What woman of Joppa gave away clothing to the widows?

11 What New Testament epistle mentions kindness to widows as a mark of true religion?

12 What parable of Jesus has a widow as the main character?

13 What infamous widow was thrown from a window after she had put on makeup?

14 What prophet revived the son of the widow of Zarephath?

15 What widow had a husband whom the Lord killed and, later, had an affair with her father-in-law?

16 What widow, the daughter-in-law of the priest Eli, had a baby named Ichabod?

(More Widows on the next page)

WIDOW WOMEN (CONTINUED)

17 What king was almost fooled by the conniving woman of Tekoa who pretended to be a poor widow?

18 Whose mother was a widow named Zeruah?

19 Which widows in Jerusalem were neglected in the daily distribution of funds?

20 What king forced 10 of his concubines to live as widows for the rest of their lives?

21 Who married King David after her drunken husband suffered a stroke and died?

22 What great city does Isaiah predict will become like a helpless widow?

The answers to the next four questions are hidden in the puzzle that follows the questions. Can you find them?

23 What book of the Old Testament is named for a famous widow who became an ancestress of David?

24 What aged prophetess in Jerusalem was a widow?

25 What city was home to the widow whose son Jesus raised from the dead?

26 Who said Christian widows were better off not to remarry?

A	N	N	A	H
W	H	I	L	T
L	U	A	P	U
D	I	N	E	R

WEDDINGS, DOWRIES, AND DIVORCES

1 Who made a wedding feast before giving the wrong bride to Jacob?

2 What gruesome objects did Saul require from David as dowry for his daughter?

3 Who prompted the Jews after the Babylonian exile to divorce their foreign wives?

4 Where was the wedding at which Jesus changed water into wine?

5 Who, according to John, is the bride of Christ?

6 Who made a seven-day marriage feast but never married the woman he intended?

7 Unscramble the letters to reveal where the first wedding recorded in the Bible took place and who gave the bride away.

FRENGONDADOEGED

— — — — — —

— — — — — —

— — —

(More Weddings on the next page)

Weddings, Dowries, and Divorces
1 Laban (Genesis 29:22-25). 2 A hundred Philistine foreskins (1 Samuel 18:25, 27). 3 Ezra (Ezra 10).
4 Cana (John 2:1-11). 5 The church (Revelation 14:10-20). 6 Samson (Judges 19:7-9). 7 Garden
of Eden; God (Genesis 2:22-24).

282   THE GOOD BOOK BIBLE TRIVIA

8 How did Boaz obtain Ruth as his wife?

9 When Shechem the Hivite asked to marry Dinah, what did her brothers ask as a dowry?

10 What did Jacob have to do to marry Rachel?

11 Which Gospel records Jesus' parable of a king's wedding feast for his son?

12 Who sent the servant woman Hagar away at his wife's urging?

13 What unscrupulous king divorced his first wife to marry his brother's wife?

14 In Jesus' parable, how many virgins were to accompany the bride and groom?

15 Who arranged Ishmael's marriage?

16 Who was the first polygamist?

17 Who said that Moses allowed divorce because of people's hardness of heart?

18 Where does the Bible prohibit polygamy?

19 What prophet spoke about Jews divorcing their wives to marry pagan women?

20 What was the levirate law?

21 What was considered proof of the bride's virginity?

22 Which Gospel states that Jesus considered adultery to be grounds for divorce?

23 According to Jeremiah, whom did God divorce?

24 What morally upright man wanted to quietly break off his engagement?

(More Weddings on the next page)

Weddings, Dowries, and Divorces
8 He purchased the property of Naomi, her mother-in-law (Ruth 3–4). **9** That all of Shechem's men be circumcised (Genesis 34:1-16). **10** Serve Laban for 14 years (Genesis 29:16-30). **11** Matthew (22:1-14). **12** Abraham (Genesis 21:9-14). **13** Herod (Matthew 14:3-4). **14** 10 (Matthew 25:1-13). **15** Hagar, his mother (Genesis 21:21). **16** Lamech (Genesis 4:19). **17** Jesus (Matthew 19:8). **18** It doesn't. **19** Malachi (2:10-16). **20** When a man died without children, his brother was expected to take his wife so as to provide descendants for the dead man (Genesis 38:8-10). **21** A bloodstained cloth (Deuteronomy 22:13-21). **22** Matthew (19:3-12). **23** Israel (Jeremiah 3:8). **24** Joseph (Matthew 1:19).

25 Which of Elkanah's wives was his favorite?

26 Who was thrown into prison for criticizing the marriage of a king?

27 Which of Paul's epistles gives the most information about marriage?

28 What Egyptian woman did Joseph marry?

29 Who was Naomi's husband?

30 What wife of David was also married to Nabal?

31 What king of Judah married a daughter of Ahab?

32 What emperor married a Jewish girl?

33 What godly priest had a wife named Jehosheba?

34 Who married a prostitute named Gomer?

35 Who was married to Zebedee, father of James and John?

36 What childless woman was married to the priest Zechariah?

37 What wicked Persian official had a wife named Zeresh?

38 What saintly woman was the wife of Cuza, the head of Herod's household?

39 What Jewish-Christian couple were probably Paul's closest married friends?

40 What husband and wife lied to Peter about their finances?

41 What Roman governor had a Jewish wife named Drusilla?

(More Weddings on the next page)

Weddings, Dowries, and Divorces
25 Hannah (1 Samuel 1:1-8).   **26** John the Baptist (Matthew 14:3-4).   **27** 1 Corinthians (7).
28 Asenath (Genesis 41:45).   **29** Elimelech (Ruth 1:2).   **30** Abigail (1 Samuel 25:3).   **31** Joram, who married Athaliah (2 Kings 8:21, 26).   **32** Ahasuerus (Esther 2:16).   **33** Jehoiada (2 Chronicles 22:11).
34 Hosea (Hosea 1).   **35** Salome (Matthew 4:21; Mark 16:1).   **36** Elizabeth (Luke 1:5).   **37** Haman (Esther 5:14; 6:13).   **38** Joanna (Luke 8:3).   **39** Aquila and Priscilla (Acts 18:2).   **40** Ananias and Sapphira (Acts 5).   **41** Felix (Acts 24:24).

42 Who took a wife who was not only nameless but ancestor-less?

43 What unnamed wife turned into a pillar of salt?

44 What judge had a Philistine wife?

45 From the choices listed, whose unnamed wife urged her husband to curse God?

A Job's   **B** Saul's   **C** David's   **D** Herod's

46 What leprous Syrian soldier had a faithful wife?

47 What prophet was married to a prophet?

48 What prophet had a wife who died suddenly?

49 What wicked priest had a harlot wife?

50 Whose wife insisted that her husband have nothing to do with Jesus?

51 Who was Moses' first wife?

52 Who was the only disciple that we know for sure was married?

EXTRA CREDIT

Who played the role of Dathan in *The Ten Commandments*?

Q&A

Edward G. Robinson

Weddings, Dowries, and Divorces
42 Cain (Genesis 4:17).   **43** Lot's wife (Genesis 19:26).   **44** Samson (Judges 14).   **45** A: Job's (Job 2:9-10).   **46** Naaman (2 Kings 5:1-4).   **47** Isaiah, whose wife was called a prophetess (Isaiah 8:3).   **48** Ezekiel (24:18).   **49** Amaziah (Amos 7:10-17).   **50** Pilate's (Matthew 27:19).   **51** Zipporah (Exodus 2:21).   **52** Peter (Mark 1:30).

MIRACULOUS PREGNANCIES

1 Who gave birth to a son when she was 90 years old?

2 What beloved wife of Jacob gave birth, after many years, to Joseph and Benjamin?

3 What elderly couple produced a child, in accordance with the words of an angel?

4 Who prophesied to the Shunemmite woman that, though her husband was too old, she would bear a child?

5 Why did God cause barrenness among the women of Abimelech's household?

6 What woman, long barren, gave birth to twins?

7 Who was taunted by her husband's other wife for being childless, though she later bore a son?

8 Whose astounded mother called herself the "the Lord's servant" when told she would bear a child?

9 Whose mother was told by an angel that she would bear a son who would deliver Israel from the Philistines?

10 What very old man remarried after his wife's death and continued to father children?

Miraculous Pregnancies

1 Sarah (Genesis 21:1-5). 2 Rachel (Genesis 30:22-24; 35:18). 3 Elizabeth and Zechariah (Luke 1:7-9, 13, 18). 4 Elisha (2 Kings 4:13-17). 5 Abimelech had taken Sarah for himself (Genesis 20:17-18). 6 Rebekah (Genesis 25:21-26). 7 Hannah, mother of Samuel (1 Samuel 1:1-19). 8 Jesus' (Luke 1:26-38). 9 Samson's (Judges 13:3, 5). 10 Abraham (Genesis 25:1-6).

286   THE GOOD BOOK BIBLE TRIVIA

BROTHER AGAINST BROTHER

1 Whose older brother refused to attend his brother's welcome home party?
2 What son of Gideon killed 70 of his brothers at once?
3 Fill in the blanks to reveal the judge, an illegitimate son, who was thrown out of the house by his brothers.

— — — — — — — —

4 Who hated his brother for taking away his birthright?
5 What did Moses rebuke Aaron for?
6 Who was the first man to murder his brother?
7 Fill in the blanks to reveal who hated his brother Ammon for what he had done to Tamar.

— — — — — — —

8 What dreamy boy was hated for being his father's favorite?
9 Fill in the blanks to reveal which of David's older brothers chewed him out for coming to watch the Israelites fighting the Philistines.

— — — — —

Brother against Brother
1 The Prodigal Son's (Luke 15:28). 2 Abimelech (Judges 9:1-5). 3 Jephthah (Judges 11:1-2).
4 Esau (Genesis 27:41). 5 Making the golden calf (Exodus 32:19-22). 6 Cain (Genesis 4:8).
7 Absalom (2 Samuel 13:22). 8 Joseph (Genesis 37:4). 9 Eliab (1 Samuel 17:28-30).

MENSERVANTS, MAIDSERVANTS

1 What runaway servant was the main subject of one of Paul's epistles?

2 Unscramble the letters to reveal who sent two of his servants to fetch Peter from Joppa.

CLUERISON

— — — — — — — — —

3 To whose servant did Peter deny any knowledge of Jesus?

4 Who, with 318 of his servants, defeated the captors of Sodom and Gomorrah?

5 Who was Elisha's servant?

6 What Egyptian official had Joseph as a servant?

7 Who was permanently crippled because a servant woman dropped him as a baby?

8 Who cut off the ear of Malchus, the high priest's servant?

9 Fill in the blanks to reveal who had a servant girl who advised him to go to Elisha to be cured of leprosy.

— — — — — —

10 What servant woman was the mother of Ishmael?

11 Whom did Abraham's eldest servant find a wife for?

12 Where did Jesus heal a centurion's servant?

13 Who was a servant to the Persian king Artaxerxes?

(More Servants on the next page)

Menservants, Maidservants
1 Onesimus (Philemon). 2 Cornelius (Acts 10:7-8). 3 The high priest's (John 18:26). 4 Abraham (Genesis 14:14-15). 5 Gehazi (2 Kings 4:12). 6 Potiphar (Genesis 39). 7 Mephibosheth (2 Samuel 4:4). 8 Peter (John 18:10). 9 Naaman (2 Kings 5:2-3). 10 Hagar (Genesis 16:1). 11 Isaac (Genesis 24). 12 Capernaum (Matthew 8:13). 13 Nehemiah (1:11).

288   THE GOOD BOOK BIBLE TRIVIA

MENSERVANTS, MAIDSERVANTS (CONTINUED)

14 What two servants of Pharaoh were in prison with Joseph?

15 Who was Laban's servant for many years?

16 Whose servant woman took Moses from the river?

17 What judge's servant killed him at his own request?

18 Fill in the blanks to reveal the names of the two servant women who bore children to Jacob.

— — — — — —

— — — — — —

19 Who made the Israelites into slaves?

20 In what parable are the servants of a landowner beaten up?

21 In what parable are servants given money to invest?

22 At whose house did Peter deny Christ to a servant girl?

23 Who was Elijah's personal servant?

24 What people were, in the time of Joshua, cursed to be Israel's servants?

25 Fill in the blanks to reveal the name of Moses' personal servant.

— — — — — —

26 Who was Jesus responding to when he told the parable of the unmerciful servant?

SPEAKING OF BEDS

1 What book of the Old Testament speaks fondly of a bed of "soft grass"?

The answers to the next six questions are hidden in the puzzle that follows the questions. Can you find them?

2 What king had a huge bed made of iron?

3 What king sulked in bed because he couldn't acquire a certain piece of property?

4 Who blessed the 12 tribes while lying in bed?

5 What prophet condemned the idle rich on their beds of ivory?

6 What king of Judah was murdered in his bed by his servants?

7 Who saved her husband, David's, life by putting an idol in his bed, covering it, and pretending it was him?

T	O	L	L	S
H	S	A	O	J
B	A	H	A	N
B	O	C	A	J
P	R	I	G	O
F	A	M	O	S

(More Beds on the next page)

SPEAKING OF BEDS (CONTINUED)

8 What church was threatened with being thrown on a "bed of suffering"?

9 What bedridden, palsied man was healed by Peter?

10 What was Jesus trying to prove when he told the lame man to take up his bed and walk?

11 According to Hebrews, what bed should be kept pure?

12 Fill in the blanks to reveal the scheming son of a king who took to his bed in order to take advantage of his sister.

— — — —

13 Whose bedridden mother-in-law was healed by Jesus?

14 Who raised a dead boy by laying him on a bed and lying on top of him?

15 What son of a king was murdered and decapitated while lying asleep in bed?

16 Fill in the blanks to reveal who tried to coax Joseph into going to bed with her.

— — — — — — — — ,   —

— — — —

17 What king of Israel was told by Elijah that he would never get up from the bed he was lying on?

18 Who put a bed in her home for the prophet Elisha?

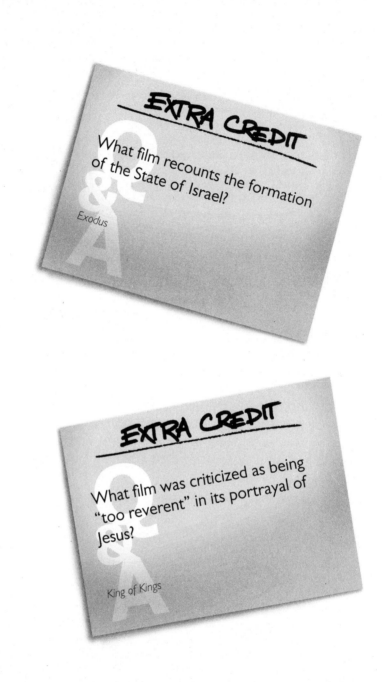

EXTRA CREDIT

What film recounts the formation of the State of Israel?

Q & A

Exodus

EXTRA CREDIT

What film was criticized as being "too reverent" in its portrayal of Jesus?

Q & A

King of Kings

PART TWELVE
THINGS TO EAT AND DRINK

FOOD, FOOD, FOOD

1 Who was famous as an eater of locusts?

2 Fill in the blanks to reveal the four faithful young men who refused to eat the rich foods of the king of Babylon.

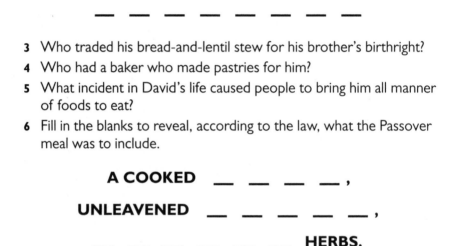

— — — — — —

— — — — — — — —

— — — — — —

— — — — — —

3 Who traded his bread-and-lentil stew for his brother's birthright?

4 Who had a baker who made pastries for him?

5 What incident in David's life caused people to bring him all manner of foods to eat?

6 Fill in the blanks to reveal, according to the law, what the Passover meal was to include.

A COOKED — — — — ,

UNLEAVENED — — — — — ,

— — — — — — **HERBS.**

7 What old man was deceived when his son dressed in goatskin gloves and presented him with a meal of cooked goat?

8 Who served cheese, milk, and veal to the Lord when he made his appearance in the form of three men?

(More Food on the next page)

FOOD, FOOD, FOOD (CONTINUED)

9 What did Ezekiel's edible scroll taste like in his mouth?

10 What judge of Israel cooked an angel a meal that included a pot of broth?

11 In what book of the Bible is Canaan first described as a land flowing with milk and honey?

12 What prized animal was killed for food when the Prodigal Son returned home?

13 Fill in the blanks to reveal the country where the Hebrews fed on cucumbers, melons, leeks, onions, and garlic.

    __   __   __   __   __

14 Fill in the blanks to reveal the food that Jacob's sons brought with them as a gift for Joseph on their second trip to Egypt.

    __   __   __   __   __   __   __

15 What prophet, who was a herdsman and fruit picker by trade, had a vision of a basket of ripe fruit?

16 Fill in the blanks to reveal who ate honey out of a lion's carcass.

    __   __   __   __   __   __

17 What miraculous food resembled coriander seed?

18 What prophet purified some deadly stew and a water supply?

19 Who cursed a fig tree for not bearing fruit?

20 What ominous winged creature is described as unclean in the law?

Food, Food, Food

9 Honey (Ezekiel 3:3). 10 Gideon (Judges 6:19). 11 Exodus (3:8). 12 The fatted calf (Luke 15:23). 13 Egypt (Numbers 11:5). 14 Almonds (Genesis 43:11). 15 Amos (8:1). 16 Samson (Judges 14:5-9). 17 Manna (Exodus 16:31). 18 Elisha (2 Kings 2:19-22; 4:38-41). 19 Jesus (Matthew 21:1-4). 20 The bat (Leviticus 11:13-19).

THINGS TO EAT AND DRINK 295

SWEET, SOUR, BITTER, POISON

1 Who ate a book that tasted like honey?

2 According to Jeremiah, what kind of grape sets the children's teeth on edge?

3 What kind of herbs were the Israelites supposed to eat with the Passover meal?

4 Who posed a riddle about finding something sweet in a lion's carcass?

5 According to Jesus after the Resurrection, what would his followers be able to drink?

6 What substance—probably very bitter—did Moses make the people of Israel drink?

7 Who ate a book that was sweet at first but turned bitter afterwards?

8 According to Proverbs, what kind of water is sweet?

9 What sweet substance was part of John the Baptist's diet?

10 What prophet made some poison stew edible by pouring meal into it?

11 According to Proverbs, what kind of bread is sweet to a man?

12 What did Moses do to make the bitter waters of Marah drinkable?

13 Who told the repentant people of Israel to go home and enjoy sweet drinks?

14 In Revelation, what falls on the earth's waters to make them bitter?

15 From the choices listed, according to Proverbs, what sort of person thinks even bitter things are sweet?

A Poor   B Rich   c Hungry   D Dying

Sweet, Sour, Bitter, Poison

1 Ezekiel (2:9–3:3).   2 Sour (Jeremiah 31:29).   3 Bitter herbs (Exodus 12:8).   4 Samson (Judges 14:14).   5 Poison (Mark 16:17-18).   6 Gold dust from the golden calf Moses had destroyed (Exodus 32:20).   7 John (Revelation 10:9-10).   8 Stolen water (Proverbs 9:17).   9 Honey (Matthew 3:4).   10 Elisha (2 Kings 4:41).   11 Bread of deceit (Proverbs 20:17).   12 Threw a piece of wood into the water (Exodus 15:25).   13 Nehemiah and Ezra (Nehemiah 8:10).   14 A star (Revelation 8:10).   15 C: Hungry (Proverbs 27:7).

STARVATION DIETING

1 Which of the four horsemen in Revelation spreads famine on the earth?

2 Who moved with Naomi to Moab to escape famine?

3 Who was a food-storage supervisor in Egypt when famine came?

4 What nation was the victim of a seven-year famine during Elisha's ministry?

5 Where did Abram go when famine struck?

6 What New Testament prophet predicted a worldwide famine?

7 Who went to live with the Philistines during a famine?

8 What two plagues probably caused famine in Egypt?

9 What king's reign saw a three-year famine, which ended when Elijah said rain was coming?

10 What figure in a parable found himself the victim of famine?

11 What king endured famine because Saul had slain the Gibeonites?

12 In the time of the judges, what marauders plundered so many crops and livestock that they probably caused famine in Israel?

13 What Babylonian king caused famine in Jerusalem?

14 Who sent his sons to Egypt because of famine in the land?

SPREADING A FEAST

1 What king had a feast where a mysterious hand wrote on the wall?

2 Who threw a royal feast where his wife disobeyed him?

3 Fill in the blanks to reveal who put on a delicious spread for some angels at the oaks of Mamre.

— — — — — — —

4 Who gave a wedding feast and then pulled a trick on his son-in-law?

5 Whose children were killed while attending a feast?

6 Who told a bizarre riddle at his wedding feast?

7 What Pharisee had a feast that Jesus attended?

8 In Revelation, what holy figure has a wedding feast?

9 Where did Jesus have a post-Resurrection fish dinner with seven of his disciples?

BY THE SEA OF

— — — — — — —

10 What dweller in Sodom had a meal prepared for angelic visitors?

11 What Egyptian official had a feast prepared for his kinsmen from back home?

12 What ruler threw a lavish feast where his wife's daughter danced?

13 At the last feast mentioned in the Bible, what is to be the gruesome food?

(More Feasting on the next page)

Spreading a Feast
1 Belshazzar (Daniel 5). 2 Ahasuerus (Esther 1:3-12). 3 Abraham (Genesis 18:1-8). 4 Laban (Genesis 29:22-23). 5 Job's (Job 1:13). 6 Samson (Judges 14:10-14). 7 Simon (Luke 7:36-50). 8 The Lamb (Revelation 19:9). 9 Galilee or Tiberias (KJV) (John 21:1-13). 10 Lot (Genesis 19:3). 11 Joseph (Genesis 43:16-34). 12 Herod (Mark 6:21). 13 The flesh of people and horses (Revelation 19:17-18).

SPREADING A FEAST (CONTINUED)

14 In what village did Jesus have his first dinner after his resurrection?

15 What child was given a feast on the day he was weaned?

16 What city had a wedding feast where Jesus' first miracle was done?

17 What prophet served his team of oxen at his ordination feast?

18 What tax collector had a feast for Jesus?

19 What army man was given a feast when he joined the side of David?

20 Who gave a feast for the evil Haman?

21 Who was given a three-day feast when he began to reign over all Israel?

22 Who held a long feast when the Jerusalem Temple was dedicated?

23 In the parable of the wedding feast, what is the fate of the man who did not put his best clothes on?

24 What town was the scene of the feast where Jesus was anointed with expensive perfume?

25 Who was given a banquet by King Ahasuerus when his beauty contest was over?

26 Who was given a feast where the entrée was a fatted calf?

27 Who gave his officials a feast after God had spoken to him in a dream?

FASTS AND BREAKING OF FASTS

1 What did Jesus eat after his resurrection to prove he was not a mere phantom?

2 Who fasted for 40 days on Mount Sinai?

3 Who had a Passover meal with his followers in the upper room?

4 Who received meals at the hands of birds?

5 Who was raped after bringing a meal to her supposedly sick brother?

6 What meat was eaten at the Passover meal?

7 Who sold his birthright for a bowl of soup?

8 Who humbled himself and fasted when accused of Naboth's murder?

9 Who fasted until his child by Bathsheba died?

10 How many men had bound themselves by an oath to fast until they had killed Paul?

11 Who prepared a meal for two angels in Sodom?

12 Who obtained his father's blessing by preparing him a meal and pretending to be his brother?

13 What was the first sinful meal?

14 Who fasted for 40 days after his baptism?

15 Who was on a ship with 275 passengers who fasted for 14 days?

16 What Roman official was fasting and praying when an angel told him to send for Peter?

17 Who read the prophecy of Jeremiah when the people of Jerusalem gathered for a fast?

(More Fasting on the next page)

18 What prophet's preaching drove the people of Nineveh to fast?

19 Who fasted before leaving Babylonia for Jerusalem?

20 Who angered his father by unwittingly breaking a fast while pursuing the Philistines?

21 What two apostles prayed and fasted as they chose elders for the churches?

22 What king of Judah proclaimed a fast when the Moabites attacked?

23 What pagan king fasted after Daniel had been thrown into the lions' den?

24 Who proclaimed a day of fasting as part of the scheme to get Naboth's vineyard?

25 What, according to Jesus, do prayer and fasting accomplish?

26 Who was Paul waiting for while he fasted three days in Damascus?

27 What king fasted all day and night while unsuccessfully inquiring of the Lord?

28 What official in the Persian court fasted before presenting his case to the king?

29 Who fasted and wore sackcloth as he prayed for the liberation of his people from Persia?

30 What church's elders fasted before sending Paul and Barnabas out as missionaries?

31 Where were the Israelites when Samuel had them fasting because of their idolatry?

32 In what country were the Jews when they fasted after learning of an executive order to have them all killed?

33 Whose death caused the people of Jabesh-Gilead to fast for seven days?

34 After Ezra had read the law to the people, what was the main sin that caused them to fast?

Fasts and Breaking of Fasts

18 Jonah's (3:4-10). **19** Ezra (8:21-23). **20** Jonathan (1 Samuel 14:24-27). **21** Paul and Barnabas (Acts 14:23). **22** Jehoshaphat (2 Chronicles 20:1-4). **23** Darius (Daniel 6:18). **24** Jezebel (1 Kings 21:8-10). **25** Driving out demons (Matthew 17:21). **26** Ananias (Acts 9:9). **27** Saul (1 Samuel 28:20). **28** Nehemiah (1:1-4). **29** Daniel (9:3-4). **30** Antioch's (Acts 13:1-3). **31** Mizpah (1 Samuel 7:3-6). **32** Persia (Esther 4:1-3, 15-16). **33** Saul and Jonathan's (1 Samuel 31:13). **34** Marrying foreigners (Nehemiah 9:1-3).

THINGS TO EAT AND DRINK   301

FRUIT OF THE VINE

1 What did Paul recommend as a substitute for wine?

2 Who was called a glutton and a wine guzzler?

3 What prophet spoke of God putting Israel into a winepress?

4 What part of the body did Paul recommend wine for?

5 Where was the one place the priest could not enter after drinking wine?

6 What group of Israelites was never supposed to drink wine?

7 According to Paul's advice, what church official must not be a wine drinker?

8 What was mingled with the wine Jesus was offered on the cross?

9 What judge threshed wheat by his winepress to hide it from the Midianites?

10 According to Jesus, what do people prefer, old wine or new wine?

11 What kind of person, according to Proverbs, should be given wine?

12 According to what Jesus said at the Last Supper, when would he drink wine again with his disciples?

13 Who murdered the Midianite Zeeb at his winepress?

14 How many jars of water did Jesus turn into wine?

15 What, according to Jesus, happens when new wine is put into old wineskins?

16 What drinkers did Isaiah condemn?

17 According to Romans, what good reason is there to avoid wine?

UNDER THE INFLUENCE

1 What husband, the victim of David's adulterous scheming, was made drunk by the king?

2 What man was seduced by his daughters while he was drunk?

3 Who dropped dead as a stone on hearing bad news the morning after being drunk?

4 Fill in the blanks to reveal the virtuous man, who later married a virtuous woman, who passed out in a heap of grain while intoxicated.

— — — —

5 Absalom wanted to avenge the rape of his sister, Tamar, so he waited until the rapist was very drunk. Who was this drunk, later slain by Absalom's men?

6 What king of Israel, who ruled barely two years, was assassinated while drunk?

7 What Syrian king was getting drunk at a time when he was supposed to be making war on the Samaritans?

8 Nehemiah waited until this Persian king was softened up with wine before he asked the king to let the Jews return to their homeland. Who was the king?

9 What Persian queen refused to obey her drunken husband's order that she appear before his besotted guests?

10 Job's sons and daughters were so busy eating and drinking that they failed to notice that disaster was about to strike. What killed them?

11 The arrogant Babylonian king Belshazzar, drunk at his feast, committed an outrage when he asked for new drinking vessels to be brought in. What were these vessels that led to so much trouble for the king?

EXTRA CREDIT

Who created the Latin translation of the Bible known as the Vulgate?

Q & A

Jerome

EXTRA CREDIT

What English king ordered William Tyndale's execution?

Q & A

Henry VIII

PART THIRTEEN
MATTERS OF LIFE AND DEATH

STRANGE WAYS TO DIE

1   Who is the first individual killed by God for being wicked?

2   What devoured Aaron's sons, Nadab and Abihu, when they offered "strange fire" to the Lord?

3   What Canaanite captain was killed when Jael, a Hebrew woman, drove a tent peg through his skull?

4   Who was killed for touching the Ark of the Covenant?

5   The Lord sent a pestilence on Israel that killed 70,000 people. What act of King David brought this on?

6   God sent fire from heaven to kill the soldiers who came to capture what prophet?

7   What husband and wife dropped dead after it was revealed they had lied about the price of the possessions they had sold?

8   Who was hanged on the very gallows he had prepared for Mordecai?

9   What people were killed by great hailstones from heaven?

10 Who, along with his household, was swallowed up by the earth for rebelling against Moses?

11 What man, reluctant to produce children with his widowed sister-in-law, was slain by God?

12 What two cities were rained on by fire and brimstone?

13 What did God do when the Israelites began to complain about the death of Korah and his followers?

14 What was the last plague sent upon the Egyptians?

15 What son of Saul was murdered by two servants who stabbed him in the belly and carried his severed head to David?

BACK FROM THE DEAD

1 What prominent leader of Israel was summoned up from the dead by a witch?

2 Fill in the blanks to reveal who raised Eutychus from the dead.

— — — —

3 What prophet revived the son of the Zarephath widow?

4 Who raised Dorcas from the dead?

5 What man of Bethany was raised from his tomb by Jesus?

6 Fill in the blanks to reveal what prophet's buried bones brought a man back to life.

— — — — — —

7 What was the name of the town where Jesus raised a widow's son from the dead?

8 Fill in the blanks to reveal what marvelous event, according to Matthew, occurred in conjunction with Jesus' death on the cross.

MANY HOLY — — — — — —

CAME — — — **OF**

THEIR — — — — — — .

9 Whom did Elisha raise from the dead?

10 Whose daughter did Jesus bring back to life?

SEVEN SUICIDES

1 What judge of Israel had his armor-bearer kill him so he would avoid the disgrace of being killed by a woman?

2 According to Matthew's account, Judas committed suicide by hanging himself. How, according to Acts, did Judas die?

3 What king of Israel, who reigned only seven days, killed himself by burning down the palace with himself inside?

4 What king killed himself by falling on his own sword?

5 What strong man killed himself along with a houseful of Philistines?

6 What friend of Absalom was so disgraced when Absalom did not follow his advice that he went and hanged himself?

7 Who refused to obey the king's request to kill him, then followed the king in committing suicide?

EXTRA CREDIT

What are the oldest existing Old Testament fragments called?

The Dead Sea Scrolls

Seven Suicides
1 Abimelech, who had a millstone dropped on his head by a woman of Thebez (Judges 9:54). 2 He fell headlong in a field and burst open (Acts 1:18). 3 Zimri (1 Kings 16:18). 4 Saul (1 Samuel 31:5). 5 Samson (Judges 16:30). 6 Ahithophel (2 Samuel 17:23). 7 Saul's armor-bearer (1 Samuel 31:5).

308 THE GOOD BOOK BIBLE TRIVIA

PEOPLE GETTING STONED

1   Who pelted David and his men with stones while he accused David of being a violent man?

2   What son of a priest was stoned to death by order of King Joash?

3   What owner of a vineyard was stoned after being falsely accused in front of Ahab?

4   Who was stoned by an irate mob while trying to carry out the orders of King Rehoboam?

5   Which of Jesus' parables talks about the stoning of a landowner's servant?

6   Who was in danger of being stoned after the Amalekites dragged off the wives and children of Ziklag?

7   What shepherd boy felled a giant with a single stone?

8   Who stoned the Amorites while Joshua led an attack on them?

9   Who was stoned for holding back some of the loot from Jericho?

10 For what seemingly minor offense did the Israelites stone a man while in the wilderness?

11 In what city did some Jews persuade the people to stone Paul?

12 Who fled from Iconium when they heard of a plot to stone them?

13 What deacon became the first Christian martyr when the Jews stoned him?

14 What Gospel mentions Jesus miraculously passing through a crowd that intended to stone him?

15 Who intended to stone the woman caught in adultery?

ALL OF THESE DISEASES

1 What afflicted the Philistines when they captured the Ark of the Covenant?

2 Where did Jesus encounter a woman who had had an unnatural flow of blood for many years?

3 What king of Judah suffered from a painful boil?

4 What apostle's mother-in-law had a fever?

5 What was the affliction of the government official's son healed by Jesus?

6 What righteous man suffered from boils?

7 According to Revelation, what afflicts those who have the mark of the beast?

8 What king of Judah suffered from a crippling foot disease?

9 In the parable of Lazarus and the rich man, what was Lazarus's affliction?

10 What son of Jonathan was crippled because he had been dropped by his nurse as a baby?

11 What man was healed of dysentery by Paul?

12 Who healed Aeneas of paralysis?

13 What was the affliction of the man let down through a roof by his friends?

14 What prophet said that all of Israel was covered with sores, wounds, and bruises?

15 From the choices listed, what did Moses toss in the air to produce boils on the Egyptians?

A His staff   **B** Sand   **C** Ashes   **D** Sticks

All of These Diseases

1 Tumors (1 Samuel 5:6).   2 Capernaum (Matthew 9:20).   3 Hezekiah (2 Kings 20:7).   4 Peter's (Matthew 8:14-15).   5 Fever (John 4:52).   6 Job (2:7).   7 Painful sores (Revelation 16:2).   8 Asa (1 Kings 15:23).   9 Running sores (Luke 16:20).   10 Mephibosheth (2 Samuel 4:4).   11 Publius's father (Acts 28:8).   12 Peter (Acts 9:33).   13 Paralysis (Luke 5:18).   14 Isaiah (1:6).   15 C: Ashes (Exodus 9:9-10).

310   THE GOOD BOOK BIBLE TRIVIA

SOME LEPERS

1 What king of Judah was a leper until the day of his death?

The answers to the next three questions are hidden in the puzzle that follows the questions. Can you find them?

2 What leper of Bethany entertained Jesus in his home?

3 Who put his hand into his bosom and, drawing it out, found it leprous?

4 What is the greatest number of lepers Jesus healed at any one time?

P	E	T	E	R
N	O	M	I	S
K	N	E	T	A
M	O	S	E	S

5 What captain of the armies of Syria was a leper?

6 Who became a leper after he lied to the prophet Elisha?

7 Who told Moses to send lepers away from the Israelite camp?

8 What prophetess became a snow-white leper for a short time?

Some Lepers

1 Uzziah (2 Chronicles 26:21). 2 Simon (Mark 14:3). 3 Moses (Exodus 4:6). 4 Ten (Luke 17:12). 5 Naaman (2 Kings 5:1). 6 Gehazi (2 Kings 5:27). 7 The Lord (Numbers 5:1-4). 8 Miriam (Numbers 12:10).

BODIES NOT FULLY FUNCTIONAL

1 Who healed the crippled man at the Beautiful Gate in Jerusalem?

2 Where was Jesus when a handicapped man's friends lowered him through the roof?

3 What grandson of Saul was crippled in both feet?

4 Which Gospel mentions the healing of the man by the pool at Bethesda?

5 Whose servant did Jesus heal without even being physically near the man?

6 Whom did Jesus heal in a synagogue on the Sabbath?

7 Who healed the paralytic Aeneas?

8 What apostle healed the man in Lystra who had been crippled since birth?

9 What was the affliction of the man Jesus healed in a Galilean synagogue?

10 Who had so much faith in Jesus' healing power that she touched the hem of his robe?

11 What blind man of Jericho did Jesus heal?

12 What was the affliction of the man at the pool of Siloam?

13 When Jesus healed the blind man of Bethsaida, what did the man say was the first thing he saw?

14 What person, suffering from deafness, was healed by Jesus after the disciples failed to heal?

(More Bodies on the next page)

Bodies Not Fully Functional
1 Peter and John (Acts 3:2).   2 Capernaum (Mark 2:5-12).   3 Mephibosheth (2 Samuel 4:4).   4 John (5:8).   5 The centurion's (Matthew 8:13).   6 A crippled woman (Luke 13:10-13).   7 Peter (Acts 9:33).   8 Paul (Acts 14:8).   9 He had a withered hand (Matthew 12:13).   10 The woman with the issue of blood (Matthew 9:22).   11 Bartimaeus (Matthew 20:34).   12 Blind from birth (John 9:7).   13 Men, who looked like trees walking (Mark 8:25).   14 The boy near Mount Hermon (Mark 9:25).

312   THE GOOD BOOK BIBLE TRIVIA

BODIES NOT FULLY FUNCTIONAL (CONTINUED)

15 What healing led to Jesus' being accused of demon possession?

16 What patriarch became so blind he couldn't tell his sons apart?

17 What sinful city entertained visitors that struck the men with blindness?

18 What priest, 98 years old, was blind?

19 What army did Elisha strike with blindness?

20 What sorcerer, an opponent of Paul, was struck blind?

21 Who was blind for three days after seeing a great light?

22 What judge was blinded by the Philistines?

23 Who had King Zedekiah of Judah blinded?

24 What father of 12 sons was blind in his old age?

25 What did Jesus put in the eyes of the blind man at the pool of Siloam?

26 What blind prophet received the wife of King Jeroboam?

27 What book says that blind animals must not be sacrificed to God?

28 What righteous man claimed that he acted as eyes to the blind?

Bodies Not Fully Functional
15 The healing of a mute man in Galilee (Luke 11:14). 16 Isaac (Genesis 27:1). 17 Sodom (Genesis 19:11). 18 Eli (1 Samuel 4:15). 19 The Syrians (2 Kings 6:18). 20 Elymas (Acts 13:7-12). 21 Paul (Acts 9:9). 22 Samson (Judges 16:21). 23 Nebuchadnezzar (Jeremiah 39:7). 24 Jacob (Genesis 48:10). 25 Mud (John 9:1-7). 26 Ahijah (1 Kings 14:4). 27 Leviticus (22:22). 28 Job (29:15).

A TIME TO WEEP

1 Who wept at thinking her son would die of thirst in the desert?

2 Who wept over the death of his rebellious son Absalom?

3 What Old Testament woman is pictured as "weeping for her children and refusing to be comforted"?

4 At whose death did Abraham weep?

5 Who wept at seeing the new Temple that was built after the exiles' return from Babylon?

6 Whose second husband, Phaltiel, wept as he watched her return to her first husband, David?

7 Fill in the blanks to reveal what caused Nehemiah to weep.

HE HEARD THE __ __ __ __ __

OF __ __ __ __ __ __ __ __ __

WERE IN __ __ __ __ __

8 Who cried as he begged Isaac for his rightful blessing?

9 Who wept because her husband's other wife taunted her for being childless?

10 Who wept because he realized David had a chance to kill him but chose not to?

(More Tears on the next page)

8 Esau (Genesis 27:38).   9 Hannah (1 Samuel 1:7).   10 Saul (1 Samuel 24:16).
6 Michal's (2 Samuel 3:16).   7 He heard the walls of Jerusalem were in ruins (Nehemiah 1:4).
4 Sarah's (Genesis 23:2).   5 Old men who remembered the glory of Solomon's Temple (Ezra 3:12).
1 Hagar, mother of Ishmael (Genesis 21:16).   2 David (2 Samuel 18:33).   3 Rachel (Jeremiah 31:15).
A Time to Weep

11 Who said, "If only my head were a pool of water and my eyes a fountain of tears"?

12 Who wept when he thought Joseph was dead?

13 Jacob wept with love and joy over what beautiful woman?

14 Who cried in Egypt when his brothers did not recognize him?

15 What judge's wife wept in front of him?

16 What three men wept when they saw Job's misery?

17 What prophet mentions women weeping for the god Tammuz?

18 What New Testament epistle mentions the priest Melchizedek weeping?

19 Whom did Jesus tell not to weep for him?

20 What king's decree for extermination caused the Jews to weep?

21 Who said, "I pour out my tears to God"?

22 What king of Israel wept in front of the prophet Elisha?

23 What two male friends wept together?

24 When Saul was king, what caused the people of Gibeah to wail in despair?

25 What prophet cried when he realized what Hazael of Syria would do to the people of Israel?

(More Tears on the next page)

A Time to Weep

11 Jeremiah (9:1). 12 Jacob (Genesis 27:35). 13 Rachel (Genesis 29:11). 14 Joseph (Genesis 42:24). 15 Samson's (Judges 14:16). 16 Eliphaz, Bildad, and Zophar (Job 2:12). 17 Ezekiel (8:14). 18 Hebrews (5:6-7). 19 The daughters of Jerusalem (Luke 23:28). 20 Ahasuerus's (Esther 4:3). 21 Job (16:20). 22 Joash (2 Kings 13:14). 23 David and Jonathan (1 Samuel 20:41). 24 The threat of attack by the Ammonites (1 Samuel 11:4). 25 Elisha (2 Kings 8:11).

A TIME TO WEEP (CONTINUED)

26 What king of Judah cried because of his terrible illness?

27 Who wept with relief when he realized all his sons had not been killed?

28 The elders of what church wept over Paul?

29 Where was Paul when his friends wept at hearing the prophecy that Paul would be handed over to the Gentiles?

30 Who wept bitterly after denying Jesus?

31 What baby was crying when he was discovered by a princess?

32 Who wept at her husband's feet and tried to dissuade him from listening to the advice of his assistant?

33 Who was reading the words of the law when the people began to weep?

34 To whom did Jesus say, "Don't cry!"?

35 What friend did Jesus mourn for?

36 What king received approval from God for weeping and tearing his clothes in repentance?

37 Who wept and said to Jesus, "I do believe, but help me overcome my unbelief"?

38 Who wept on seeing what the Amalekites had done to the people of Ziklag?

39 Who discovered the widows of Joppa weeping over the dead Tabitha?

40 Where was Jesus when the sinful woman wiped his feet with her tears?

A Time to Weep

26 Hezekiah (2 Kings 20:3). **27** David (2 Samuel 13:36). **28** Ephesus (Acts 20:37). **29** Caesarea (Acts 21). **30** Peter (Matthew 26:75). **31** Moses (Exodus 2:6). **32** Esther (8:3). **33** Ezra (Nehemiah 8:9). **34** The widow of Nain (Luke 7:13). **35** Lazarus (John 11:35). **36** Josiah (2 Chronicles 34:27). **37** The father of the boy with an evil spirit (Mark 9:24). **38** David (1 Samuel 30:4). **39** Peter (Acts 9:39). **40** The home of Simon the Pharisee (Luke 7:38).

316 THE GOOD BOOK BIBLE TRIVIA

SAD RAGS—SACKCLOTH AND ASHES

1 What rich man sat in a pile of ashes?

2 What pagan city wore sackcloth as a sign of repentance?

3 Who wore sackcloth when he heard Joseph had perished?

4 What prophet declared that the people of Jerusalem should put on clothes of mourning in view of the coming destroyer?

5 What prophet in Babylon wore sackcloth while seeking the Lord?

6 What prophet told the people to mourn like a bride dressed in black, mourning her dead husband?

7 What king was confronted by a prophet who had disguised himself with ashes?

8 What book pictures the elders of Jerusalem sitting silently on the ground and wearing sackcloth?

9 What Syrian king had his servants wear sackcloth and grovel before King Ahab?

10 Who said, "I wear burlap to show my grief. My pride lies in the dust"?

11 What two cities did Jesus say would have repented in sackcloth and ashes if they could have seen his miracles?

12 Who put ashes on her head after being sexually assaulted by her lecherous half brother?

13 Who put on sackcloth when he learned of a government plan to wipe out the Jews?

14 Who was Job speaking to when he said, "I take back everything I said, and I sit in dust and ashes to show my repentance"?

RENDING THE GARMENTS

1 What momentous finding caused King Josiah to tear his clothes?

2 Who tore his clothes when Jesus spoke of being seated at the right hand of God?

The answers to the next five questions are hidden in the puzzle that follows the questions. Can you find them?

3 Reuben and what other relative of Joseph tore their clothes when they heard he had been killed?

4 Who tore his clothes when he heard his sons and daughters had all died at once?

5 Who tore his clothes when he heard of the intermarriages of Jews with foreigners?

6 Who, along with Joshua, tore his clothes when the Israelites murmured against the Lord about going into Canaan?

7 What abused sister tore her clothes after being raped by Amnon?

B	O	J	O	A
O	F	F	R	B
C	U	Z	A	E
A	E	P	M	L
J	U	M	A	A
W	A	I	T	C

(More Rending on the next page)

8   Who tore their clothes when Joseph's cup was found in Benjamin's sack?

9   Whose death caused David to order the people to tear their clothes?

10   What queen tore her clothes when she was put out of power by Jehoiada the priest?

11   Who tore their clothes when the people of Lystra began to worship them as gods?

12   What judge tore his clothing when his hasty words came back to haunt him?

13   Whose oration caused King Hezekiah to tear his clothes?

14   Who rent his clothes when he heard Absalom had taken revenge on Amnon?

15   What man's assassination caused 80 men to come to Jerusalem with torn clothes and offerings of grain and incense?

16   What leper's plea for a cure caused the king of Israel to tear his clothes?

17   What warrior's death caused David and his men to tear their clothes in grief?

18   What friend of David, loyal during Absalom's rebellion, met David with a torn robe and ashes on his head?

19   Who tore his clothes when Elijah was taken to heaven?

20   Who tore their clothes on seeing Job's pitiful condition?

GRAVE MATTERS

1 What beheaded prophet was buried by his disciples?

2 What prophet's buried bones worked a miracle?

3 Who is the only person in the Old Testament mentioned as being buried in a coffin?

4 Who was buried in the cave of Machpelah?

5 What is the first burial of a servant mentioned in the Bible?

6 Who buried Moses?

7 What prophet, after being mourned by all Israel, was buried at Ramah?

8 What rebel was buried by Joab in a great pit in the forest?

9 What king's bones were, after his body was burned, buried at Jabesh?

10 What was placed over Achan's body after the Israelites stoned him?

11 What leader was buried "in the land he had been allocated, at Timnath-serah"?

12 Who was buried with Manoah, his father?

13 What judge died at a ripe old age and was buried in the grave of Joash, his father?

14 What wicked king, the son of a godly king, was buried in the garden of Uzza?

15 What evil king of Judah was buried, like his father, in the garden of Uzza?

16 Where were Joseph's bones finally buried?

17 What king's servants buried him with his forefathers in Jerusalem?

(More Graves on the next page)

Grave Matters

1 John the Baptist (Matthew 14:11-12). 2 Elisha's (2 Kings 13:20-21). 3 Joseph (Genesis 50:26). 4 Abraham, Sarah, Isaac, Rebekah, Jacob, and Leah (Genesis 49:30-31; 50:13). 5 Deborah, Rebekah's nurse (Genesis 35:8). 6 The Lord (Deuteronomy 34:6). 7 Samuel (1 Samuel 25:1). 8 Absalom (2 Samuel 18:17). 9 Saul's (1 Samuel 31:12-13). 10 Heaps of stones (Joshua 8:29). 11 Joshua (24:30). 12 Samson (Judges 16:31). 13 Gideon (Judges 8:32). 14 Manasseh (2 Kings 21:18). 15 Amon (2 Kings 21:26). 16 At Shechem (Joshua 24:32). 17 Ahaziah (2 Kings 9:28).

GRAVE MATTERS (CONTINUED)

18 What leper king was buried in a special field?

19 What did the chief priests buy with the silver Judas returned to them?

20 What did Jesus say to the man who wanted time to bury his father?

21 Who begged the Canaanites for a place to bury his dead?

22 Who begged his son to bury him somewhere else besides Egypt?

23 What book says, "Blood has flowed like water all around Jerusalem; no one is left to bury the dead"?

24 Who said, "I go to the grave and make my bed in darkness"?

25 What book says that in the grave there is no work, no planning, no knowledge, and no wisdom?

26 Who said, "The dead cannot praise you; they cannot raise their voices in praise"?

27 What apostle said, "O death, where is your victory?"

28 What prophet, speaking the words of the Lord, asked, "Should I ransom them from the grave"?

29 What figure is portrayed in these words by Isaiah: "He was buried like a criminal; he was put in a rich man's grave"?

30 To whom did the Israelites say, "Why did you bring us out here to die in the wilderness? Weren't there enough graves for us in Egypt?"

31 What Gospel records the graves opening after Jesus' death on the cross?

(More Graves on the next page)

32 Who said, "The time is coming when all the dead in their graves will hear the voice of God's Son"?

33 What people did Jesus refer to as "hidden graves"?

34 According to Psalm 5, what is like an open grave?

35 According to Jesus, the Pharisees built tombs for whom?

36 Who gave his rock-cut tomb as a burial place for Jesus?

37 Fill in the blanks to reveal who infuriated Isaiah by building an elaborate tomb for himself.

__ __ __ __ __

38 What man who hanged himself was buried in his family tomb?

39 Whose burial at Hebron caused the grief of David?

40 According to the law, when was a hanged man's body supposed to be buried?

41 What wicked queen did Jehu send his men to bury, though she had already been devoured by dogs?

42 Who erected a memorial pillar for himself during his own lifetime?

43 What king had his body cast at the city gate with stones heaped on it?

44 What two liars were buried by the early Christians?

45 According to Jeremiah, what king was destined to have the burial of a donkey?

46 What woman, according to Jesus, prepared him for burial?

(More Graves on the next page)

Grave Matters
32 Jesus (John 5:28). **33** The scribes and the Pharisees (Luke 11:44). **34** The enemies' mouths (Psalm 5:9). **35** The prophets (Matthew 23:29). **36** Joseph of Arimathea (Luke 23:50-53). **37** Shebna (Isaiah 22:15-16). **38** Ahithophel (2 Samuel 17:23). **39** Abner's (2 Samuel 3:31). **40** The same day as the hanging (Deuteronomy 21:23). **41** Jezebel (2 Kings 9:34-37). **42** Absalom (2 Samuel 18:18). **43** The king of Ai (Joshua 8:29). **44** Ananias and Sapphira (Acts 5:6, 10). **45** Jehoiakim (Jeremiah 22:19). **46** The woman with the perfume (Matthew 26:12).

GRAVE MATTERS (CONTINUED)

47 Who brought myrrh and aloes for the burial of Jesus?

48 According to Revelation, whose bodies would lie in the streets for three and half days without burial?

49 Fill in the blanks to reveal the two epistles that compare baptism with burial.

— — — — — —

— — — — — — — —

50 Who buried Stephen?

51 Who did God promise would be buried at a ripe old age?

52 Fill in the blanks to reveal the two people who buried Abraham.

— — — — —

— — — — — —

53 According to Jeremiah, who would not be buried or mourned?

54 What priest did Jeremiah tell he would be buried in Babylon?

55 Fill in the blanks to reveal the two people who buried Isaac.

— — — —

— — — —

56 What prophetess died and was buried at Kadesh?

(More Graves on the next page)

57 What priest died and was buried at Moserah?

58 What judge of Israel was buried at Shamir?

59 What king was buried in Jerusalem after being killed by Pharaoh's armies?

60 What wicked king who had sacrificed his son was refused burial in the kings' cemetery?

61 What king of Judah, murdered by his servants, was refused burial in the royal cemetery?

62 What judge of Israel was buried in Gilead?

63 Who moved the bones of Saul and Jonathan to their final burial place?

64 Who was the first king to be buried in Samaria?

65 What king was killed by Jehu and then cast into Naboth's field?

66 How long had Lazarus been in his tomb when Jesus came?

67 What king desecrated the tombs at Bethel, burning the bones on an altar?

68 What disturbed man lived among burial caves?

69 What group of people told Abraham that they would not refuse him burial in their tombs?

70 In John's Gospel, who is the first person to see Jesus' empty tomb?

71 According to Matthew, who ordered the guard at Jesus' tomb?

72 What prophet referred to his unusual prison as "the land of the dead"?

(More Graves on the next page)

Grave Matters

57 Aaron (Deuteronomy 10:6). **58** Tola (Judges 10:1-2). **59** Josiah (2 Chronicles 35:24). **60** Ahaz (2 Chronicles 28:27). **61** Jehoash (2 Chronicles 24:25). **62** Jephthah (Judges 12:7). **63** David (2 Samuel 21:12-13). **64** Omri (1 Kings 16:28). **65** Jehoram (2 Kings 9:25). **66** Four days (John 11:17). **67** Josiah (2 Kings 23:16). **68** The Gadarene demoniac (Mark 5:2). **69** The Hittites (Genesis 23:5-6). **70** Mary Magdalene (John 20:1). **71** Pilate (Matthew 27:65). **72** Jonah (2:2).

73 What prophet pictures the Lord preparing a grave for Nineveh?

74 What book compares the power of jealousy to the power of the grave?

75 What book says that the grave is one of the four things that can never be satisfied?

76 Who is the only person in the Bible pictured as wearing his grave clothes?

77 What wife of Jacob had a pillar erected upon her grave?

78 In the New Testament, what young man was raised from the dead while on his way to be buried?

79 What prophet heard God describing the armies of the heathen nations gathered around their own graves?

80 What prophet complained that his mother's womb should have been his grave?

81 In Luke's Gospel, who is the only apostle to actually investigate the empty tomb?

82 In Matthew's Gospel, who moved the stone from Jesus' tomb?

DEATH IN MASSIVE DOSES

1 What nation saw 185,000 of its soldiers slaughtered by an angel of the Lord?

2 What judge and his men killed 120,000 Midianites?

3 When the Israelites lost 30,000 soldiers in the time of Samuel, whom were they fighting?

4 What king headed up the slaying of 47,000 Syrians?

5 When the Jews were allowed to defend themselves against the Persians, how many Persians were killed?

6 What king of Israel killed 20,000 men of Judah in one day because they had forsaken the Lord?

7 For what offense did the Lord kill 50,070 men of Beth-Shemesh?

8 For what sin of David did the Lord kill 70,000 Israelites with a plague?

9 What king of Judah led an army that killed 500,000 soldiers of Israel?

10 What Syrian king fled when 100,000 of his soldiers were killed by the people of Israel?

EXTRA CREDIT

What Bible was the one most likely used by the Pilgrims?

The Geneva Bible

KILLED BY THE BEASTS

1 What sinister creature came in droves and killed the people of Israel in the wilderness?

2 What son of Jacob was, according to his brothers, killed by a wild animal?

3 Which book mentions people being devoured by lions?

4 What prophet saw two female bears devour the children who had poked fun at his baldness?

5 Unscramble the letters and find a common nickname as well as the actual name of the animal that devoured the foreigners who had moved into Israel.

GEKOSITFINALSNOBS

__ __ __ __ __ __

__ __ __ __ __ __

__ __ __ __ __

6 For what strange offense was a prophet killed by a lion?

7 What animal killed a man for disobeying the old prophet of Bethel?

Killed by the Beasts
1 Fiery serpents (Numbers 21:6).   2 Joseph (Genesis 37:33).   3 Daniel (6:24).   4 Elisha (2 Kings 2:24).   5 King of beasts; lions (2 Kings 17:24-25).   6 He refused the request of another prophet to hit him (1 Kings 20:35-36).   7 A lion (1 Kings 13:20-32).

EXTRA CREDIT

Who produced the textus receptus, an edition of the Greek New Testament used in later Bible translation?

Erasmus

EXTRA CREDIT

What Bible translation, still popular today, was published in 1611?

The King James Version

PART FOURTEEN
. . . AND THINGS LEFT OVER

ACROSS THE BIBLICAL SPECTRUM

NOTE: There may be some variance in the answers because the names of colors differ in different Bible translations.

1 What color was the hideous seven-headed dragon in Revelation?

2 What is the first color mentioned in the Bible?

3 What doting father gave his favorite son a coat of many colors?

4 What New Testament woman was a seller of purple cloth?

5 What book describes a handsome man whose hair is black like a raven?

6 What prophet had a vision of four chariots pulled by different colored horses?

7 According to Isaiah, what color does the Lord wear?

8 According to Isaiah, what color are sins?

9 What color was the sun in Revelation when it became like sackcloth?

10 What animal is mentioned as churning up white foam in the sea?

11 In 2 Peter, who had a place of deep blackness reserved for them?

12 What evil woman was dressed in purple and scarlet and covered with jewels?

13 According to Joel, what fateful day would be a day of blackness?

14 Which Old Testament book mentions the color blue the most?

15 According to Psalms, what color is the sinner after being washed by God?

16 What color was the cloth draped over the Ark of the Covenant?

17 Who sang a victory song that mentions "white donkeys" (NIV)?

(More Colors on the next page)

Across the Biblical Spectrum

1 Red (Revelation 12:3).   2 Green (Genesis 1:30—"I have given every green plant as food.").   3 Jacob (Genesis 37:3).   4 Lydia (Acts 16:14).   5 Song of Songs (Song of Solomon (5:11).   6 Zechariah (6:1-3).   7 Red (Isaiah 63:2).   8 Scarlet (Isaiah 1:18).   9 Black (Revelation 6:12).   10 Leviathan (Job 41:32).   11 False teachers (2 Peter 2:17).   12 Babylon, the great harlot (Revelation 17:4).   13 The Day of the Lord (Joel 2:2).   14 Exodus (because of the many references to the Tabernacle furnishings).   15 Whiter than snow (Psalm 51:7).   16 Blue (Numbers 4:6).   17 Deborah and Barak (Judges 5:10).

ACROSS THE BIBLICAL SPECTRUM (CONTINUED)

18 What Gospel mentions Jesus commenting on the red sky as a weather omen?

19 In Mark's Gospel, what color was the robe Jesus wore when the soldiers mocked him?

20 Fill in the blanks to reveal what three colors were used for the curtain for the Holy of Holies in the Temple.

— — — —

— — —

— — — — —

21 What Jew wore the royal purple garments in a foreign court?

22 What prophet talked about idols dressed in blue and purple garments?

23 Fill in the blanks to reveal who had a vision of a heavenly being with white hair and white clothing.

— — — — — —

24 What people defeated by Gideon wore purple garments?

25 What book speaks of an industrious wife who wears clothes of fine purple linen?

26 Fill in the blanks to reveal what prophet saw a drought end when the sky grew black.

— — — — —

27 What book mentions people who had worn purple while pawing through the garbage of Jerusalem?

(More Colors on the next page)

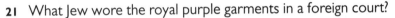

Across the Biblical Spectrum

18 Matthew (16:2).   **19** Purple (Mark 15:17).   **20** Blue, red, and purple (2 Chronicles 3:14).
21 Mordecai (Esther 8:15) or Daniel (5:29).   **22** Jeremiah (10:9).   **23** Daniel (7:9).   **24** The
Midianites (Judges 8:26).   **25** Proverbs (31:22).   **26** Elijah (1 Kings 18:45).   **27** Lamentations (4:5).

ACROSS THE BIBLICAL SPECTRUM (CONTINUED)

28 What servant of a prophet had his skin turned white as snow?

29 What colors were the fabrics used inside Solomon's Temple?

30 Which of Jesus' parables has a rich man dressed in purple robes?

31 What insect invasion made the Egyptian ground black?

32 Who prayed that the day he was born would be covered with blackness?

33 Who had a vision of horsemen with breastplates that were yellow like sulfur?

34 How many times does the Bible mention brown?

35 What book mentions an immoral woman covering her bed with colored sheets from Egypt?

36 What prophet saw a multicolored eagle carrying off the top of a cedar tree?

37 What disease was considered to be healed if healthy black hair was growing on the skin?

38 What creature eliminated every green thing from the land of Egypt?

39 In Revelation, what did the rider on the red horse bring to the earth?

40 What kind of pastures are mentioned in Psalm 23?

41 According to Proverbs, what kind of person thrives like a green leaf?

42 What prophet says that God is like a green tree giving shelter to those who trust him?

43 In Revelation, what caused earth's green grass to be burned up?

44 What color do the armies of heaven, described in Revelation, wear?

(More Colors on the next page)

Across the Biblical Spectrum
28 Gehazi, Elisha's servant (2 Kings 5:27). **29** Blue, red, and purple (2 Chronicles 2:14). **30** The parable of the rich man and Lazarus (Luke 16:19). **31** Locusts (Exodus 10:15). **32** Job (3:5). **33** John (Revelation 9:17). **34** Once (the color of a horse) (Zechariah 1:8). **35** Proverbs (7:16). **36** Ezekiel (17:3). **37** Leprosy (Leviticus 11:31, 37). **38** The locusts (Exodus 10:15). **39** War (Revelation 6:4). **40** Green pastures. **41** A righteous person (Proverbs 11:28). **42** Hosea (14:8). **43** Hail, fire, and blood poured on the earth (Revelation 8:7). **44** White (Revelation 19:14).

45 What color rope was Rahab supposed to tie to her window so the Israelites would recognize her home?

46 In Revelation, what did the rider on the black horse bring to the earth?

47 What book mentions a woman with lips like a scarlet ribbon?

48 What color was the horse in Revelation that carried a rider with a pair of scales in his hands?

49 According to Job, what animal searches for green things to eat in the mountains?

50 According to Matthew's Gospel, what color was the robe the Roman soldiers put on Christ when they mocked him?

51 What evil woman in Revelation rode on a scarlet beast?

52 In Revelation, what fallen city is noted as having dressed itself in scarlet and purple?

53 Where are black sheep mentioned in the Bible?

54 Who practiced genetic engineering by using green and white branches in his flocks' drinking water?

55 What color were the clothes of the person who held seven stars in his hand?

56 What color hair was considered a symptom of leprosy?

57 What color was the cloth over the altar in the Tabernacle?

58 What king promised purple robes for the man who could explain a strange inscription?

59 What book advises people always to wear white clothing?

60 Who, according to Lamentations, had their skin blackened after the fall of Jerusalem?

(More Colors on the next page)

Across the Biblical Spectrum

45 Scarlet (Genesis 2:18). **46** Famine (Revelation 6:6). **47** Song of Songs (Song of Solomon) (4:3). **48** Black (Revelation 6:5). **49** Wild donkeys (Job 39:8). **50** Scarlet (Matthew 27:28). **51** The great harlot (Revelation 17:3). **52** Babylon (Revelation 18:16). **53** Genesis 30:35—Laban had them in his flock. **54** Jacob (Genesis 30:37-42). **55** White (Revelation 1:14). **56** White (Leviticus 13:3). **57** Blue (Numbers 4:11). **58** Belshazzar (Daniel 5:7). **59** Ecclesiastes (9:8). **60** The princes (Lamentation 4:8).

61 Where was Jesus when his clothes became radiantly white?

The answers to the next six questions are hidden in the puzzle that follows the questions. Can you find them?

62 Who raised the question about whether there was flavor in the white of an egg?

63 According to Proverbs, we should avoid looking at wine when it is what color?

64 What color horse did Death ride?

65 What color stone was promised to the faithful people at the church of Pergamum?

66 Which of Jacob's sons was described as having teeth whiter than milk?

67 What Gospel says that the transfigured Jesus wore clothes whiter than anyone could ever wash them?

D	B	O	J	M
E	L	I	U	E
R	T	V	D	L
C	N	I	A	A
A	S	A	H	P
K	R	A	M	W

(More Colors on the next page)

Across the Biblical Spectrum

61 The Mount of Transfiguration (Matthew 17:2). **62** Job (6:6). **63** Red (Proverbs 23:31). **64** Pale (or pale green, depending on your translation) (Revelation 6:8). **65** White (Revelation 2:17). **66** Judah (Genesis 49:12). **67** Mark (9:3).

334 THE GOOD BOOK BIBLE TRIVIA

68 According to Isaiah, what color would God change the scarlet sins to?

69 What church was told to buy white clothes to cover its nakedness?

70 What color clothes were the 24 elders in Revelation wearing?

71 According to David, which leader had clothed the women of Israel in fine scarlet robes?

72 What color cow was to be burned so that its ashes could be used in removing uncleanness?

73 What color thread was tied around the arm of the firstborn of Tamar's twins?

74 Who complained that his skin had turned black?

75 What color were the pomegranates around the hem of the high priest's robes?

76 What people did Jesus compare to whitewashed tombs?

77 What person did Paul call a "whitewashed wall"?

78 Whose name means "red"?

79 What color were the cords on the tassels the Israelites were commanded to put on their garments?

80 What sea was parted by a wind from God?

81 In the law, what color ram's skin was acceptable as an offering?

82 What color horse did Faithful and True ride?

83 According to Moses, what color is a grape's blood?

84 What people were frightened away when they mistook the redness of the morning sun on water for blood?

(More Colors on the next page)

Across the Biblical Spectrum

68 White (Isaiah 1:18). **69** Laodicea (Revelation 3:18). **70** White (Revelation 4:4). **71** Saul (2 Samuel 1:24). **72** Red (Numbers 19:2). **73** Scarlet (Genesis 38:28). **74** Job (30:30). **75** Blue, red, and purple (Exodus 28:33). **76** The scribes and Pharisees (Matthew 23:27). **77** Ananias the high priest (Acts 23:3). **78** Edom (Esau's other name) (Genesis 25:30). **79** Blue (Numbers 15:38). **80** The Red Sea (Exodus 13:18). **81** Red (Exodus 25:5). **82** White (Revelation 19:11). **83** Red (Deuteronomy 32:14). **84** Moabites (2 Kings 3:22).

... AND THINGS LEFT OVER   335

85 Whose face turned red with weeping?

86 What color was the first of the four horses in Revelation?

87 Who warned his followers that they could not change the color of their hair by worrying?

88 What color was the stew Esau begged Jacob to give him?

89 According to Nahum, what city was attacked by soldiers in scarlet uniforms and carrying scarlet shields?

90 In Revelation, what did the rider on the white horse bring to the earth?

91 What prophet mentioned a harlot cavorting with soldiers in purple uniforms?

92 Who had a vision of ravenous locusts that devoured foliage and made the trees' branches white?

93 What color did the moon become when the sixth seal was broken open?

94 What color were the clothes of the angel that stood by Jesus' tomb?

95 What prophet mentions multicolored carpets?

96 Who had a throne with purple cushions?

97 What prophet said that prophets had whitewashed a pile of loose stones?

98 What sweet food was white like coriander seed?

99 What book mentions making robes white by washing them in blood?

100 What curious object was in the hand of the person sitting on the white cloud in Revelation?

Across the Biblical Spectrum

85 Job's (16:16). **86** White (Revelation 6:2). **87** Jesus (Matthew 5:36). **88** Red (Genesis 25:30). **89** Nineveh (Nahum 2:3). **90** Conquest (Revelation 6:2). **91** Ezekiel (23:6). **92** Joel (1:7). **93** Blood red (Revelation 6:12). **94** White (Matthew 28:3). **95** Ezekiel (27:24). **96** Solomon (Song of Songs (Song of Solomon) (3:10). **97** Ezekiel (13:10). **98** Manna (Exodus 16:31). **99** Revelation 7:14—The blood of the Lamb makes them clean. **100** A sickle (Revelation 14:14).

GOING TO EXTREMES

1 Who was the youngest king mentioned in the Bible?

2 What was the largest army assembled?

3 From the choices listed, what king of Judah had the longest reign?

    A Manasseh **B** David **C** Hezekiah **D** Josiah

4 What king of Israel had the shortest reign?

5 What is the shortest prayer in the Bible?

6 What are the two shortest verses in the Bible?

7 What is the longest verse as recorded in the King James Version?

8 What is the longest prayer in the Bible?

9 What is the biggest animal mentioned in the Bible?

10 What is the smallest animal mentioned in the Bible?

11 What is the longest book in the Bible?

12 What is the longest book in the New Testament?

13 Fill in the blanks to reveal what the longest chapter in the Bible is.

    — — — —   — — —

14 What word, the name of Isaiah's son, is the longest word in the Bible?

Going to Extremes

1 Joash (or Jehoash), who began his reign at the age of seven (2 Chronicles 24:1). 2 One million men, brought by Zerah the Ethiopian against Asa of Judah (2 Chronicles 14:9). 3 A: Manasseh. He ruled for 55 years (2 Kings 21:1). 4 Zimri, who ruled for seven days after usurping the throne (1 Kings 16:15). 5 "Lord, save me," uttered by Peter while sinking (Matthew 14:30). 6 "Jesus wept" (John 11:35) and "Eber, Peleg, Reu" (1 Chronicles 1:25). 7 Esther 8:9 with 90 words. 8 Probably Nehemiah 9:5-38. 9 The whale (Genesis 1:21). 10 The gnat (Matthew 23:24). 11 Psalms. 12 Luke. 13 Psalm 119. 14 Maher-shalal-hash-baz (Isaiah 8:1).

HAIRSBREADTH ESCAPES

1 Paul, newly converted to Christianity, enraged the Jewish leaders in a certain city, so they decided to murder him. His friends let him down in a basket through the city wall. What city was it?

2 The judge Ehud stabbed the fat Moabite king Eglon while they were alone together. What simple maneuver did Ehud use to evade the king's guards?

3 Nebuchadnezzar breached the walls of Jerusalem, but the king and many others escaped. How?

4 The king of Sodom escaped his attackers by hiding where?

5 In Mark's Gospel, a young man who was following Jesus on the night of his betrayal just barely escaped from being apprehended himself. What was the sole garment the young man was wearing, and how did he escape?

6 Where did Joseph take Mary and the infant Jesus in order to escape the wrath of King Herod?

7 Where did Moses, still living in the royal household of Egypt, take refuge after killing an Egyptian?

8 When a violent storm caused the death of all of Job's children, how many people in the household escaped the tragedy?

(More Escapes on the next page)

9 Jesus was threatened with stoning by people gathering in Jerusalem for the Feast of Dedication. How did he escape?

10 Of the many times Saul tried to kill David, one of the closest calls was when he threw a spear at David. What did David do?

11 How did Michal, David's wife, fool the messengers who came to fetch the runaway David?

12 Running from Saul, David took refuge in Gath, where the king was worried at having a popular folk hero in town. How did David keep himself from being a victim of the king's anger?

13 When Absalom was trying to usurp the crown from his father, David, a woman helped David by hiding two of his messengers from Absalom's men. How did she hide them?

EXTRA CREDIT

Who published a translation of Paul's epistles called Letters to Young Churches?

J. B. Phillips

Hairsbreadth Escapes

9 We don't know; the Gospel account gives no explanation (John 10:22-39). **10** He merely sidestepped the spear so it went into a wall (1 Samuel 19:10). **11** She placed an idol (presumably human sized) in David's bed and told the messengers he was sick (1 Samuel 19:11-18). **12** He pretended to be crazy (1 Samuel 21:10-15). **13** She hid them in a well, spread a covering over the well, and spread grain over the covering to hide it (2 Samuel 17:17-21).

HUGS AND KISSES

1 What two hostile brothers met and kissed each other, weeping all the way?

2 Whom did Joab murder while kissing?

3 What prophet talked about kissing calves?

4 Who kissed Barzillai, an old man who had provided supplies for the army?

5 Who kissed Absalom after his two years in exile?

6 Who poured oil on Saul's head and kissed him?

7 What aged father kissed one son, mistaking him for the other?

8 Who met Moses in the wilderness and kissed him?

9 When Jacob died, who wept over him and kissed him?

10 What bereaved woman kissed her daughters-in-law goodbye as she left to return to her own country?

11 What rebel was so magnetic in personality that the men of Israel couldn't help kissing him?

12 Who kissed David when he was fleeing from Saul?

13 Who met Moses by the mount of God and kissed him?

14 Who kissed his brothers in a tearful family reunion?

15 Who kissed and blessed Ephraim and Manasseh, Joseph's sons?

16 Who kissed his nephew the first time they met?

17 Who returned home after making peace with his son-in-law and kissing his grandchildren good-bye?

(More Hugs on the next page)

Hugs and Kisses

1 Jacob and Esau (Genesis 33:4).   2 Amasa (2 Samuel 20:9-10).   3 Hosea, who was referring to calf idols (13:2).   4 David (2 Samuel 19:39).   5 David (2 Samuel 14:33).   6 Samuel (1 Samuel 10:1).   7 Isaac, who kissed Jacob instead of Esau (Genesis 27:27).   8 Jethro, his father-in-law (Exodus 18:5, 7).   9 Joseph (Genesis 50:1).   10 Naomi (Ruth 1:9).   11 Absalom (2 Samuel 15:5-6).   12 Jonathan (1 Samuel 20:41).   13 Aaron (Exodus 4:27).   14 Joseph (Genesis 45:15).   15 Jacob (Genesis 48:10, 20).   16 Laban, Jacob's uncle and future father-in-law (Genesis 29:13).   17 Laban (Genesis 31:55).

18 What book begins "Kiss me and kiss me again, for your love is sweeter than wine"?

19 What book says "An honest answer is like a kiss of friendship"?

20 Who had a tearful farewell, with many kisses, at the city of Miletus?

21 Which epistle says "Greet one another with a kiss of love" (NIV)?

22 According to Proverbs, whose kisses are deceitful?

23 Where was Jesus when the sinful woman kissed his feet and anointed him?

24 Which epistles end with Paul's admonition to greet fellow Christians with a "holy kiss" (NIV)?

25 Where is a kiss described as lustful?

26 Who kissed Jesus as a supposed sign of friendship?

27 Who kissed the Prodigal Son?

28 Which book says "Kiss the Son, lest he be angry" (NIV)?

29 Who kissed Rachel almost as soon as he met her?

30 What prophet protested men kissing the image of Baal?

31 To whom did Job speak about kissing the hand as an act of homage?

Hugs and Kisses

18 Song of Songs (Song of Solomon) (1:2). **19** Proverbs (24:26). **20** Paul (Acts 2:36-38).
21 1 Peter (5:14). **22** An enemy's (Proverbs 27:6). **23** The home of Simon the Pharisee (Luke 7:36-43). **24** Romans (16:16), 1 Corinthians (16:20), 2 Corinthians (13:12), and 1 Thessalonians (5:26).
25 Proverbs 7:13. **26** Judas (Matthew 26:48). **27** His father (Luke 15:20). **28** Psalms (2:12).
29 Jacob (Genesis 29:11). **30** Elijah (1 Kings 19:18). **31** Eliphaz, Bildad, and Zophar (Job 31:27).

FOOT COVERINGS

1 Who was told by God to take his shoes off because he was standing on holy ground?

2 Who told people that he was not worthy to carry the Messiah's sandals?

3 During what historic event were the Hebrews instructed to keep their shoes on and be ready to travel?

The answers to the next four questions are hidden in the puzzle that follows the questions. Can you find them?

4 Who told a king that he would not accept a gift of shoelaces? Where did this king rule? (Both answers are hidden in the puzzle.)

5 What book mentions the custom of giving a person one's shoe as a sign of transferring property?

6 How many years did the best-made shoes in the Bible last?

7 Who was told by an angel to put on his clothes and shoes?

R	E	T	E	P
S	H	Y	L	A
O	I	T	B	K
D	J	R	U	A
O	A	O	N	R
M	H	F	A	T

(More Shoes on the next page)

Foot Coverings
1 Moses (Exodus 3:5). 2 John the Baptist (Matthew 3:11). 3 Passover (Exodus 12:11). 4 Abram; Sodom (Genesis 14:23). 5 Ruth (4:7). 6 Forty (Deuteronomy 29:5). 7 Peter (Acts 12:8).

342   THE GOOD BOOK BIBLE TRIVIA

FOOT COVERINGS (CONTINUED)

8 What nation did God "toss his sandal" upon?

9 Whom did Jesus tell not to carry sandals with them on their journey?

10 The people of what town tricked Joshua by putting on worn-out shoes when they went to meet him?

11 What sea, according to Isaiah, would be dried up by the Lord so that men could walk over it in their shoes?

12 What prophet, once he had taken his shoes off, walked around barefoot for years?

13 According to Ezekiel, what city did God put leather sandals on?

14 Who was told not to take his shoes off after his wife died?

15 Which prophet accused the people of Israel of selling the poor people for a pair of sandals?

16 What book has a devoted lover praising a woman's sandaled feet?

17 Who was told by the commander of the heavenly army to take off his shoes?

18 Who ordered a pair of sandals for his son's feet?

19 For what crime could a man have his shoe taken away and his face spit in?

20 Who prophesied that soldiers' boots would be used as fuel for burning?

Foot Coverings

8 Edom—"Upon Edom I toss my sandal!" (Psalm 60:8, NIV). 9 The disciples (Matthew 10:10).
10 The people of Gibeon (Joshua 9:5). 11 The Egyptian sea (Isaiah 11:15). 12 Isaiah (20:2).
13 Jerusalem (Ezekiel 16:10). 14 Ezekiel (24:17). 15 Amos (2:6). 16 Song of Songs (Song of Solomon (7:1). 17 Joshua (5:15). 18 The Prodigal Son's father (Luke 15:22). 19 Refusing to marry the widow of his deceased brother (Deuteronomy 25:9). 20 Isaiah (9:5).

STONES, ROLLING AND NONROLLING

1 Who suggested that stones could be turned to bread?
2 Who used a stone for a pillow?
3 What enemies of Joshua were pelted by stones from the Lord?
4 In what humiliating way was Abimelech murdered?
5 Who had a vision of an angel casting an enormous stone into the sea?
6 Who erected a large pillar of stone and called it Ebenezer?
7 What shepherd boy went into battle with a bag of stones?
8 Who built an altar of stone that was consumed by fire from heaven?
9 Unscramble the letters to reveal the names of the patriarch and his father-in-law who heaped up stones as a sign of their covenant together.

CLANBABAJO

__ __ __ __ __

__ __ __ __ __

10 Who sat on a stone while the Amalekites fought the Israelites?
11 Who had a dream about a giant statue struck by a stone?
12 Which disciple was called a rock?
13 In Revelation, what did the Spirit promise to the churches that would overcome?

(More Stones on the next page)

14 Who set up a commemorative stone after the Israelites covenanted to serve the Lord?

15 Which of Paul's epistles speaks about a "spiritual rock" that was Christ?

16 Who rolled the stone across the tomb when Jesus was buried?

17 Who spoke of a rejected stone becoming the chief cornerstone?

18 What friend of Jesus had a stone rolled over the front of his tomb?

19 Who rolled a stone from off a well so that Laban's flocks could be watered?

20 Who sealed up five Amorite chieftains in a cave by rolling large stones across the entrance?

21 Who was thrown into a den of wild animals that was sealed with a stone?

22 Who brought costly stones for the foundation of the Temple in Jerusalem?

23 Whom did Jesus tell that the stones would cry out if the people were silenced?

24 Who set up a commemorative pillar of stone at Paddan-Aram?

25 Who struck a rock and brought water from it?

26 Who prophesied that there would not be one stone of the Temple that would not be thrown down?

27 Who picked up 12 souvenir stones from the dry path across the Jordan River?

28 Who had a garment with two onyx stones engraved with the names of the children of Israel?

29 Who wrote on tablets of stone for Moses?

(More Stones on the next page)

Stones, Rolling and Nonrolling

14 Joshua (24:27). 15 I Corinthians (10:4). 16 Joseph of Arimathea (Matthew 27:59-60). 17 Jesus (Matthew 21:42). 18 Lazarus (John 11:38-40). 19 Jacob (Genesis 29:10-11). 20 Joshua (10:16-18). 21 Daniel (6:17). 22 Solomon (1 Kings 5:17). 23 The Pharisees (Luke 19:40). 24 Jacob (Genesis 35:9, 14). 25 Moses (Exodus 17:6). 26 Jesus (Mark 13:1-2). 27 Joshua (4:4-8). 28 Aaron (Exodus 28:9-12). 29 God (Exodus 24:12).

30 Who had a breastplate with 12 precious stones in it?

31 What precious jewel is mentioned by Jesus in a parable about the Kingdom?

32 What city is decorated with 12 precious stones?

33 What did Jesus say should not be cast before swine?

34 What did Job say was so precious it could not be purchased with gems?

35 What, according to Proverbs, is more precious than rubies?

36 What prophet said that Jerusalem would have walls made of jewels?

37 What city has gates made of pearl?

38 What epistle says that Christian women should not wear pearls?

39 What prophet talks about nine precious stones adorning the king of Tyre?

40 Which psalm says that the stone rejected by the builders becomes the chief stone?

41 Who questioned Job about the cornerstone of the earth?

42 Who spoke about God laying a precious cornerstone for Jerusalem?

43 Which epistle refers to Christ as a living stone?

44 Which epistle says that the apostles and prophets are a foundation and Christ is the chief cornerstone?

45 Whom was Peter addressing when he spoke of Jesus as the cornerstone?

BOATS AND OTHER FLOATING THINGS

1 What king's household was carried in the only ferryboat mentioned in the Bible?

2 What was the material used in making the basket the infant Moses was floating in?

3 Who joined with wicked King Ahaziah of Israel in building a navy to go to Tarshish?

4 What nervous prophet actually requested that he be thrown off a storm-tossed ship at sea?

5 What king of Israel had two navies?

6 What was Jesus doing when a storm struck the boat carrying him and his disciples?

7 What was the only ship in the Bible mentioned by name?

8 What was the name of the island where Paul and his companions landed after the shipwreck?

9 Who used a ship as a pulpit?

10 What two prophets predicted attacks from the warships of Chittim?

11 What New Testament author uses the symbol of a ship's rudder to describe the power of the human tongue?

12 Who sent timber, in the form of rafts, to King Solomon?

13 What prophet predicted a glorious day when God's people would not be threatened with attacking ships?

14 What was Noah's ark made of?

THEM BONES, THEM BONES

1 What weapon did Samson use to kill a thousand men?

2 Whose bones were buried under a tree at Jabesh?

3 Who was made from a single bone?

4 Who was spared having his bones broken because he had already died?

5 Who had a vision of a valley filled with men's dry bones?

6 What saintly king desecrated a pagan altar by burning human bones on it?

7 What prophet's bones had sufficient power to raise another man from the dead?

8 What leader, carefully buried in an Egyptian coffin, had his bones transported out during the Exodus and was buried at Shechem?

9 Which psalm contains a lament that passersby can count the psalmist's bones?

EXTRA CREDIT

What Bible was created by Ken Taylor to help his children understand it?

The Living Bible

Them Bones, Them Bones

1 The jawbone of a donkey (Judges 15:15). 2 Saul's and his sons' (1 Samuel 31:11-13). 3 Eve (Genesis 2:21-22). 4 Jesus (John 19:33, 36). 5 Ezekiel (37:1-14). 6 Josiah (2 Kings 23:16). 7 Elisha's (2 Kings 13:20-21). 8 Joseph (Joshua 24:32). 9 Psalm 22:17.

THINGS IN BASKETS

1 What king received 70 human heads in baskets?
2 What apostle owed his life to a basket?
3 What ill-fated servant had a dream of three breadbaskets?
4 Solve the math problem below to reveal how many basketsful of leftover food were collected after the feeding of the five thousand.

$$4 \times 23 - 30 \div 7 - 60 + 3 = \underline{\quad}$$

5 Who had a vision of two baskets of figs in front of the Temple?
6 What prophet had a vision of a basket of summer fruits?
7 Who had a vision of a wicked woman rising up out of a basket?
8 What future liberator was found floating in a basket in the river?
9 Who served an angel a young goat in a basket?
10 How many baskets full of food were collected after the feeding of the four thousand?

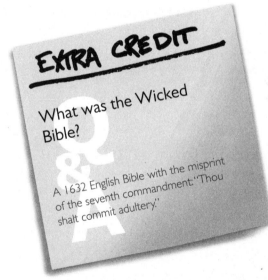

EXTRA CREDIT

Q What was the Wicked Bible?

A A 1632 English Bible with the misprint of the seventh commandment: "Thou shalt commit adultery."

Things in Baskets
1 Jehu (2 Kings 10:7).   2 Paul (Acts 9:25).   3 Pharaoh's baker (Genesis 40:16-17).   4 Twelve (Matthew 14:20).   5 Jeremiah (24:1).   6 Amos (8:1).   7 Zechariah (5:7).   8 Moses (Exodus 2:3-5).   9 Gideon (Judges 6:19).   10 Seven (Matthew 15:37).

. . . AND THINGS LEFT OVER   349

AS A REMINDER

1 What was given as a reminder that the world would never again be destroyed by a flood?

2 What ritual was to be a reminder of Christ's body and blood?

3 What day of the week is a reminder of God's completed creation?

4 What was the manna put into the Ark of the Covenant a reminder of?

5 What festival was to be a memorial of the Jews' salvation from the wicked Persian Haman?

6 What feast was to be a reminder of the simple homes the Israelites had in Egypt?

7 What feast was a reminder of the death angel killing the Egyptian firstborn?

8 Who hammered bronze incense burners into an overlay for the altar to remind the people of Israel that no one except Aaron's descendants should serve as priests?

9 What woman did Jesus say would have her story remembered for doing a kindness to him?

10 Who set up 12 stones to remind the people of God's power in bringing them across the Jordan?

A SIGN UNTO YOU

1 What was given as a sign that the shepherds had found the baby Jesus?

2 What gift was given to Christians as a sign of God's power to unbelievers?

3 What day was a sign of completion and rest?

4 According to Jesus, what prophet's sign would be given to the unbelieving Jews?

5 Who received a wet fleece as a sign of God's approval?

6 Who prophesied a virgin conceiving a child as a sign of God's presence?

7 Who saw a "slow" sundial as a sign of Hezekiah's recovery from illness?

8 Why did Joshua set up 12 stones as a sign of God's parting of the Jordan?

9 What nation suffered 10 plagues that were signs of God's power?

10 From the choices listed, what food was a sign of the deliverance from Egypt?

    A Manna   **B** Unleavened bread   **C** Quails   **D** Lamb

11 What king saw an altar broken as a sign that God was speaking through a prophet?

12 What prophet advised building a signal fire as a sign of the coming invasion of Babylon?

A Sign unto You

1 The swaddling clothes and the manger (Luke 2:12).   2 Tongues (1 Corinthians 14:22).   3 The Sabbath (Exodus 31:13).   4 Jonah's (Matthew 16:4).   5 Gideon (Judges 6:36-38).   6 Isaiah (7:14).   7 Isaiah (2 Kings 20:8-11).   8 To represent the twelve tribes of Israel (4:5).   9 Egypt (Exodus 10:2).   10 B: Unleavened bread (Exodus 13:7-9).   11 Jeroboam (1 Kings 13:5).   12 Jeremiah (6:1).

LAMPS, CANDLES, ETC.

1 Who had a vision of Jesus walking among seven gold lampstands?

2 Who told a story about 10 women lighting their lamps to meet a bridegroom?

3 Who saw a torch from God pass between the animals he had brought to sacrifice?

4 Which psalm says "Your word is a lamp to guide my feet and a light for my path"?

5 Who was told to make a seven-branched candlestick to place inside the Tabernacle?

6 According to Jesus, where do we never put our light?

7 What king sang, "O LORD, you are my lamp. The LORD lights up my darkness"?

8 Unscramble the letters to form three words that identify the man who, when he saw his headquarters collapse, called for a light to check on Paul and Silas.

NAPHTALIRIPEJEHIPIL

— — —

— — — — — —

— — — — —

9 What judge confused the Midianite army by having his men break the jars they were using as lanterns?

10 According to the New Testament, what city has no need of lamps or candles?

11 In Jesus' parable, what was the woman who searched her house with a lantern looking for?

Lamps, Candles, Etc.
1 John (Revelation 1:12). 2 Jesus (Matthew 25:1). 3 Abraham (Genesis 15:17). 4 Psalm 119 (verse 105). 5 Moses (Exodus 25:31-37). 6 Under a bushel (Matthew 5:15). 7 David (2 Samuel 22:29). 8 The Philippian Jailer (Acts 16:29). 9 Gideon (Judges 7:16-21). 10 The new Jerusalem (Revelation 22:5). 11 A lost coin (Luke 15:8).

352   THE GOOD BOOK BIBLE TRIVIA

THREADS AND ROPES AND CHAINS

1 What hyperactive person broke all the chains that had been used to bind him?

2 Who dropped a scarlet rope from her window to aid the Israelite spies?

3 Who made chains strung with pomegranates to decorate the Temple?

4 Who put a chain of gold around Daniel's neck?

5 What people had golden chains around their camels' necks?

6 What apostle had his chains removed by an angel?

7 Who bound King Zedekiah in chains and blinded him?

8 Who gave birth to twins, one of which had a scarlet thread tied around it by the midwife?

9 Who put a golden chain around Joseph's neck?

10 What judge was bound up in cords by the Philistines?

11 What prophet was bound up in chains, along with the others who were carried away as captives?

12 What figure in the New Testament is bound up for a thousand years by a chain?

13 Who arrived in Rome bound by a chain?

14 Who wore an ephod with gold chains on it?

15 Whose servants put ropes on their heads and begged Ahab for mercy?

16 What apostle was on a ship where the ropes holding the lifeboat were deliberately cut?

Threads and Ropes and Chains

1 The Gadarene demoniac (Mark 5:3-4). 2 Rahab the harlot (Joshua 2:15-19). 3 Solomon (2 Chronicles 3:16). 4 Belshazzar (Daniel 5:29). 5 Midianites (Judges 8:26). 6 Peter (Acts 12:6-7). 7 Nebuchadnezzar (Jeremiah 39:7). 8 Tamar (Genesis 38:28). 9 Pharaoh (Genesis 41:42). 10 Samson (Judges 16:6-9). 11 Jeremiah (40:1). 12 Satan (Revelation 20:1-2). 13 Paul (Acts 28:20). 14 Aaron (Exodus 28:14). 15 The servants of Ben-hadad (1 Kings 20:31). 16 Paul (Acts 27:30-32).

THINGS ON WHEELS

1   What prophet's exit is associated with chariots of fire?

2   Who sent back the Ark of the Covenant on a cart pulled by a cow?

3   What king had 1,400 chariots and 12,000 horses?

4   What foreign official was in his chariot when Philip came to him?

5   Who had a vision of four chariots driven by angels?

6   What king burned the idolatrous chariots of the sun?

7   Who took off in his chariot when his tax collector was stoned by the people?

8   Who got to ride in Pharaoh's second chariot?

9   What tribe was given six covered wagons in which to haul the Tabernacle and its furnishings?

10   What mighty nation had its chariots ruined in the Red Sea?

11   What king rode into battle in a chariot but was fatally wounded by an Assyrian arrow?

12   Who sent wagons to Canaan to carry back his father and his in-laws?

13   What Syrian leper rode up to Elijah's house in a chariot?

14   What king of Israel was noted as a fast and furious chariot driver?

15   What king, fatally wounded while fighting the Egyptians, was brought back to Jerusalem in a chariot?

16   Whose servant saw a hillside covered with chariots of fire?

17   Who had a vision of wheels that looked to be made of beryl?

ABOUT THE AUTHOR

Trivia master J. Stephen Lang is the author of more than thirty books, including the best-selling *The Complete Book of Bible Trivia* and *The Big Book of American Trivia*. His other books include *The Bible on the Big Screen, Know the Bible in 30 Days, What the Good Book Didn't Say,* and *Everyday Biblical Literacy.* He writes the Bible IQ feature for *Today's Christian* magazine and is a regular contributor to *Discipleship Journal* and *Christian History.* He lives in Seminole, Florida.